STORMING EAGLES

Parachuting into action:
the revolutionary new form of
warfare. Here a Fallschirmjaeger
descends on his RZ1 parachute
during a training jump.
Ironically, the élite paratroops
were destined to parachute into
action but rarely after the
climax of the Crete invasion.
(Brian L. Davis)

Below: Two heavily armed
Fallschirmjaeger after landing in
Crete, May 1941. (Brian L.
Davis)

STORMING EAGLES

German Airborne Forces in World War Two | James Lucas

GUILD PUBLISHING
LONDON

This book is dedicated, in general, to all the British Army's former opponents – opponents but never enemies – in the German Airborne formations during the Second World War. Specifically, it is dedicated the those against whom I fought in Tunisia. To Paul Beck, who took me prisoner, to Hans Teske, who now serves with me on the British Section of La Confédération européenne des Anciens Combattants, to Franz Josef Kugel, Rudi Hambuch, Willi Keuter, all of whom served in the Sturm Regiment Koch/Schirmer; as well as to Guenther Raebiger, a very special friend and to all of his Regiment who fought against mine at Cassino.

First published in Great Britain in 1988 by Arms and Armour Press,
Artillery House, Artillery Row, London SW1P 1RT.

This edition published 1988 by Guild Publishing by arrangement with Cassell.

CN 8698

Front of jacket illustration: items provided by Brian L. Davis; photograph by Michael Dyer Associates, London.

The illustrations in this book have been collected from many sources, and vary in quality owing to the variety of circumstances under which they were taken and preserved. As a result, certain of the illustrations are not of the standard to be expected from the best of today's equipment, materials and techniques. They are nevertheless included for their inherent information value, to provide an authentic visual coverage of the subject.

Designed and edited by DAG Publications Ltd.
Designed by David Gibbons; edited by Michael Boxall; layout by Anthony A. Evans; typeset by Ronset Typesetters Ltd., Darwen, Lancashire; camerawork by M&E Reproductions, North Fambridge, Essex; printed and bound in Great Britain by the Bath Press, Avon.

Contents

Acknowledgements

My interest in the Fallschirmjaeger extends back more than four decades, to the years of the Second World War. I met German paratroops in combat first in North Africa and then during the Italian campaign. Over the long span of years since the end of the Second World War, it has been my privilege to attend their reunions and a pleasure to greet them at the Museum in which I formerly worked. More than a decade ago, plans for writing this book were formulated and on the basis of my own experiences as well as correspondence entered into, conversations recalled and anecdotes remembered, the book began to take shape. It is, however, around the generous response of the Fallschirmjaeger to my requests for help that so much of the text has been constructed.

Inevitably, among the replies received in response to my appeal, there were a great many letters which recorded the same incident in a battle or a campaign. In order to avoid repetition I have either incorporated the details supplied so that they form part of the text of the book, or have amalgamated various elements of them so as to create a single narrative. This means that in such instances, where only fragments of letters or snippets of discussions have been used, the correspondents have not been mentioned by name.

Inevitably, the greatest number of those former Jaeger who wrote and told me of their experiences are not acknowledged. I regret this, but assure them all that their contributions were as vital to the writing of the book as were the accounts of those whose names are recorded.

To all those who sent photographs, maps and other memorabilia I am deeply grateful. In particular it is a pleasure to acknowledge the outstanding generosity of Oberst Busch, Reinhold Hoffmann, Rudi Hambuch, Michel Klein, Adolf Strauch, Hans Teske, Brian Davis and George Harper.

I am also grateful to those archives and museums, both here and in Germany, whose staff have been of outstanding help. To the staff of Arms & Armour Press; to Beryl, David and Tony, who produced a book from the typescript; and to my agents, Sheila Watson and Mandy Little, go also my sincere thanks for their skill and patience.

No work of mine can ever be begun or completed without the encouragement and support of my beloved wife Traude, whose help I acknowledge together with that of our eldest granddaughter, Victoria, who carried out a great deal of the research.

It is, however, to all ranks of the Fallschirmjaeger organization that my chief thanks go, for their comradeship and support in helping to produce this record of their service.

James S. Lucas London, 1988

Right: The author (right) with Paul Beck, who took him prisoner in April 1940 in Tunisia; here they meet again at a Para Reunion at Lich in 1986.

Preface

On a star-filled night in April 1943, I was one of a three-man reconnaissance patrol in the Oued Zarga hills of Tunisia. Lieutenant Sidney Keyes, the patrol leader, gave a sudden urgent hand-signal at which Corporal Gibson and I dropped to the dew-wet grass. Through the stillness of the night I heard our officer giving orders in German. He stopped and then called Gibson and me forward to where a figure was seated on a rock. It was an enemy soldier. His alert attitude suggested that he was still alive, but on closer inspection it was clear that he had been dead for some time. His right hand gripped tightly the upper part of his rifle barrel. His left arm was a prop that held him erect on the rock upon which he had died.

In the afternoon of the following day the Corporal and I went out again into the valley below the crest of Oued Zarga to bring back any documents which the dead German might have in his pockets. The corpse sat as we had seen him by starlight; head erect as if on the alert. There was no wound to show how he had died – no blood,

no torn clothing. From his attitude it was clear that this soldier had met death in those bleak and barren hills with complete calm and fearlessness. He must have died alone with no comrade to comfort him as he passed, for the identity disc was unbroken. Under his overcoat I noticed that the uniform jacket carried above the right breast pocket, not the standard, square winged Army eagle, but the more expressive and natural, free-flying Luftwaffe variant. His jacket shoulder straps were bordered in green. I was looking at the first German paratrooper I had ever seen.

Only weeks later a counter-attack launched by men of the 5th Fallschirmjaeger Regiment against my unit, 'C' Company of 1st Battalion, The Queen's Own Royal West Kent Regiment, killed, wounded or captured that Company. During our few weeks of captivity, for we were soon liberated, we prisoners talked a lot about the events of that particular morning; of the fury of the German attack and of the skill with which it had been carried out.

After Tunisia, I met the Fallschirmjaeger again. Not just in war-time situations in Italy, but more frequently, in post-war years, when groups of them visited me at the Imperial War Museum or when I attended their regimental reunions. The Fallschirmjaeger ex-Service Association is without doubt the best-organized and attended in Germany, for the loyalty, the comradeship, each to the other, which once bound those soldiers in war has been maintained undiminished across more than four decades of civilian life.

This book is the fulfillment of the long-held wish; to tell the story of the German airborne soldiers in their own words, since much of the narrative is from their letters or has been taken from conversations with them. To write this book has been a double pleasure. First, because the Fallschirmjaeger were an élite force who were given the hardest military tasks to perform and, as a consequence, have the most exciting stories to tell. Secondly, because these men have been my comrades for many decades now and what greater pleasure can there be for a writer than to describe the exciting stories of his friends?

Introduction
'WE WEAR THE STORMING EAGLE ON OUR TUNIC'

I n the autumn of 1935, Archibald Wavell, an officer of the British Army, attended the Red Army man-oeuvres in Soviet Russia. The report which he wrote at the end of those exercises included the sentence, 'If I had not seen it for myself, I should not have believed such a thing to be possible.' The military operation that had moved a highly experienced and much decorated soldier of the Great War to use such words was a combined, mass airborne one, the first that he had witnessed. What he had seen was 1,000 men dropping by parachute and the airlanding of transport planes carrying another 2,500 fully armed men together with their heavy weapons. These two types of airborne soldier had then carried out conventional infantry attacks covered by fire from machine-guns, mortars and light artillery.

These had not been the first Red Army manoeuvres in which airborne troops had been used. There had been earlier ones, but in those former operations small groups had been landed and had operated more in the role of commandos and less as standard infantry. The idea of placing a large body of troops inside enemy territory was not a new one. As early as 1918, Brigadier General Mitchell of the US Army had proposed that, to break the deadlock of the Western Front, parachute battalions should be raised and landed behind the German lines. Allied High Command calculated that the complexities of such unique operations would take six months to plan, organize and equip, for there were not enough aircraft immediately available to carry the paratroop battalions in a single lift, nor were there enough parachutes. The plan came to nothing and the Armistice of November 1918 brought the war to an end.

The idea of such operations then lay fallow for more than a decade until it was reactivated in the Soviet Union. By the autumn manoeuvres of 1935, the Red Army's progress in airborne techniques enabled it to carry out a combined mass parachute drop and an airlanding opera-tion. The Red Army had demonstrated that wars of the future would have a new dimension. To the former ones of depth and width was now added that of height. On future battlefields vertical envelopment would create another and very vulnerable flank which would need to be covered. In Western countries governmental cowardice in the face of vociferous pacifism cut the spending of money on modern weapons, on research and new military tech-niques. This was not the case in the dictatorships. In Russia, as we have seen, airborne warfare had been tested in theory and proved in practice. The Soviet airborne forces were expanded. In Nazi Germany the strategic possibilities of the new idea were quickly appreciated. Money was made available for research and instruction. Parachute training schools and research institutions had been set up by the end of 1936. There had been activity even earlier than that. Among those who advocated the formation of parachute units was one of the leaders of Hitler's new Germany, Hermann Goering. He had been an air-ace who had succeeded to the command of the élite von Richthofen squadron and had also been awarded the highest Prussian decoration, the Pour le Mérite. Goering was a man of talent, vigour and ability. In February 1933, in his capacity as Chief of the Prussian police, he ordered a Major Wecke of that Force, to raise a very special, law enforcement, anti-terrorist group. The establishment of 'Police Group Wecke' was fourteen officers and 400 men.

Wecke's group was soon in action and raided one of the principal headquarters of the illegal Communist Party. That initial success was followed up by a series of attacks upon other left-wing cells. A story, apocryphal but widely accepted as true, described the way in which Goering's unconventional methods of attack defeated the revolu-tionary groups. The Red Cells in inner city areas were protected by an elaborate screen of watchers who raised the alarm when numbers of police were seen in the nearby streets. As the result of the timely warning by the street watchers the revolutionary leaders could make good their escape or be safely hidden. Goering's method of defeating the Red watchers, it was said, was to land his policemen by parachute directly on to the houses in which the revolutionary cells were operating.

Wecke's unit and the successes it achieved earned it the

reputation of a crack formation and it was presented with its own Standard. Just before Christmas 1933, the name of the detachment changed to 'Provincial Police Group Goering' and then to 'General Goering Regiment'. Goering, who had been created Supreme Commander of the Luftwaffe and who was aware of the advances in airborne techniques which the Red Army had made, converted his élite police regiment to an Air Force one. In an order of 29 January 1936, he directed that one of its battalions be trained and equipped in a paratroop role so that it could serve as the cadre for a future airborne organization. In earlier years Goering had declared that it was his intention to produce from his Prussian police force a weapon '. . . equal to that of the Reichswsehr' (the German Armed Forces). That goal had been achieved and in the short time that had elapsed from the Nazi assumption of power in January 1933, Goering had transformed a group of provincial policemen into a crack regiment, one of whose battalions possessed parachuting skills, an ability unique at that time in the German armed forces. From such a small beginning was to develop the airborne arm of service, eleven Divisions strong, which began and ended as a volunteer Force.

At the end of January 1936, a Luftwaffe Paratroop Training School was set up on the Stendal-Bostel airfield and on 11 May 1936, Major Brauer commanding the 'Hermann Goering' parachute battalion became the first soldier of the German airborne arm to make a parachute descent. He was followed within weeks by other graduates of the Stendal school, but these did not jump from an aircraft wing as Brauer had done, but through the side doors of a transport aircraft, a method of exit which had been evolved and which, in time, became standard in the airborne units of most countries.

In contrast to the Luftwaffe, the German Army did not have as its Commander-in-Chief a man with the same drive as Goering, or with the same ease of access to the Fuehrer. It can, therefore, be understood why it was not until the spring of 1937, that Army High Command (OKH) obtained authority to create a Para Rifle Company. The Army had no para training establishment of its own; the soldiers were sent to the Luftwaffe school at Stendal.

In October 1936, a platoon of the 'Hermann Goering'

Below: A 'stick' of paras leaving a Ju 52 during a training flight. The picture is interesting because it shows the development of the unfolding of the canopy. (Brian L. Davis)

Para battalion carried out the first public demonstration of a paratroop drop during the autumn manoeuvres in Lower Saxony. The whole battalion was dropped at the 1937 manoeuvres, and the Army's Para Company also carried out a demonstration. The Army unit was expanded to battalion strength in June 1938. The anomalous situation in which two separate Service branches each controlled airborne troops was resolved during 1939, when an official order was published amalgamating the Army battalion with the Luftwaffe organization. An earlier start towards a common identity had been made when the Army pattern airborne proficiency badge was withdrawn at the end of 1938, and that of the Luftwaffe became the recognized emblem of a trained paratrooper.

It is interesting to note, at this point, the different concepts held by the Army and the Air Force High Commands as to the employment of airborne forces in war. The Army saw that role very much in the way that General Mitchell had proposed, that is the landing of a large body of men behind enemy lines who would carry out conventional infantry attacks in the enemy's rear. For that role the 22nd Infantry Division was selected and trained in airlanding operations.

The Luftwaffe concept was for the employment of small commando-type units which would attack and destroy special and important targets. Basing its training upon that framework, the Luftwaffe laid stress on military engineering skills, particularly in demolition techniques. When the two para arms of service amalgamated each submitted its evaluation of airborne techniques and employment to the Armed Forces High Command (OKW). That body then issued a Directive in 1938, of which the paragraphs given below are a summary. There were two types of airborne mission:

1. Strategic airlanding missions carried out in conjunction with the Army.

'The scope and execution of an airlanding operation depends upon both the military situation and the intention behind the operation. In addition to the air-landed troops other Luftwaffe units, fighters and fighter-

bombers are to be employed. This type of mission must be closely linked to Army operations. The Luftwaffe will be responsible for the preparation and execution of the battle plan as well as for air supply drops. The Army will only assume command of the airlanded formations once contact has been established between those men and our own ground forces.

2. Airlanding operations within the framework of a Luftwaffe mission.

'In this connection what is implied are sabotage or demolition units landed on to objectives which have been nominated by the Luftwaffe because it had not been possible totally to destroy or severely damage them by aerial bombardment.'

The difference in the tactical concepts of the Army and the Luftwaffe on the use of airborne troops was that the Army believed a point of maximum effort (Schwerpunkt) should be quickly established by means of a mass air-landing too large for the enemy to counter. The Luftwaffe proposal was known as the 'drops of oil' technique. In this,

simultaneous para drops, each of a small number of men, would combine to form perimeters which would threaten the enemy line at a number of places. Those perimeters, which offered the greatest potential for exploitation, would be reinforced and expanded until they had joined up to create the Schwerpunkt.

While the conceptual differences were being discussed there was a continuing expansion of the airborne force and amalgamations of its units until a point was reached at which the disparate groups needed to be formed into a single major formation. On 1 July 1938, the Luftwaffe High Command (OKL) ordered that the para, glider and air transport units under its command be formed into 7th Flieger Division. Tempelhof in Berlin became the headquarters for the new formation and Major-General Kurt Student was named as the commander. He was a tireless officer with great organizational ability whose ideas on the employment of airborne troops in a strategic capacity were revolutionary at that time.

Despite Student's drive and the fact that the building of

Left: Hitler's birthday parade, 20 April 1939: the new Fallschirmjaeger units march past. Shown here is the 1st Battalion with its colour. (Brian L. Davis)

Right: Major-General Kurt Student, shown here as a Colonel-General. First commander of the parachute arm, he was wounded in Holland; later he commanded Fliegerkorps XI in the Eastern Mediterranean. (Author's collection)

the German airborne force was pushed forward as quickly as possible, it had still not been possible to complete the raising of 7th Flieger Division, or complete the traning of Army's 22 (Airlanding) Division by the outbreak of war in September 1939.

At this point it is, perhaps, relevant to explain the distinction between the roles and purposes of these two formations. The 22nd was a standard Army infantry formation whose regiments would be brought in by air in Ju 52 machines. There were sufficient aircraft on the strength of 7th Flieger Division's Special Operations Air Transport Group to move 5,000 men in a single 'lift'. The operational method was for the Jus to carry units of the 22nd and land them on airfields behind enemy lines, which paratroops and/or glider units would have already captured and secured. Once the soldiers of the 22nd Division had deplaned they would capture their given objectives using standard infantry methods.

The airborne units of 7th Flieger Division would be landed by parachute or brought in by glider. The para-troops (Fallschirmjaeger), carried usually twelve in a JU 52, would be transported to the dropping zone and would there jump from the aircraft. As the drops were made from altitudes of between about 800–400 feet (250–120 metres), the method of exiting from the plane was for the soldier to throw himself forward in an almost horizontal dive, thereby achieving the optimum results; a quick opening of the canopy and reduced swing which would enable the parachutist to make a controlled descent. It was usual, in those early days, for the para rifleman to be armed only with a pistol and hand-grenades. Other weapons were carried in containers which were dropped at the same time as the troopers. The alternative method of bringing the airborne soldiers to an objective was by glider, usually the Gotha DFS 230, which carried either nine men or a thousand kilograms of supplies, ammunition or equipment.

Thus, the German airborne arm was made up of three types of unit: those which would drop on to the target area by parachute; others which would be carried to the objective by glider and, third, the airlanding regiments which would be brought to their objectives, usually enemy airfields, by transport aircraft.

The Order of Battle of 7th Flieger Division as at November 1938, was:

Divisional headquarters (Tempelhof)	Major-General Student, GOC
1st Battalion, 1st Parachute Rifle Regiment (Stendal)	Lieutenant-Colonel Brauer
Parachute Infantry Battalion (Braunschweig)	Major Heidrich
Air Landing Battalion, 'General Goering' (Berlin)	Major Sydow
Infantry Gun Company (Gardelegen)	First-Lieutenant Schram
Medical Company (Gardelegen)	Major Dieringshofen
Glider Detachment (Prenzlau)	Lieutenant Kiess
Signals Company (Berlin)	First-Lieutenant Schleicher
Training School (Stendal)	Major Reinberger
Air Transport Groups I and II	Captain Morzik

At the beginning of 1939, there was a complete reorganization of the airborne detachments. The loose framework that had hitherto sufficed needed to be replaced by a more formal establishment if 7th Flieger was to become a Division in the full sense of that term.

The establishment of a standard German Infantry or Rifle Division, was for three regiments, each of three battalions. The 7th Flieger had, at the beginning of 1939, only one regiment with one battalion. True, there were on divisional strength Heidrich's Para Infantry Battalion and Sydow's Airlanding Battalion of the 'General Goering Regiment', but these had not been formally established as part of the regiment. When that amalgamation was carried out Heidrich's had become the 2nd Battalion and Sydow's the 3rd Battalion of 1st Regiment. A headquarters was established and Brauer assumed command of the 1st Regiment. He was succeeded in the post of commander of 1st Battalion by Major von Grazy. With the formal establishment of the first of the Division's three regiments at last completed, work was then begun, in June 1939, on forming the 2nd Regiment and by the end of July, two battalions had been raised. With the prospect of a European war, efforts were made to complete the divisional establishment.

On 1 September 1939, the German Armed Force marched into Poland. The Second World War had begun. In that brief campaign neither 7th Flieger nor the 22nd Air Landing Divisions were used in the roles for which they had trained. To preserve the secret of a German airborne force, no parachute operation was carried out by any unit of 7th Division. There were, however, airlanding operations undertaken towards the end of the Polish campaign when 1st Battalion of 2nd Regiment was put down on the Deblin airfield and 2nd Battalion was landed on other airfields as well as near the Dukla Pass. In every case the missions were flown to speed the dissolution of the Polish Army and to prevent its senior officers from escaping by air to allied countries. Some units from 2nd Battalion 1st Regiment saw active service in the ground battles and it was in Poland, at Vola-Guloska, fighting against a Polish artillery regiment, that the first Fallschirmjaeger fell in action – the first of a great many.

1940

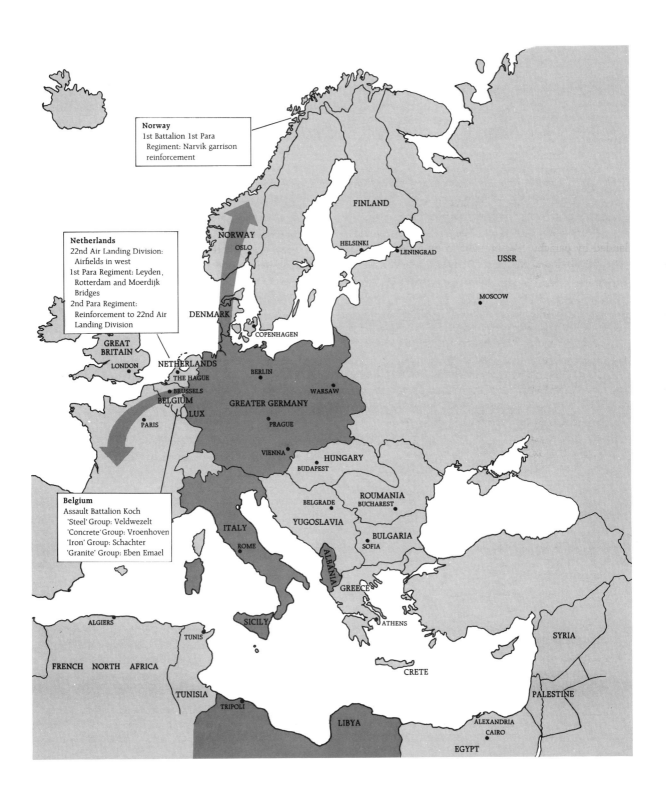

Norway
1st Battalion 1st Para
 Regiment: Narvik garrison
 reinforcement

Netherlands
22nd Air Landing Division:
 Airfields in west
1st Para Regiment: Leyden,
Rotterdam and Moerdijk
Bridges
2nd Para Regiment:
Reinforcement to 22nd Air
Landing Division

Belgium
Assault Battalion Koch
'Steel' Group: Veldwezelt
'Concrete' Group: Vroenhoven
'Iron' Group: Schachter
'Granite' Group: Eben Emael

FINLAND

HELSINKI

LENINGRAD

USSR

MOSCOW

NORWAY
OSLO

DENMARK

COPENHAGEN

GREAT
BRITAIN
LONDON

NETHERLANDS
THE HAGUE
BRUSSELS
BELGIUM
LUX

BERLIN

WARSAW

GREATER GERMANY

PRAGUE

PARIS

VIENNA

HUNGARY
BUDAPEST

ROUMANIA
BELGRADE
BUCHAREST

YUGOSLAVIA

BULGARIA
SOFIA

ITALY
ROME

ALBANIA

GREECE

ATHENS

ALGIERS

TUNIS

SICILY

SYRIA

FRENCH NORTH AFRICA

CRETE

PALESTINE

TUNISIA

TRIPOLI

LIBYA

ALEXANDRIA
CAIRO

EGYPT

1. The Northward thrust into Denmark and Norway
APRIL 1940

The airlanding operations which had been carried out in Poland in September 1939, were similar to those which had been undertaken in March, when Germany had invaded the rump of Czechoslovakia. In that mission three Jaeger battalions, together with the headquarters group of 7th Flieger Division, were airlanded at Prague aerodrome to suppress any opposition by the Czech Army to the German invasion. In the event there was none and a week later all the units returned to their bases in Germany. That use of airlanded battalions during the crisis aroused little if any comment. For years past many of the world's major military forces had deployed troops by that means. Britain had used aircraft to move troops in Iraq and Persia as had the French in North Africa, and Fascist Italy in Libya and Abyssinia.

From the end of the war with Poland in September 1939, there were no further German military operations until 9 April 1940 when the forces of the Third Reich attacked both Denmark and Norway.

Norway obsessed Hitler's mind. To capture it he launched a major operation and to hold it he committed huge numbers of men who might have been employed on either the Western or the Eastern Fronts. His attack in Scandinavia was prompted, perhaps, less by the need to secure Swedish iron ore deposits coming through the Norwegian port of Narvik, than to prevent Britain and France from outflanking Germany to the north – a threat which Hitler took very seriously indeed.

The consequence of the Fuehrer's obsession was Operation 'Weseruebung' a simultaneous attack upon both Denmark and Norway. There was to be the highest level of secrecy about the operation, particularly since much of the invasion force for Norway would be carried by ship through areas in which the submarines of the Royal Navy were known to operate. The German Navy would undertake a major strike against six of Norway's principal ports. At those places the Army units would be disembarked and would go into action against the Norwegian Army. Air superiority, another vital part of the battle plan, could be guaranteed by the Luftwaffe re-

deploying its squadrons. The capture of airfields in southern Norway would enable the Luftwaffe to operate against the central parts of that country, and in turn the occupation of the central parts would enable operations to be flown against the northern areas.

Everything depended upon the speedy capture of the airfields in Denmark and southern Norway and this task was given to Captain Walther's 1st Battalion of 1st Jaeger Regiment. A para drop would secure the airfields and on to them would land the Junkers aircraft carrying the airlanded contingents. Walther had four principal tasks to accomplish, two of which were in Denmark and the other two in Norway. They would also have to be undertaken more or less simultaneously.

The first operation was for Captain Gericke's No 4 Company to airdrop and capture the very long Stoerstrom bridge which linked the islands of Falster and Seeland at whose end was the capital, Copenhagen. It was Gericke's task to hold that bridge intact until German troops arrived. His sixty men dropped on each side of the bridge and within minutes it had been taken. The second part of the Danish operation was for a platoon to seize the airfield at Aalborg in the north of Denmark. The mission ran without fault. The detachment dropped and seized its objective within thirty minutes and less than two hours later the first Luftwaffe fighters were using Aalborg as a forward air base.

While, during that blustery April morning, Gericke's units were capturing their objectives in Denmark, Lieutenant von Brandis's No. 3 Company was *en route* to the Stavenger/Sola airfield in the west of Norway. The appalling weather, high wind and a low cloud ceiling, made the approach a hazardous one for both the transport pilots and the men who would jump. As the Ju 52s approached the airfield the cloud base was down to thirty feet. Suddenly the murk lifted to disclose clear skies and at correct operational height Brandis's Company jumped. They were met by small arms fire from defensive positions around the airfield perimeter and that opposition kept them from retrieving the weapons containers for more than half an hour. Junkers transports brought in the Army back-up units which went on to secure the area and the harbour.

Captain Walther, his battalion headquarters group and No. 2 Company of the 1st Battalion arrived over the Oslo-Fornebu airfield in conditions of poor visibility. At Fornebu there was to be no parachute air drop and the Junkers went straight in to land on the runway. Norwegian defensive fire forced the transports to abort the mission, but the pilots of the Messerschmitt aircraft, who had been strafing the field, landed and opened fire with their machine-guns. Under that fire the Junkers put down, the Company deplaned and went into action. Half an hour later the airfield was secured.

On 14 April, No. 1 Company of 1st Regiment dropped at Dombas intending to block the northern road through the hills and to hold it against a British Infantry Brigade which had landed at Aandalesnes and was striking southwards. Bad weather affected the outcome of the operation, forcing the aircraft to fly and drop the Jaeger from heights too low for their parachutes to open. Many were killed. The survivors took up defensive positions and held out for five days and nights, isolated and unsupported. At last, with all food and ammunition gone and with a growing number of casualties, Lieutenant Schmidt surrendered the remnants of his Company to the Norwegians.

The campaign in Norway had been the first active service test of the new Airborne force and it had proved itself. One single battalion had captured four, widely separated strategic objectives within a single day. The subsequent operation at Dombas, which had been a failure, could not detract from the victory which the Jaeger had gained. The campaign in Norway continued using Army ground forces and while they were fighting for the iron-ore railway at Narvik in the north of Norway, the great mass of the German Army was preparing to undertake a war in the West – Operation 'Gelb'.

Below: Fallschirmjaeger in the north of Norway: men of the 1st Battalion touch down to reinforce the Mountain Troops facing the Allies at Narvik in June 1940. (M. Klein)

Two dramatic views during the first seconds after exiting the aircraft. The parachute is about to be pulled open by the static line; the Fallschirmjaeger prepares himself for the shock of deceleration by spreading his limbs so that his body becomes horizontal and the harness can absorb the forces evenly. The crosses on the ground mark the target area. (Brian L. Davis)

2. I know a grave in Flanders...'
BELGIUM AND HOLLAND, MAY 1940

The role of the German airborne forces was vital to the successful opening moves of Operation 'Gelb', and it can be claimed that that success was dependent upon the fighting ability of fewer than 500 men, the soldiers of Assault Battalion Koch.

It must be explained that the German Army has always laid great emphasis upon assault or storm troops. Although each trained paratroop soldier of 7th Flieger Division was a physically and mentally fit fighting man, a conference of senior officers of the Airborne force, held in June 1939, concluded that there was a need for an assault unit within their élite Division. The senior commanders realized that there was a requirement for men willing to undertake operations involving the highest risk and that such men would need very special training and specialist equipment. Almost concurrent with the conclusion that a storm-troop élite was needed were the discussions on airborne tactics.

These were determined by the parachute's design which in turn was dictated by the low altitude at which the soldiers jumped. To reduce to a minimum the time spent hanging defenceless in the air, a canopy was needed that would open swiftly and land them quickly. The RZI-pattern chute, designed for and issued to the Fallschirmjaeger, opened automatically by means of a static line fitted inside the aircraft. To absorb the tremendous force produced when the canopy opened it was essential that when it did the soldier was horizontal in the air with legs and arms outspread. Failure to achieve this position might result in broken ribs. The exit position in the open door of the aircraft was with legs and arms apart and braced. A hefty push using hands and feet against the open door-frame forced the trooper out of the aircraft in the required position. Since both hands were needed to achieve the push, the soldier was unable to carry a weapon, but he had a pistol worn on his waist-belt. Rifles, machine-pistols and machine-guns were stowed in containers under the aircraft's wings and were dropped together with the troops. Thus, the Fallschirmjaeger were almost defence-less until they could retrieve the containers.

The time of greatest weakness for troops who had parachute landed was immediately after touchdown when they were scattered and before they had armed and grouped themselves into a fighting force. Under best possible conditions a stick of twelve paratroopers evacuating an aircraft in seven seconds, would be dispersed over an area of 900 square metres. Between leaving the plane and concentrating on the drop zone, so much time might be lost that the enemy could recover from the surprise assault and begin to react. Discussions at senior officer level determined the fact that in certain circumstances dispersal of the Fallschirmjaeger could result in failure of the mission. Clearly what was needed was for the entire detachment to be carried directly to the target and landed as a single, concentrated force. The carrier could only be an aircraft's fuselage, but not that of a conventional aircraft because they were noisy, expensive, of robust, metal construction and had too high a landing speed. The solution was the silent, cheap, glider. These were easy to assemble, had low landing speeds and flimsy walls which could be quickly torn open for a speedier exit. There were a great many civilian glider clubs in Germany and from the best pilots of these clubs a Luftwaffe glider detachment was formed and taken on to the divisional establishment.

In November 1939, acting upon the need for a glider-borne élite force, Luftwaffe High Command grouped three airborne units into a specialist detachment whose true role was concealed under the name, 'Test Section Friedrichshafen'. The principal components of the 'Test Section' were No. 1 Company of 1st Battalion, 1st Para Regiment; the Pioneer Platoon of 2nd Battalion, 1st Para Regiment; and a glider group. The 'Test Section' was commanded by Captain Koch, with Lieutenants Witzig and Kiess leading the Pioneer Platoon and the Glider Section respectively. The unit name was changed within months to 'Assault Battalion Koch'.

With the campaign in Poland concluded and antici-pating correctly, the rejection by the Western Allied governments of his peace offers, Hitler decided, as early as

9 October 1939, that a campaign in the West should begin on 12 November. His Generals made him realize that such a demand at such short notice was unfeasible. Nevertheless, throughout the winter of 1939–40, there were frequent alarms and massive troop movements. In every case Hitler, who had demanded that an operation be launched, was also the man who cancelled it. But his intention was clear. He was determined to destroy France and Great Britain.

The eastern frontier of France was protected for much of its length by a vast complex of permanent defences, the Maginot Line, and the training of Koch Battalion was directed towards the task of creating and exploiting breaches in fixed defences of that pattern. In the Adler Mountains of Czechoslovakia there were Maginot-type fortifications and it was upon these that the Assault Battalion practised ground attacks using conventional explosives. In other parts of Germany Koch's glider pilots were undergoing training that would enable the whole group to land their machines in an area little larger than that of a tennis-court.

At Supreme Command level the forthcoming campaign was being planned. The first proposal put forward was that Army Group 'B' attack westwards through Holland and Belgium and reach a point in its advance from which it could drive southwards into France. During that southern strike Army Group 'A' would enter the battle and the combined force of both Army Groups would drive the Allied armies back on to the guns of Army Group 'C'. This first plan was in essence a re-run of the 1914 Schlieffen Plan in which the main thrust or Schwerpunkt was in the Low Countries and the subsequent thrust-line was north/south, from Flanders down to the Somme.

During the planning stage the Chief of Staff of Army Group 'A', General von Manstein, proposed an alternative Schwerpunkt and thus an alternative thrust-line. The attack in Holland and Belgium would be retained, but this would be the secondary and not the principal strike. The main drive would go in from the Ardennes and the thrust-line would be east/west from the Ardennes to the Channel. Manstein anticipated that the Allies would react to early German moves in Holland and Belgium by sending their best units northwards to meet what they would see as the German main attack. Therefore, Manstein's proposed thrust through the Stenay Gap in the Ardennes would be made out of an area from which the Allies would anticipate no attack and would meet only the limited

Right: Practising the parachute roll. Since the parachutist had no control over the parachute, his landing was also uncontrolled. The jarring effect of landing in this way could result in broken bones, even on flat ground, so the parachutist had to absorb the impact throughout the length of his body. All paratroops have had to learn this technique: a carefully timed roll at the very moment of landing. (Brian L. Davis)

opposition of second-line units. These would be brushed aside and through the rupture which had been made in the French line von Kleist's Panzer Group (or Army) would head westwards to gain the Channel ports. This Panzer drive would pass behind the Allied armies in Flanders and Holland and would separate them from the forces positioned south of the Somme. The Franco-British armies in Belgium would first be crushed between Army Groups 'A' and 'B', and when that had been accomplished the German host would go on to drive the remaining Allied forces towards Army Group 'C'.

Manstein's daring plan was not at first accepted by his superiors who pointed out that the Ardennes was difficult country with a network of poor, secondary roads. His plan was saved by the fact that Hitler accepted it and backed it. The reluctant acceptance by OKW of the plan determined the use of both airborne and airlanded units in the forthcoming operation in the west. His westward thrust would be made by a massed Panzer force whose northern flank would be covered by Sixth Army, a mainly infantry force. Nothing must impede the south-westerly drive by that Army if it were to keep pace with the Panzers. But in the path of Sixth Army lay the strong Belgian fortress complex – Eben Emael – whose guns dominated the Albert Canal bridges across which Sixth Army must pass. It was imperative that the fortress and the bridges be taken. If they were not, Sixth Army would be held up and the northern flank of the Panzer force would be open to an enemy counter-thrust. The Belgian objectives must be taken in a swift assault and this could only be an airborne operation.

Colonel-General von Bock, commanding Army Group

'B', then produced a demand for airborne operations in Holland. In his opinion the German attack upon the Netherlands would result in a British sea-borne landing on the coast of Flanders. If the British advance reached Antwerp the Dutch Army would be reinforced. To prevent that link-up von Bock demanded that the bridges across the Diep and in the area of Moerdijk, Rotterdam and Dordrecht be seized quickly. The speediest method of assault was a parachute drop and the Fallschirmjaeger must hold their objectives until relief arrived. To ensure that the lightly armed airborne detachments were not too long isolated, von Bock strenghtened Eighteenth Army by posting to it the 9th Panzer Division. He was also aware that the Dutch heartland, 'Fortress Holland', would be protected by a combination of flooding and permanent defences and that to fight a way through those obstacles might take so much time that the British/Dutch link-up might be achieved. Von Bock's demand increased the number of tasks which the Airborne would have to undertake. In addition to the bridges to be captured, other para units would drop and seize airfields in the west of Holland where 22nd Division would be airlanded. A strong German force would, therefore, have vaulted both the Peel defence lines and the water obstructions and would be firmly established inside the 'Fortress Holland'. A landing so close to the Dutch capital would also lead to the capture of the Royal family and the government who would be held hostage for the good behaviour of the population.

To summarize the situation: in order that the opening moves of the war in the west succeeded, units of 7th Flieger and 22nd Air Landing Divisions would be used. The vital task of capturing the fortress of Eben Emael and of seizing the Albert Canal bridges would be undertaken by Koch's Assault Battalion. It was upon the success of that unit's 500 men that the timing of the German war in the west depended. Once Koch's battalion had gone into action there would be para drops over the Dutch targets leading to the capture of bridges and of airfields. On to the latter the 22nd Division would be brought in.

Of all the objectives the capture of Eben Emael was the most important. It stood on a 150-foot-high ridge, protected to the east and north-east by the River Maas and the Albert Canal. On its southern and south-westerly sides it was defended by anti-tank ditches and field fortifications. The fortress guns, many set in retractable, rotating cupolas, dominated the area for miles around. It was the one objective which had to be taken without fail. If it were not, the German battle plan would be jeopardized. So vital, indeed, was the capture of Eben Emael and the adjacent bridges that it was not until five minutes after the gilders had touched down that the

general assault by the German Army would begin. Not until thirty minutes after the landings at Eben Emael and the Albert Canal would the airborne operations in Holland open.

High Command having produced a battle plan, then passed its orders down the chain of command to the subordinate units. General Student, commanding 7th Flieger Division, received his. These read, in part, that the principal task of his Division was to '. . . enable Sixth Army to pass without delay . . .' It was a key sentence repeated, indeed emphasized, in every set of orders and at every conference. Although Koch's battalion was not told exactly where it would carry out its part of the operation, the officers and men now knew that they were training to attack a specified and vital objective; their intensive training had had a definite purpose. In the early spring of 1940, the paratroops and the glider pilots carried out joint exercises, perfecting their skills in conditions of total secrecy. Glider practice was carried out in the Hildesheim area and when the training exercises had been completed the machines were broken down and taken away in furniture vans. All the sub-units of the battalion underwent frequent moves and changes of name to confuse enemy Intelligence agents. From the first days unit badges and distinctive insignia had been removed, no leave was permitted for any reason and the troops were forbidden to leave the barracks. Utmost secrecy was essential.

The Eben Emael operation would depend upon the glider pilots being able to land the eleven machines of the group, more or less simultaneously, on to a very small area. During training it had been established that the glider landing run was too long and this was reduced by barbed wire wrapped round the nose-skid. So proficient were the pilots that they were soon able to bring their machines to within twenty yards of a given objective. Each glider would carry a group of 7–8 men, armed with a variety of equipment, including flame-throwers and special explosives. These latter were so secret that they were only tested upon fortifications at Gleiwitz in Germany and not upon the Czech forts.

Let us see the Eben Emael objective as the glider troops saw it. The assault teams would have landed on what was the roof of the diamond-shaped fortress complex, an area only 800 yards (900 metres) long and 650 yards (700 metres) wide. This was covered with artillery positions, some fitted with short-range guns for local defence and others for long-range fire. There were also well-designed, all-round fortifications of pillbox design along the 13 foot (4 metre) wall surrounding the fortress. On the north-eastern side of the complex a cliff 130 feet (40 metres) deep dropped sheer into the Albert Canal and gave complete protection against a conventional attack from

Right: One of the 7.5cm gun cupolas at the fortress of Eben Emael. (M. Klein)

that direction. To the north-west the ground might be flooded and if it were the ground assault would have to be made through water and mud against bunkers which would be set on higher ground.

The ground beneath the fort was honeycombed with tunnels connecting individual turrets to the command centre, the hospital, the living-quarters and the ammunition stores. A power-station provided the electricity to work the guns, to provide illumination, to power the wireless network and to work the air-purifying system. The Belgian garrison was said to number 2,000 men.

The para detachment whose task it was to be to take out this major objective was headed by two officers, Witzig and his second in command Delica, with 83 rank and file, of whom eleven were glider pilots. After landing these would form part of the ground assault teams. In addition to the conventional explosives in general Service use, Witzig's Pioneer platoon was equipped with the secret explosive devices mentioned above. These were hollow-charge grenades in two weights. The 50kg charge, which could bite through 25cm of armour plate and the 12.5kg charge which was especially effective against gun barrels.

The chief problem which Witzig's group would face was time. Although there would be no declaration of war to warn the Belgian authorities and although it was antici-pated that the noiseless approach of the gliders swooping out of the dawn sky would give the attackers the advantage of surprise, this would last at the most 60 minutes. Thereafter, the enemy's growing strength both inside and outside the fort would come into play. The German plan was to take out within that short period of one hour all infantry anti-aircraft positions, and as many as possible of the twenty individual cupolas or artillery positions and to block all entrances and exits to the subterranean areas. But at all costs, the long-range guns which dominated the bridges to the north and south had to be put out of action. The most vital period of that 60-

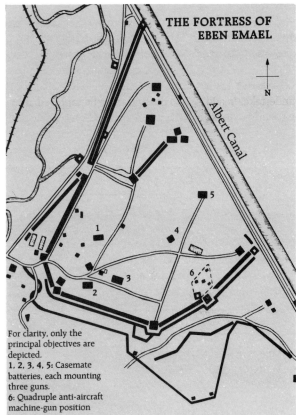

THE FORTRESS OF EBEN EMAEL

Albert Canal

N

For clarity, only the principal objectives are depicted.
1, 2, 3, 4, 5: Casemate batteries, each mounting three guns.
6: Quadruple anti-aircraft machine-gun position

minute advantage was the first ten minutes. Destruction of the guns was expected to be virtually complete within ten minutes – 600 seconds. Inside that time the individual Troops had to break out of their gliders, orientate themselves, cover the distance to their principal targets, fix the heavy charges in position and detonate them. Before the 9-second fuzes had detonated the Troop would be in action against their second objective. It was upon the depth and extent of their intensive training that the mission depended.

Once Eben Emael had been taken Witzig's group was to hold it until relieved by the Engineer Battalion of 151st

Infantry Regiment, which would cross the Albert Canal at Canne.

Koch's orders to Witzig's group, code-named 'Granite', were direct '... you will put out of action the armoured cupolas ... destroy the enemy's resistance and defend the gains you have made until relieved'. Three other detachments of Koch's battalion were to drop and land at the same time to seize the Albert Canal bridges at Veldwezelt, Vroenhoven and Canne. Those groups were code-named 'Steel', 'Concrete' and 'Iron'.

The battalion, for reasons of security, lay dispersed in its several locations in the Rhineland area. During the evening of 9 May preliminary orders were received which put the detachments on to full war alert and ordered them to concentrate. Shortly after the groups had arrived in their concentration area a second message arrived. Operation 'Gelb' was to begin at 05.25 on 10 May.

The battalion took off from Cologne's two principal airfields at 04.30 hours. In the darkness of the May night 42 gliders carrying 493 officers and men, were lifted off and shortly after the armada of towing planes and gliders was airborne it swung out on a southerly course to gain height. Once the correct altitude had been reached the aircraft took up attack formation and began the approach run to the objective. Strict radio silence had been ordered. This meant that the crews of the tug aircraft received no navigational directions but followed instead a chain of fires pointing westwards towards Belgium. The strict radio silence also meant that the senior airborne commanders could not be told that the tow-ropes on two gliders had snapped. One of the luckless pair of machines was carrying Witzig and the Reserve Troop, the men who would exploit gains made, who would reinforce a detachment that had suffered heavy loss or who would restore momentum to a failing assault. The second glider was carrying his No. 2 Troop.

In both cases the tow-rope had broken during the wide southward sweep, and as neither glider had gained sufficient height to reach the target area they were put down as quickly as possible inside Germany. Witzig had his group transferred to a new glider. Another towing aircraft was found and the young commander's detachment flew westwards, towards the objective.

Hidden in the pre-dawn darkness the armada of gliders was cast off at 7,000 feet, an altitude sufficient for them to cover the twenty miles to the objectives. The towing aircraft climbed, banking steeply, taking a course eastwards back to the airfields from which they had set off less than an hour earlier. The gliders had been cast off this distant from the target area so that the noise of aircraft engines would not alert the Belgians.

When their tow-ropes were slipped the gliders dipped suddenly and began to fall but were corrected to bring them to the trim of a 1 in 12 dive, sufficient to carry them to the Albert Canal. Near the target a steeper angle was chosen and swooping out of the lightening eastern sky the gliders of Koch's battalion, partially shrouded in the dawn mist of a beautiful spring day, reached their objectives.

The black gliders swooped down one after the other and touched down. An alert sentry manning the quadruple anti-aircraft machine-gun position, Objective No. 29, situated in the south-eastern sector of the diamond, opened fire as the gliders skidded past him across the small grassy area of the roof of the fortress.

As each of the gliders reached the end of its run the order was given 'Doors open. Cockpit cover away!' and the

Left: Part of the fortresses of Eben Emael after its capture by Witzig's 'Granite' group. Flamethrowers have left evidence of their effectiveness. (M. Klein)

Troops broke out of the fuselage doors to begin their first attacks. A fast assault against Objective No. 29, still the only Belgian post in action, was quickly successful. The belief that its guns had been neutralized proved false when the Belgian defencers manned them again and re-entered the battle. For a second time the position was attacked and to prevent any resurgence of Belgian opposition the quadruple-mounted guns were blown up.

It had been anticipated that 'Granite' would have an hour before Belgian reaction became serious and that the first ten minutes of that hour would be the crucial ones. Within those ten minutes the nine Troops of the 'Granite' group, no more than 55 men in all, attacked and destroyed a number of objectives. There were two main concentrations of defences: in the north and in the south of the complex. The fighting to take out those objectives was carried out by two individual groups of Fallschirmjaeger, each of which was working to its own schedule, almost independent of the other. In the absence of Lieutenant Witzig, control of the entire group was exercised by Lieutenant Delica who led in the south. Command of the northern group was with Sergeant Wenzel, who gained there his reputation as the 'cupola smasher of Eben Emael'.

It is possible to describe the course of the fighting of that first intense hour only by detailing what each Glider/Troop did. Remember, all that is described in the following paragraphs happened simultaneously. Consider also that that in that first hour at Eben Emael a military revolution occurred with the adding of a vertical flank to battlefield dispositions. The concepts of warfare were changed and the events of that day in May 1940, ushered in the era of the highly skilled, SAS-type, all-round warrior of today's army.

Glider No. 1, carrying Lieutenant Delica's Troop, came to a halt within yards of Objective No. 18, an artillery observation casemate fitted with three 75mm guns. This was a main target for it was the closest turret to the fort's Command Centre. The young Para lieutenant crippled one of the guns with a light charge, and the detonation of a 50kg charge placed on the roof of the objective smashed both it and the observation dome completely. The fortress had lost one of its eyes.

Glider No. 3 – it will be remembered that Glider No. 2 was one of the pair which had broken its tow-rope – attacked and destroyed Objective No. 12, a pair of 12cm guns mounted in a traversing turret. Objective No. 26, in the east of the complex, and fitted with three 75mm guns, was attacked by the Troop of No. 5 Glider, but the Paras did not completely destroy the position and within minutes one of the three guns was back in action and had opened fire. No. 5 Troop broke off the attack they had been making against their secondary objective and

smashed the defiant gun. Objective No. 26 was now dead.

The Troop in No. 8 glider took out two targets in the south-eastern sector of the fortress: Objective 31, a pair of 75mm guns in a retractable cupola and Objective No. 25, a barracks occupied by men of the Belgian garrison. The target, known as Objective No. 24, occupied a dominant position in the southern central sector. It was a twin turret with 12cm guns mounted in a rotating cupola and was considered to be too large for a single Troop to destroy. A combined force from gliders 6 and 7 were put in to take it. Assault sections from each of the two Troops raced forward and under covering fire, fixed hollow-charge grenades on the armoured dome. The force of these, powerful though they were, could not destroy the huge metal disc, but they shook the garrison and while the concussion held the Belgian soldiers inactive, other Paras from Nos. 6 and 7 Troops attacked and smashed the gun barrels.

While these actions were being carried out against the southern concentration of guns, similar scenes were being repeated in the north. Objective No. 13, the target of No. 9 Troop, consisted of a casemate holding multiple machine-guns whose arc of fire covered the defences along the whole western side of the fortress. The Fallschirmjaeger team deputed to destroy it used a flame-thrower to force back the Belgian soldiers from the pillbox embrasures. Covered by the arc of fire other men of the assault team charged forward and smashed the armour turret with a 50kg charge. The Troop in Glider No. 4, went in against and destroyed Objective 19, whose observation cupola was fitted with machine-guns. Objectives 15 and 16, the other two principal targets in the northern half of the complex, were found to be dummy installations.

Within ten minutes of the gliders touching down inside the walls of Eben Emael the principal objectives, both in the south and in the north, had been taken in one fierce blaze of conquest. An unexpected complication then arose. It had not been thought necessary to take out Objective 23, a pair of 75mm guns set in a retractable cupola, for it had not been considered that the fire from those guns could affect the progress of the attack. That assumption was soon shown to be false for the guns of Objective 23 opened fire and their rapid bombardment forced the Paras to take cover. Excellent wireless communication between Lieutenant Delica and a Stuka squadron soon brought the Ju 87s screaming down and although no direct hit was scored the bomb explosions caused the Belgians to retract the cupola and to keep it retracted throughout the rest of the fighting.

It will be recalled that the Para officers planning the operation had considered that the surprise assault might give Witzig's force a 60-minute advantage. Thereafter,

Left: Sergeant Wenzel's detachment of 'Granite' Group. Wenzel, with bandaged head, was reported to have sat astride the gun barrels of the fortress, stuffing explosives down the barrels. (M. Klein)

Left and **below left**: Witzig's 'Granite' group return in triumph to the Assault Battalion's headquarters in Maastricht, on 11 May 1940. (M. Klein)

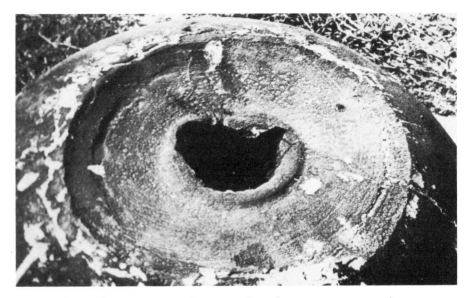

Right: Stark witness to the power of hollow-charge grenades: a crater and hole punched through one of the cupolas. All the occupants would inevitably have been killed or injured by the blast and by the whirling fragments of metal and concrete in the confined cupola. (M. Klein)

Belgian reaction would increase against the small German group. Those projections proved correct. Belgian resistance did grow but it was too late. Within the 60 projected minutes the principal and secondary tasks of 'Granite' Group had been accomplished. The main armament of the fortress had been put out of action. Subsequent and unco-ordinated Belgian counter-moves were limited initially, to sporadic artillery fire from guns within the fortress area; of nuisance value only and not strong enough to affect the passage of Sixth Army across the Albert Canal. Not that Sixth Army had yet reached the canal. Away to the east, on the river Maas, Belgian engineers had destroyed three vital bridges across that river and well-directed arillery fire was holding the German advance in check. Until all-out assault forced the Maas or until bridges had been built, Sixth Army could not advance westwards.

Meanwhile Altmann's 'Steel' Group landed and took out the bridge at Veldwezelt, Schacht's detachment 'Concrete', captured that at Vroenhoeven. In both cases surprise had been total and the bridges were captured intact. At Canne, however, Schaechter's 'Iron' detachment had the frustration of seeing the target destroyed before it could be taken. The failure to seize that bridge intact, the nearest one to Eben Emael, caused the attackers most concern. Not only had it been blown, but the Belgian defenders put up a desperate resistance throughout the day and flung back the many efforts of 51st Engineer Battalion to cross the Albert Canal and relieve the 'Granite' assault group. The staunch defence of the Belgians at Canne was supported by the defenders in Eben Emael's No. 17 blockhouse, who poured enfilading fire into the Engineer

Battalion's assault craft attempting to cross the waterway.

At Eben Emael the attack had succeeded brilliantly. Thanks to the high standards of training the loss of the two gliders, although a serious blow to 'Granite' was not a disastrous one. All the troops had been trained to take over the tasks of any other Troop. Flexibility – the keyword in the intensive training – was needed at Eben Emael in the first daylight hour of that May day.

The relief which had been promised to Koch's units was thus delayed. At Vroenhoven, and in Veldwezelt where the assault groups had created small bridgeheads, heavy machine-gun teams had been parachuted in at H-Hour plus 40. Together with the original attackers the reinforcements fought off the Belgian infantry assaults until, during the afternoon, men of 51st Engineer Battalion having forced a crossing of the Maas followed this with a swift advance up to the east bank of the Albert Canal.

Meanwhile, Belgian opposition from outside the fortress was growing and was causing concern. Then Witzig's glider landed at 08.30 hours and his arrival was timely. There is a phase during every battle when the nervous tension which has animated the soldiers at the outset begins to ebb. It is then that a galvanizing force is needed to re-inspire the flagging spirits. Witzig supplied that energy and under his direction patrols were soon in action dominating the Belgian garrison and holding its soldiers confined within the shattered galleries of the fort. Other Para groups beat back the Belgian infantry attacks against the north-western sector of the fortress many of which were made without proper artillery support. Those assaults were soon crushed by the machine-gun fire of 'Granite' Group. The one objective which Witzig's force had been unable to destroy was No. 17, a machine-gun and searchlight position which, as stated earlier, had sup-

Left: Recruits were taught to pack their own parachutes: the safety of the drop thus depended upon their own skill. Made of light, soft silk, which would unfold easily from the pack, parachutes were normally of a 'natural white' colour, and the belief grew among the Fallschirmjaeger that coloured 'chutes (which were used for canisters) inhibited opening. Here parachutes are being packed, while others hang ready in order to prevent tangling. (Brian L. Davis)

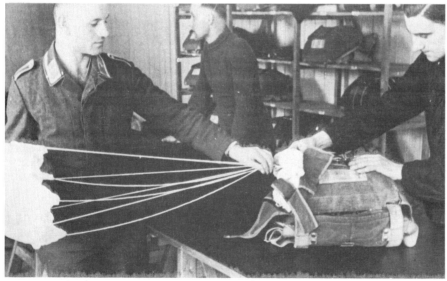

Left: Packing the parachute. The static line tugged the parachute from the pack; the consequent delay in opening resulting from the length of the static line gave time for the parachutist to drop well away from the aircraft so that the 'chute would not be fouled by the tail of the Junkers. (Brian L. Davis)

ported the Canne bridge defenders, and had forced the 51st Engineer Battalion to make its crossing of the Albert Canal via a smaller bridge north of Canne. With the relief of Witzig's group at 07.00 hours on 11 May, the operations mounted by Koch's battalion were at an end and it had contributed to the German Army's successes in the opening moves of Operation 'Gelb'.

To complete the story of the German airborne assault in the west, we must go back to the morning of 10 May, and to the mass of 1st Para Regiment which had emplaned on airfields in the Dortmund, Muenster and Paderborn areas of Westphalia to undertake the assaults in Holland. Take-

off was timed so that the Ju 52s arrived over their drop zones some 30 minutes after Koch's battalion had landed on its Belgian objectives. It will be recalled that the task of the airborne forces in northern Holland was to leap over the Peel defences and reach 'Fortress Holland', while other detachments were to speed the advance of Eighteenth Army. To ensure the success of these separate missions units from both 7th Flieger Division and 22nd Air Landing Division were to be employed. Some para groups of 1st and 2nd Regiments were to be dropped to seize a number of important bridges between Leyden and Rotterdam and to hold those until 9th Panzer Division and the

Leibstandarte SS 'Adolf Hitler' reached the bridges, and relieved them. Meanwhile other groups from the two Fallschirmjaeger regiments would drop and seize a number of airfields on to which the divisional back-up groups and the bulk of 22nd Division would land.

Captain Prager's 2nd Battalion of 1st Para Regiment dropped, landed and seized the Moerdijk bridge, beating down opposition from its Dutch defenders in a short but intensive fire-fight. The regiment's 1st Battalion, commanded by Captain Walther, those target was the bridge at Dordrecht, captured it before the Dutch had had time to blow it, but suffered heavy casualties in the action. The 3rd Battalion of 1st Para Regiment dropped and captured the Waalhoven aerodrome near Rotterdam and then the bridge across the Maas.

During the course of 10 May, reinforcements from 2nd Battalion of 2nd Para Regiment were airlanded on the Waalhoven aerodrome together with anti-tank, anti-aircraft and light artillery units which went into action in support of the hard-pressed Para perimeters at Moerdijk, Dordrecht and Rotterdam.

The anti-tank unit, a single Company, had been formed only in June 1939, and had been unable to find prime movers. There was nothing in the German Army's vehicle lists small enough to be carried in the Ju 52 and yet powerful enough to tow the guns. Attempts were made to use motor cycle combinations, but these had proved unsatisfactory. It seemed as if there were no other solution than for the crews to tow the pieces into action. Stories have been wide-spread that the Paras used dogs, ponies or small horses, but there is no evidence in the post-battle reports to support this claim, and the Anti-tank Company went to war without having found a solution to its problems.

Below: Ground training for the Fallschirmjaeger recruits laid emphasis on correct 'exiting' from the open doorway of the Ju 52. Note in this illustration the static lines of those who had already jumped; also the heavy gauntlets and the side-laced boots. (Brian L. Davis)

Below: Unlike the parachutes used by Allied paratroops, the German chutes suspended the wearer by one single support point, which meant that he could not reach the rigging lines and control his attutude during descent except by a sort of swimming motion using the arms and legs. (Brian L. Davis)

During the morning of 10 May 1940, Major Goetzel's Anti-tank Company, equipped with the 3.7cm Pak, paraded on the airfield at Paderborn waiting to be flown into Holland with 22nd Division's second-wave units. During the long hours of waiting the airborne men saw that the Jus which had flown the first wave into Wallhaven were marked with bullet holes and had shrapnel tears in their fuselages and wings. It was clear that the receptions they would receive upon touchdown in Wallhaven would be a lively one. Eventually the waiting Para gun crews and the infantry of 22nd Division embarked and the armada took off, but the aircraft had barely covered half the distance to the target when a wireless message recalled them. Divisional Headquarters had learned that the target airfield had not been captured and the senior officers were unwilling to risk more men until the situation improved. After two hours of waiting on Paderborn airfield the 'all clear' was given and for a second time the Jus headed westward in a cloudless blue sky.

'From the small windows of our transport we could see some of the air activity connected with this first operational mission by airborne troops. On either side there were the Jus of our group holding formation with our machine. On either flank, as well as above and below us,

we had fighter escort. Then a long chain of Jus passed us, heading eastwards, flying back to their start 'dromes to load up and to bring in more men. Whole squadrons of fighters roared back to refuel and to return to the battle and still higher above us were machines which were identified as He IIIs. I had never seen so impressive a demonstration of German air power. It was a most emotional experience.'

Touchdown brought reality. Waalhaven airfield was under artillery fire and was being constantly raided by RAF bombers flying at low level. Under the spur of bombardment from the air and from heavy guns, every attempt was made to unload the transports quickly, but the removal of such bulky pieces as the Pak took time and while these were being unloaded another air raid came in during which two of the guns were knocked out and the Company suffered its first casualties. In addition to these losses, eight of the 32 transports of the second wave, which had landed on Wallhaven airfield, were destroyed on the ground.

The Pak Company was a divisional unit, to be deployed where the Commander felt its guns would be most effective. The guns were towed, using captured Dutch trucks as prime movers, to the school in the south of Rotterdam where Student had set up his headquarters.

Left: On the road to Waalhaven, a member of the reconnaissance group who has looted a bicycle waits by the side of the road for orders to advance. (M. Klein)

Right: Fallschirmjaeger with an MG 34. This light machine-gun was replaced by the MG 42 later in the war. (M. Klein)

The situation in which the 7th and 22nd were placed was not good. Although 3rd Battalion of 1st Regiment had finally captured Wallhaven airfield, thus allowing reinforcements to be brought in, the attacks by elements of 22nd Division and two battalions of 2nd Regiment to the north of Rotterdam had failed with heavy loss. The best efforts of the troops in that sector had failed to seize the airfield which was their objective, but the flexibility of the German Command system was demonstrated when, taking advantage of the numerous canals and waterways, troops were flown in seaplanes to land near an island on the Maas near Rotterdam. These seaplane-landed units quickly set up a bridgehead, extended it and went on to assault and capture the airfield north of the city. Student sent out one anti-tank gun northwards into Rotterdam and this was soon in action – not against tanks – but firing at Dutch motor torpedo-boats which had entered the battle. Another Pak gun was sent off to strengthen the defence of the Maas island where the seaplanes had landed.

During 12 May, the Dutch Light Division, one of the élite formations of that country's army, arrived from the Peel defence positions in the east of Holland where it had been obstructing the advance of Eighteenth Army. The Dutch plan was that the Light Division should return quickly to Rotterdam and smash the isolated airborne units quickly before returning to the Peel Line to take up its post in the Dutch main defence system. Powerful attacks by the battalions of this very competent formation began to drive in the German perimeters and the Dutch success posed a serious threat to the airborne divisions. The greatest threat was to the bridge at Moerdijk and, on 14 May, Student assembled a battle group and sent this down to strengthen the perimeter there. Two and a half Companies, which were all the Jaeger he could spare, moved by truck, together with six mountain guns and three anti-tank guns, up to the start-line of their attack. The battle group arrived to find heavy fighting in progress and the units at Moerdijk at the end of their strength. The group roared forward in support.

The guns were unlimbered and went immediately into action. Covered by their fire the Jaeger fought their way forward against the Dutch opposition and the fury of the battle only died away at last light. Reinforcement to the perimeter came in during the night of 14/15 May, and with that support the Moerdijk garrison was able to fight off the attacks of a new Dutch formation which had entered the fight mounted on bicycles. The airborne men, who had landed on 10 May and had been continually in action, were by this time totally exhausted and short of

ammunition. Their part in the operation was soon to end for relief was at hand. In the early afternoon of 18 May, a reconnaissance group of armoured cars and tanks, the advance guard of Eighteenth Army, rolled into the battle zone and with their support the Dutch were finally forced back. As more and more German units arrived, the Moerdijk perimeter grew in size until the whole of the southern area of the city had been captured, and where Dutch resistance flared, it was beaten down by the Panzers and the, now, highly mobile Pak of Goetzel's Company. There had been little opportunity for the weapons to be used against Dutch armoured fighting vehicles, but firing high-explosive shells they had acted as close-support artillery to the Jaeger units. Their losses had not been light. Five of the gun commanders were among the men who had been killed during the short campaign in Holland.

As we have seen, the operations carried out by 1st Para Regiment were everywhere successful while those which had been initiated by units of 2nd Regiment were almost everywhere a disaster. In several cases this was the fault of the Ju 52 pilots who had failed to identify the correct dropping zones around the airfields and had dropped the Paras instead over areas which were strongly defended.

Captain Noster's three Companies, which should have parachuted in and captured both Valkenburg and Ypern-berg airfields, had been dropped too far away from their objectives and had not been able to capture them.

Lieutenant von Roon's Company, which should have parachuted over Ockenburg, was dropped at the Hook of Holland, and only one platoon managed to fight its way to the objective and capture a small part of the airfield. The Dutch fought hard and skilfully and opened fire upon the follow-up aircraft bringing in 22nd Air Landing Division. As the Jus made their approach runs they were raked with machine-gun and shellfire which drove off most and which left others wrecked or ablaze. In view of that failure the plan to capture the Dutch Royal family and government could not succeed.

There was to begin with a limited success at Katwijk where the men of No. 6 Company of 2nd Regiment seized the airfield and were followed in by units of the 22nd Division. That gain was slight and of brief duration. Dutch

Above: Student (in soft cap), Koch (to his left) and Witzig (behind him) congratulate officers and men of Battalion Koch after their signal contribution to the success of the German offensive in the west. (M. Klein)

reaction was swift and overwhelming and the airlanded troops, together with the 6th Company of Fallschirm-jaeger, had soon been driven back from Katwijk to Valkenburg where they linked up with other German units fighting desperately against superior numbers.

Eighteenth Army, racing across Holland to relieve the airborne troops, had been so obstructed by tenacious Dutch defence that not until 13 May did their spearhead detachments gain touch. The War Diary of the SS Leibstandardte 'Adolf Hitler', reported that its advance guard detachments met and destroyed patrols from the Dutch 1st Hussar Regiment near Nijkerk as these searched for German paratroops. On the following day (14th) the Standarte moved out at 04.00 hours towards Dordrecht, crossed the Moerdijk bridge and relieved the men of 2nd Battalion of 1st Regiment, who had held the objective for four days against the enemy's furious assaults.

The Commander of 9th Panzer Division then ordered the SS attack to resume so as to relieve the troops who

had been airlanded and were now surrounded at Delft and Rotterdam. A swift drive brought the SS unit into the city at 07.00 hours on the 14th, where they gained touch with No. 11 Company of the 16th Air Landing Regiment. Slowly, the Fallschirmjaeger were being relieved of the burden of the battle.

'Panzer' Meyer, Commander of the SS Motorcycle Company sent to relieve the Paras, led his SS motor cycle Company through the streets of Rotterdam, still blazing from the German bombing of the city, and drove into Overschie where the Dutch had raised the canel foot-bridge to delay the advance. Meyer ordered a heavy recce vehicle to be driven up the wooden slope and under that weight the footbridge was soon down to road level. The SS motorcyclists roared across it with machine-guns blazing and saw all round them as they advanced evidence of bitter fighting between the Dutch and the Paras. On the broad concrete autobahn along which they were driving lay the wrecks of a great number of Ju 52s. The pilots of many aircraft bringing in 22nd Air Landing Division, unable to land on their target airfields, had sought the nearest flat spaces and had touched down on the wide motorway, only to be shot up by Dutch infantry and artillery fire. The whole area was littered with smashed aircraft and dead soldiers. The SS War Diary records that no living German soldier was met until just before Delft when one officer and ten men were found, still holding out. By 21.00 hours the Standarte had gained touch with and had relieved all the Airborne units surrounded in that town.

It was also on the 14th that the Dutch forces surrendered and in one of the last fire-fights General Student was struck in the head and seriously wounded. Hearing the sounds of gunfire he had walked across to the windows of the Rotterdam house which he was using as a temporary headquarters, he was hit and was out of action for months. It was an unfortunate end to a battle in which his airborne troops had played so distinguished a part.

The missions undertaken by the Fallschirmjaeger and Air Landing units had been concluded and because of the speed of subsequent military operations the regiments were not called upon for the battle for France.

In Norway the campaign was still being fought and German Supreme Command, now with élite troops available, could reinforce the Mountain Troop and Naval garrison at Narvik. The 1st Battalion of 1st Para Regiment was selected, but could not be dropped in a single lift because of the shortage of transport aircraft. As a result the dropping operations, which had begun on 26 May, were not concluded until 1 June. Fighting for the iron ore terminal ended on 9 June, when the Allied troops withdrew from the Narvik area. German troops then occupied the town.

With the French, Belgians and Dutch out of the war, with Denmark and Norway subjugated and with Spain, Sweden and Switzerland neutral, there was no other country in continental western Europe to challenge Germany's supremacy. Hitler was the master of western Europe. There remained, however, one island off that continent, Great Britain, which was still at war with Germany and which had not been defeated. The overtures for peace which Hitler made were rejected by Churchill's government and, angered by that rejection, the Fuehrer gave orders for an invasion of Great Britain to be planned. The operation was code-named 'Sealion'.

Below: Hitler's heroes: the Fuehrer poses with the victors of Eben Emael after awarding Knights Crosses. Second from the left is Witzig; third is Koch. (Brian L. Davis)

3. 'We are sailing against England...'
OPERATION 'SEALION', SUMMER 1940

The most astonishing fact concerning Operation 'Seeloewe' ('Sealion'), was that the German Army commanders considered the crossing of the English Channel to be only marginally more difficult than the storming of a rather wide river. Unshakeable in that conviction they failed to understand the opposition of the German Naval commanders to the OKH proposed battle plan which foresaw an assault landing of nine Divisions along an area from Ramsgate to Lyme Bay. So far as the Army was concerned the landing should be made on the widest possible front. In that way the British forces would be overstretched and a breakthough of their battle line MUST take place. The OKH, believing its Army to be more flexible in thought and operation than the British, would then concentrate at that breakthrough point faster than the enemy and make the maximum effort there. Once the Panzers began rolling and the *Blitzkrieg* was under way, the British would be defeated.

It was believed that there was little the British could put into the field against the battle-tested German Army. 'Foreign Armies West', the OKH Department responsible for gathering information on Germany's western European enemies, detailed the military units available in the United Kingdom. Of the fourteen Divisions with which she had begun the war, most had been brought back through Dunkirk having suffered defeat in the battle for Flanders. In that disastrous operation these Divisions had lost their vehicles and most of their artillery and anti-tank weapons. The defence of Great Britain thus rested, according to the Intelligence reports of 'Foreign Armies West', upon those remnants of the British Expeditionary Force together with a number of Territorial Army Divisions. This, largely immobile force, had at its disposal one armoured Division. The Royal Air Force, so it was confidently predicted by the Luftwaffe High Command, would soon be swept from the skies. With air supremacy gained the Army, extended on a front from the Thames estuary to Dorset, would land and establish beachheads. The Kriegsmarine would be responsible for furnishing and protecting the troop convoys.

The chagrin of the OKH officers can well be imagined when the commanders of OKM, the German Navy, pointed out that there were insufficient ships to take across the great number of troops and equipment, including thousands of horses, which Army demanded. There were, in addition, too few warships to escort the troop convoys and, to demonstrate that fact, OKM reported that it had only four destroyers in commission and no capital ships at all. Oberkommando der Marine demanded a reduction in the width of the landing area and of the number of assault Divisions. That proposal was brusquely rejected by Army whose commanders asserted that such a reduction in assault width and numbers would be tantamount to putting the invading troops through a mincing-machine.

On 16 July, Hitler issued Directive No. 16, 'Regarding the preparations for a landing operation in England,' based chiefly upon the Army plan of battle. Army Group 'A' would carry out the invasion using Sixteenth Army as the right wing of the assault and Ninth Army as the left wing. The troops of both armies then set to work on strict training schedules, assault landings, cliff-scaling exercises and infantry attacks upon field fortifications and villages. Elsewhere Panzer units were practising assaults from the sea using submersible vehicles. The gunners were busy in the construction of rafts on which field artillery could be mounted to support the initial landings.

The German Supreme Command realized that there would be a need for spearhead troops, other than infantry, in the vital opening stages of 'Seeloewe', OKW planned to use the airborne battalions which had demonstrated their considerable abilities and skills in the initial moves of Operation 'Gelb'. Both paratroops and gliderborne units would be used in their opening attacks and these would be followed up by the 22nd Airlanding Division. OKW saw it as the most obvious task to attack and secure an airfield. That at Lympne, on Romney Marsh, was selected and thus became the target for the operations to be mounted by 7th Flieger and 22nd Airlanding Divisions.

In the pre-dawn dark of X-Day, while the sea convoys

were making their slow way towards the coast of Britain, on airfields in northern France the Junkers aircraft would be waiting. Some paratroops would emplane, others would climb into the gliders and the aerial armada would set off. A rough sketch-map of the proposed operation is held in the Department of Documents of the Imperial War Museum and from that and from other documents it is possible to build up the Fallschirmjaeger battle plan. Two minutes after sunrise it was proposed that Major Meindl's battalion would be dropped around Hythe while units of Colonel Brauer's regiment jumped over Paddlesworth and Etchinghill. The common objective was Sandgate. While those units were moving towards the target area the transport machines would be flying back to France there to reload and to bring back Major Stenzler's battalion. That wave of paratroops would drop around the villages of Sellinge and Postling, would reinforce the first waves and together with them would begin to surround the airfield. When the Jus returned with the next wave the encirclement would be completed and the area would be consolidated. A ground and gliderborne attack would then go in, first against the airfield and then to seize and hold the high ground beyond it. With an airfield in their possession the German forces could begin to bring in 22nd Division whose battalions would thicken the perimeter and take out new objectives. Also from the captured airfield of Lympne the Luftwaffe's advanced striking force of fighter aircraft would operate in close support of the ground forces.

With hindsight we can see that the premises upon which the whole of Operation 'Seeloewe' were based were faulty. So far as this book is concerned, those faults are evident in the role foreseen for the airborne units. Admittedly, the losses which both 7th Flieger and 22nd Air Landing Divisions had suffered during Operation 'Gelb', had been made good by volunteer replacements but time is needed to produce a fighting team, particularly in paratroop units, and there had been little time for such production. It was, perhaps, a measure of Supreme Command confidence in the ability of the airborne units, given the splendid results obtained in Holland and Belgium, that the half-formed 7th Flieger Division should be given tasks which would have been beyond its capabilities had the invasion actually taken place. That the officers, NCOs and men of the airborne units would have done their utmost to achieve the stated objectives is not the point – the pre-conditions for a successful undertaking did not exist. The units had not undergone the training exercises which convert groups of soldiers into crack battalions; there were too few transport aircraft, too few dispatchers – in short too few and too little of almost everything. The overriding question was one that must

have been uppermost in the minds of the unit commanders: 'How long will we be without support?' It will be appreciated that the weight and space limitations of aircraft in those early days did not allow heavy weapons to be brought in. The maximum weight which a glider could carry was one ton and this limited carrying capacity forbad the 'lifting' of even armoured cars or the standard anti-tank guns. The airborne troops holding their positions on Romney Marsh, would, therefore, be without adequate support until fully armed, infantry or Panzer units came in. How long it might be before relief arrived from mainland Europe could only be conjecture and until that relief did arrive the lightly armed Paras would be at a disadvantage *vis-à-vis* the British defenders.

The inability to resolve the wide differences which separated the concepts of the German Army and Navy on Operation 'Sealoewe', coupled with the failure of the Luftwaffe to gain air supremacy over Britain meant that time began to run out for the Germans. These delays worked in favour of the British. Each passing month enabled them to rebuild more of their Army's shattered strength and to import from the USA and from other overseas sources the weapons which were needed. Delay which was a benison to the British was a curse to the Germans; a situation completely understood by the young officers of the Airborne arm.

Colonel Hermann Goetzel, now retired from active service, was at the time of 'Seeloewe' a Captain and a Company Commander. He recalled that by the time that the orders to prepare 'Seeloewe', had been issued much valuable time had been lost. Transferred to HQ of 7th Flieger Division as Ib (today's G4), his first tasks in the weeks immediately following the campaign in France were concerned with the raising of new airborne formations and their equipping. On 7 or 8 September, he was ordered, together with two other Para captains to undertake a recce to select airfields in Belgium and northern France from which the airborne troops could take off for 'Seeloewe'. Travelling in a light truck the group not only found eight suitable fields, chiefly in the area of Laon, from which the missions could be flown, but also a building near Laon which could serve as a Para supply base. The Luftwaffe authorities in Northern France/ Belgium were instructed to prepare the airfields for the airborne operation.

General Putzier, who had taken over leadership of 7th Division while Student was recovering from the wounds he had received at Rotterdam, agreed to Captain Goetzel's proposals and gave orders for the Laon building to be prepared as a Para supply depot. Goetzel now recalls that General Putzier and other officers took part in a war-game at Roubaix, near Lille. The object of the game, attended by

Above: Parachute harness demonstrated to visiting members of the RAD (Reichs Arbeits Dienst), the German Labour Corps, during a recruiting drive. The hook was to be placed on the static line in the aircraft from which the paratrooper would drop; on exit from the aircraft, the weight of the falling Fallschirmjaeger would cause his parachute to be tugged out of his pack. (Brian L. Davis)

Right: Emplaning. The static line hook was a potential nuisance, so the standard practice was to hold it in the mouth, leaving the hands free to haul paratrooper and bulky parachute pack ino the aircraft. (Brian L.Davis)

more than two hundred Generals and Admirals, was to determine the situation on the ground between the 4th and 6th days of 'Seeloewe'. It was assumed that by that time paratroops and airlanded troops would have created a bridgehead. It had to be established whether during the 4th to 6th day of the operation enough troops could be brought into the bridgehead to allow a successful breakout. The confidence of the Luftwaffe and Army officers that an attack would succeed was in direct contrast to the pessimism of the Navy and no firm conclusions could be drawn from the war-game. The presence of the Paratroop officers at the game was, in Goetzel's opinion, unnecessary, for their strictly airborne role would have been completed by Day 4 of 'Seeloewe'. That they would continue to be employed in a ground role as infantry was foreseen in Hitler's Directive No. 16, which ordered them to form an Assault Troop Reserve to be used wherever needed.

Within days, Goetzel, was ordered to prepare the bases in northern France and Belgium for the arrival of the paratroops. The Concentration Plan was that the troops, dispersed in their depots all over Germany, should reach the departure airfields within two days. The march routes set out that the units were to cross the Rhine between Duisberg and Mannheim. During the night of X-Day minus 2 and X-Day minus 1, part of the Para force would be east of the river while the remainder would be west of the Rhine. By the evening of X-Day minus 1 all troops would be at the airfields from which the missions would be flown. The glider group, which would be carrying a battalion of the Assault Regiment in the opening attacks, was to be brought by glider to the Advanced airfield ready for the dawn take-off. The strictest orders were issued that troops moving towards their start fields, as well as those advance parties which had moved out to prepare the airfields for the main body, and all vehicles, were to remove every indication, badge or marking that would show them to be members of 7th Flieger Division. No specialist badges were to be worn, all distinctive uniform was to be packed away and no Paratroop songs were to be sung, so that enemy Intelligence should not learn that the airborne units were preparing for action.

While Captain Goetzel was working out the movement orders for the Fallschirmjaeger units, allocating each battalion its departure airfield, organizing the supply and reinforcement details and carrying out the myriad tasks associated with the dispatch of so many men, his colleague, Major Trettner, was working on the attack orders. The demand for secrecy was so great that each officer worked in isolation, each having so great a work burden that there was no time for the normal social intecourse between the planning staffs.

Hermann Goetzel described in his letter that shortly after the movement orders were issued a situation developed which could only be described as farcical. The Para advance parties were suddenly to move quite openly, into the departure areas of northern France. No attempt was made to disguise their unit affiliation and since the orders authorizing that movement had not originated from 7th Division but from Luffwaffe High Command, Goetzel formed the opinion that 'Seeloewe' had certainly been postponed if not cancelled altogether. It was obvious that the open concentration of paratroops in northern France was a move in the war of nerves against the British and had nothing to do with the preparation for an airborne assault.

The year 1940, had been a dramatic one for the officers and men of 7th Flieger Division. A successful first operation in Scandinavia during April, had been followed in May by the sensational assault landings at Eben Emael, along the Albert Canal and in western Holland. Those missions, begun and ended quickly, had greatly assisted the opening stages of the German Army's offensive in the west and through them the world had become aware that the new, revolutionary tactic of vertical development was one which worked with terrible efficiency.

The plan to invade Great Britain had come to nothing and there seemed, in the last days of the fateful year 1940, no nation in Europe ready to challenge the might and power of the German Army. True, the British were fighting in the desert, but that war was an Italian one, as was the campaign which Mussolini was prosecuting, without success it must be said, in the mountains of western Greece.

Peace, it seemed was assured, and it was possible to reduce the hard pace of Jaeger training. There were no signs that within four months an airborne regiment would be fighting one short operation in Greece and that that mission would be followed, only weeks later, by a longer one, involving the entire Division; one in which the Jaeger regiments would be decimated.

1941

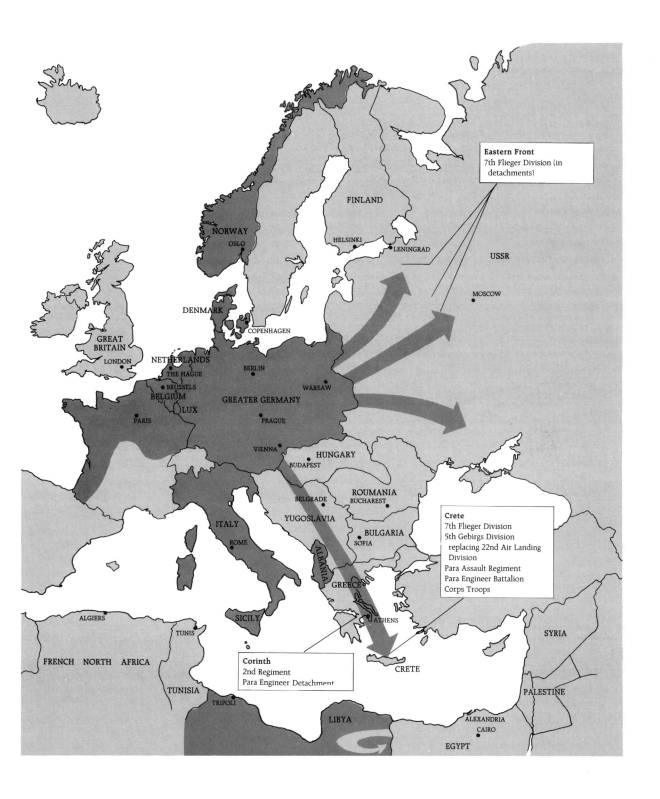

Eastern Front
7th Flieger Division (in detachments)

Crete
7th Flieger Division
5th Gebirgs Division replacing 22nd Air Landing Division
Para Assault Regiment
Para Engineer Battalion
Corps Troops

Corinth
2nd Regiment
Para Engineer Detachment

NORWAY
OSLO

FINLAND
HELSINKI
LENINGRAD

USSR
MOSCOW

DENMARK
COPENHAGEN

GREAT BRITAIN
LONDON

NETHERLANDS
THE HAGUE
BRUSSELS
BELGIUM
LUX
PARIS

BERLIN
WARSAW
GREATER GERMANY
PRAGUE

VIENNA
HUNGARY
BUDAPEST

BELGRADE
ROUMANIA
BUCHAREST
YUGOSLAVIA

ITALY
ROME

ALBANIA
GREECE

BULGARIA
SOFIA

ATHENS

SICILY

ALGIERS
TUNIS

CRETE

SYRIA

FRENCH NORTH AFRICA

TUNISIA
TRIPOLI

LIBYA

PALESTINE

ALEXANDRIA
CAIRO

EGYPT

4. 'We've swept the Tommies from the continent'
CORINTH, APRIL 1941

At the end of August 1940 Operation 'Sealion' was postponed and the battalions which might have spearheaded the invasion returned to their home stations. The next important event in the history of the German airborne forces was the OKW directive that 7th Flieger and 22nd Airlanding Divisions would be combined to form XI Flieger Corps.

To create a Corps required that Para units be taken from their parent Divisions to form cadres which would then be fleshed out with new men. In addition to the Jaeger units other detachments were taken and formed into an all-arms group known as 'Corps Troops'. By the end of August an anti-aircraft machine-gun battalion, an expanded medical group and other Service units had been detached from their Divisions to serve as Corps troops together with certain non-Divisional bodies such as Para training schools and replacement units. When Corps HQ was eventually established in 1941, with its setting-up came promotions and command changes. Student, who was named as Corps Commander, took with him into the new appointment many of the Divisional Staff Officers. General Suessmann, his successor to the post of General Officer Commanding 7th Flieger Division, had, therefore, to create a new divisional staff.

The months which elapsed between 'Sealion' and the next campaigns – those in the Balkans in 1941 – were times of growth and improvement in techniques. The campaign in Holland had highlighted the weakness of dropping paratroops without the support of heavy weapons. The Jaeger, who had dropped in the Netherlands, had fought at a disadvantage until light artillery and anti-tank guns were brought in. Post-battle experiments carried out in the summer of 1940, showed that by using multi-chute support and by enclosing gun barrels in wicker tubes it was possible to drop such weapons without damage. The success of these experiments meant that in future campaigns the Jaeger would no longer be without heavy weapons to support them in the initial stages of an operation when they were at their weakest.

Although Britain had been driven from the mainland of western Europe during the summer of 1940, it was the standing concern of the German High Command that from colonies and protectorates in Cyprus, Egypt, Palestine and Iraq, British forces might attack the long and vulnerable coastline of the northern Mediterranean, re-enter Europe and establish airfields from which the oilwells of Roumania could be bombed.

During the months spent in hospital and in convalescence as a result of his wound, Student had exercised his mind with the problem of how he could use his airborne units to prosecute the war in the Mediterranean. The solution he decided was that his Fallschirmjaeger should mount a succession of assaults upon islands in the central and eastern Mediterranean. Each new success in those areas would take the German forces into positions where they would threaten Britain's power. The final assault of that series of 'island-hopping' operations would be made against Alexandria and the Suez Canal. The whole strategic plan was bold in concept and daring in design. The only choice that needed to be made was; which island should be the first to be attacked? The invasion of Greek territory by Italian troops on 28 October 1940, set in train a series of events at the end of which the target for the airborne assault had selected itself.

One of the incentives for Hitler to open an attack in the Balkans and to invade Greece was the poor showing of the Italian army in the war which it had been waging for nearly six months without success. Another incentive was the need to drive out the expeditionary force which Churchill had sent into Greece. This British force, in the opinion of OKW, had brought the British Army back on to the mainland of Europe. Student, now returned to duty and aware of the successes which the German Army was achieving in the Greek campaign, saw that this victory could be fully exploited if his 'island-hopping' campaign were begun. In view of its strategic position Crete should be the first objective. He briefed Goering who put the idea to Hitler. The Fuehrer, who had been impressed with the work of the airborne forces in the opening stages of the

Right: A last check on the fit of harness and parachute before boarding the aircraft for a training drop. (M. Klein)

Right: Fallschirmjaeger inside a Ju 52. (M. Klein)

Right: Ground training for aircraft exit. The further one leapt the better, in order to clear the slipstream of the aircraft and the tailplane. (Brian L. Davis)

Left: The greatest danger after a Fallschirmjaeger had landed was that his wind-inflated canopy would drag him along the ground. Recruits were taught to cope with this situation. In emergencies the harness straps could be cut using the gravity knife that each man carried (M. Klein)

Left: Containers dropped with the Fallschirmjaeger delivered their arms and ammunition. For precious minutes, the para-troops would be defenceless, so speedy recovery and opening of these canisters was vital for success – and survival. The impact of landing was absorbed by a screw-on, corrugated metal-alloy cushion, seen here on the left of the picture. Mobility was afforded by a pair of wheels and a towing bar, clearly visible in this picture. (Brian L. Davis)

campaign in the west, grasped immediately the General's revolutionary strategy. On 25 April, he signed Directive No. 28, ordering Operation 'Mercury', the attack upon the island of Crete to be planned, mounted and executed before the end of May.

Although military operations in Greece were proceeding so well that by 24 April the British had been forced to retreat from their positions at Thermopylae, German High Command circles feared that the bulk of the expeditionary force might reach evacuation ports and escape by sea to fight another day. The few principal escape routes funnelled down to a single land crossing-point across the Corinth Canal; to a bridge which linked the Ionian and Aegean seas. It was the only crossing-point and if it could be captured and held not only would the great mass of the British forces in Greece be unable to cross the isthmus, but German forces could use the bridge to speed their pursuit of the retreating British forces. There was no way in which conventional German ground forces could strike, reach and take the bridge before the British had escaped. Only an airborne assault could achieve that result. In Bulgaria there was a Brigade-sized group, commanded by General Suessmann, which included the 2nd Jaeger Regiment as well as artillery, flak and engineer detachments. OKW had intended to use this Brigade detachment in an operation against Lemnos, but that island had been invaded and occupied by an Army unit. Para Detachment Suessmann, therefore was free to undertake the Corinth mission.

On 26 April, Sturm's 2nd Regiment was ordered to take the bridge across the Isthmus at Corinth. The plan was simple. Six gliders carrying 54 Para engineers would land at dawn to the north and south of the objective. Once it had been taken, the 1st and 2nd Battalions of 2nd Regiment would parachute in, one battalion at each end of the bridge, and form a defensive perimeter which they would hold until relieved.

Considered objectively the gliderborne mission seemed almost suicidal. The whole area around the bridge was known to be crammed with columns of British troops making their way in unbroken procession towards and across this single point. There was, however, one advantage. The attack would be unexpected and surprise would be complete.

During the night of 26/27 April, Ju 52s towing the gliders took off from Larissa airfield for the two-hour flight to Corinth. A short time later, 272 aircraft carrying the two Jaeger battalions, whose men formed the first wave of the attack, took off and headed southwards. Flying low through the pre-dawn darkness the Jus cast off the gliders some twelve miles (20 kilometres) from the objective, and at a launch height of 4,000 feet (1,200

metres). Out of the morning sun the gliders dropped, recovered and swept over the high ground to the north of the isthmus and touched-down as planned at each end of the bridge. The landing was accomplished for the loss of only one machine whose pilot, attempting to make a pinpoint touch-down, had crashed into one of the pillars at the end of the bridge. It broke up, injuring all the men inside it.

The assault parties of Para Engineers rushed, firing, at the sentries guarding the bridge. Even before that brief fire-fight had ended and the British posts had been overrun, two groups of Para Engineers had begun to search the bridge for explosive charges and another two groups had, in a matter of minutes, attacked and destroyed eleven anti-aircraft gun positions. Surprise had been total and the glider detachments met no initial organized resistance from Allied troops in the area. But the British and Greek officers soon realized how few in number were the Para Engineers who had seized the bridge. Allied counter-attacks, at first unco-ordinated but then more sophisticated, came in to recapture it and thereby reopen the escape road. During one counter-attack about ten minutes after the engineers had landed, a massive explosion destroyed the bridge.

The cause of this explosion has never been established. Contrary to German Army regulations, the explosive charges removed from the bridge had not been taken away by the Para Engineers, but had been left piled up on the road. There were stories on the German side that during one local Allied counter-attack two British officers were seen to rush towards the explosive charges, firing pistols so as to detonate them.

Whether a British shell had struck and exploded these charges, or whether British officers had sacrificed their lives cannot be known for certain. A series of dramatic, contemporary stills from a film shows a group of Para Engineers doubling across the bridge as if rushing forward to meet an assault and then a cloud of thick black smoke obscures everything. The road link between the Ionian and Aegean seas had been destroyed in a matter of seconds.

It was into the noise, the fury and the confusion which existed on both sides of the bridge that the Jaeger of Sturm's 2nd Regiment jumped. In the short time that the engineers had spent in clearing the explosive charges, the Jus carrying the paratroops came in, flying low over the sea and towards the drop zone. At an altitude of 350 feet (100 metres) the Jaeger leaped into the fire of British machine- and anti-aircraft guns. There were no losses from the gunfire but one group of No. 3 Company, which jumped a few seconds too soon, fell into the sea and were drowned before help could reach them. There were other

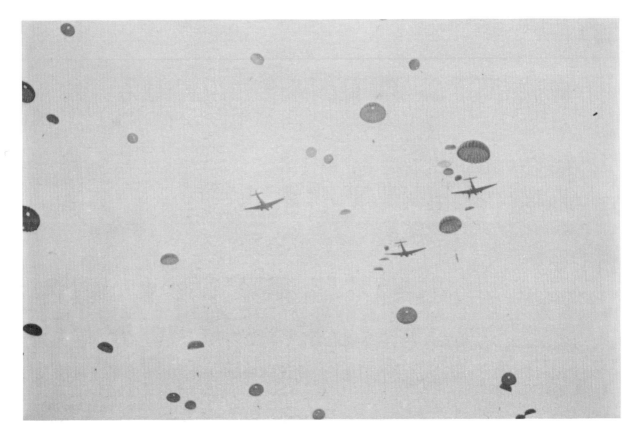

Left: The sky above the Corinth Canal fills with the parachutes of the Fallschirmjaeger, April 1941. (Adolf Strauch)

Right: Members of Strauch's company accept the surrender of British troops near the Corinth Canal. (Adolf Strauch)

Left: Strauch's company take up defensive positions near the end of the bridge. (Adolf Strauch)

Right: It is believed that this photograph shows the Corinth Canal bridge blowing up, temporarily severing the line of retreat for the British to the Peloponnese. (Brian L. Davis)

44 CORINTH, APRIL 1941

casualties, too, when one Ju stalled as it tried to gain height to clear a mountain peak. Only two men got out. The 1st Battalion had landed to the north of the bridge and was in battle.

No. 5 Company of 2nd Battalion, which dropped on the bridge's south side, was the first to jump and within minutes of landing had captured the anti-aircraft positions guarding the bridge, the railway station and a convoy of British trucks. The battalion then pushed out to set up a defensive perimeter. No. 4 Company of 2nd Battalion, which had dropped a few minutes after No. 2, went into action destroying four gun positions while No. 7 Company captured the western entrance to the canal in the face of determined resistance by British and Dominion troops. The Jaeger from Battalion Headquarters and from other Companies consolidated the area and set up TAC HQ into which the battalion commander was carried. In a bad landing on the rocky ground he had broken both ankles. Captain Schirmer took over the battalion.

Left: An 'O' group during the Corinth operation. Officers and NCOs plan the next part of the mission. (M. Klein)

Below left: The Fallschirmjaeger and the Leibstandarte SS 'Adolf Hitler' link up at the canal. (M. Klein)

Below: Looking down the canal at the site of the now-demolished bridge, April 1941.

Among the vehicles captured by 2nd Battalion was a Bren gun carrier in which men of No. 6 Company rode out on a recce patrol towards Corinth. The mayor and garrison commander were quickly persuaded to surrender the town.

The loss of the bridge meant that the mission had only succeeded in part. The objective should have been captured intact and held. To enable the Jaeger to cross from one side of the canal to the other, No. 3 Company erected an emergency bridge which was then found to be strong enough to carry artillery pieces. Across this hastily constructed bridge 2nd Battalion continued its pursuit of the retreating Allied forces.

During its operations 1st Battalion intercepted and captured more than 10,000 British and Greek soldiers. Schirmer's 2nd Battalion, on the Peleponnesian side of the isthmus, took 2,000 prisoners. The 3rd Battalion, which landed during the afternoon of the 27th, then took over the task of mopping up and securing the area. The battle had lasted only a matter of hours and for the strategic success that had been gained German losses had been comparatively light; 63 killed and 174 wounded or missing in action. The Corinth Canal bridge operation was an outstanding success, but one that was to be soon overshadowed by the even more dramatic victory of 7th Flieger Division in Operation 'Mercury', the battle for Crete.

5. 'On Crete our banners are flying'
CRETE, MAY 1941

The revolutionary concept of capturing an island from the air using glider-borne and parachute troops – the first occasion of such an enterprise being attempted – excited Hitler's imagination.

The mountainous island of Crete, some 160 miles (260 kilometres) long and between 12-30 miles (twenty-fifty kilometres) wide, is about 60 miles (100 kilometres) from the southernmost point of the Greek mainland. It lies in the eastern Mediterranean, a sea which in 1941 was dominated by the Royal Navy. Student intended to negate British supremacy at sea by overflying its warships. Just as there would be no need to consider the Royal Navy, neither would there be concern for the safety of the aircraft and gliders which would carry the invasion force. The Luftwaffe's fighter squadrons, operating from bases on the Greek mainland, would guard the transport armada on their flights from Greece to the battle area and protect them against the few British fighters which would, in any case, soon be driven from Crete and back to Egypt. The Cretan campaign falls into two distinct parts: the airborne assault to gain footholds and the break out from these perimeters by mountain troops who then went on to capture the island. In this book the airborne operations will be described.

The northern side, that on which Student intended to make the first landings, had some narrow beaches behind which a thin fertile strip of intensively cultivated land rose into foothills and then quite abruptly into high and arid mountains. On the northern side, too, there were, in 1941, three small airstrips, at Maleme, Canea and Heraklion. A single main road ran east-west on the northern side of the island and connected the principal towns.

According to German sources, particularly in post-operation accounts of the battle, the British forces were picked units from the homeland and from the Dominions, a statement not strictly accurate. The greatest number of the 25,000 defenders were men and units that had fought in, and then been evacuated from Greece, in a campaign during which all the heavy equipment had been lost. There was insufficient field or anti-aircraft artillery to

support the defence and only a few old tanks. The permanent garrison had been – until the men evacuated from Greece arrived – only three battalions of British infantry. Lacking heavy weapons, General Freyburg, the British commander, had to use inadequately supported infantry to defend the airstrips. The survivors of 5th New Zealand Brigade were deployed in the west of Crete; the 22nd Battalion around Maleme, the 23rd Battalion east of that and 28th (Maori) Battalion on the Brigade's right flank. To the right of the Maori battalion was an Australian Brigade and farther eastwards, the British brigade defended Heraklion area.

Student, commanding XI Flieger Corps, was forced to work to a very tight deadline. He had only a few weeks in which to plan and carry out the operation, and the difficulties facing him and his Staff officers were enormous. The first blow was that 22nd Air Landing Division, part of the Corps establishment, would not be available for Operation 'Mercury'. The substitute for the 22nd was 5th Alpine Division – a crack unit and one competent to fight through the mountainous Cretan terrain – but a formation with absolutely no experience of air transport operations. Then, too, XI Flieger Corps had too few transport aircraft to carry the para/gliderborne contingents in a single 'lift'. There would have to be two waves of drops; a shuttle service with all the disadvantages and delays of such an operation. A third blow was the realization that the island's airfield runways were so short that when trying to land, the Ju 52s bringing in the 5th Alpine battalions, would face unusually high risks even under the best possible conditions.

For Operation 'Mercury', Student intended to use all three Jaeger regiments plus the Assault Regiment and his Corps troops. The airborne operations would be supplemented by sea-borne landings. Certain heavy weapons and some para groups, together with battalions from 5th Alpine, would be shipped from Greece in slow-moving convoys of local vessels, known as caiques. These convoys would sail so as to arrive after the airborne landings had been accomplished. The units in the seaborne convoys, bringing in the heavy weapons, would reinforce the exploitation phase of 'Mercury'.

Tactically, Student divided his forces into three battle groups: West, Centre and East. Battle Group West, under Meindl, contained the mass of the Assault Regiment. It would form part of the first wave and would land at dawn in a simultaneous glider and Para drop around Maleme airfield. Battle Group Centre, one battalion of the Assault Regiment and the 3rd Regiment, would make the major effort and would be commanded by General Suessmann, the divisional commander. To support this principal effort would be the Corps Engineer Battalion, a company of the machine-gun battalion, and a platoon of the anti-tank battalion. The whole of Battle Group Centre would be 'lifted' in the first wave. A reinforcement to Battle Group Centre would be Sturm's 2nd Regiment which would form part of the second wave and which would drop in the early afternoon. Battle Group East, formed out of Brauer's No. 1 Regiment, would come in as part of the second wave and drop over Heraklion.

Student decided to make his principal effort at Canea, the island's capital, as well as on the Akrotiri peninsula. With those places in the hands of Battle Group Centre he would have both an airfield and a harbour through which to reinforce the battle line. The attacks by Battle Groups East and West would be subordinate to the principal

objective of seizing the capital. One object in the assault was to capture senior officials and thereby diminish the risk of any organized resistance. Appendix No. 2 to the orders issued by 3rd Regiment state. '... Immediately locate and arrest important personalities, viz the enemy divisional commander and other senior officers, the Mayor, chief of police, bishop and officials of the Cretan Government. These people may be held as hostages or be used in negotiations.'

Battle Group West had a number of tasks to fulfill. The Assault Regiment's 1st Battalion, less two Companies, would take out the anti-aircraft guns on either bank of the River Tavronitis. An assault group of men from nine gliders would land and capture the river bridge and cut the road from Maleme to Sphakia. No. 4 Company of the Assault Regiment would attack and capture Point 107, a hill dominating the Maleme airstrip. This was the most difficult task and it was thus upon No. 4 Company that the success or failure of the Maleme landings depended. The airfield itself was to be attacked by 3rd Battalion of the Assault Regiment.

Suessmann's Battle Group Centre would be landed in two waves. Heidrich's 3rd Regiment would para drop south-west of Canea, in the area around Galatas. To provide deep protection to the south, the Para Engineer Battalion, together with No. 3 Company of the Para

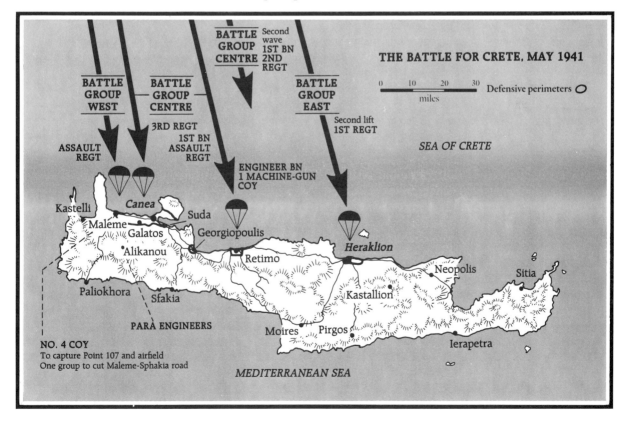

machine-gun battalion and a platoon of the Para anti-tank battalion would drop around Alikanou. Their task was to block the roads which ran north-westerly and north-easterly from that place. The 1st Battalion of 3rd Regiment was to jump over an area extending from the Canea road to Suda Bay. The 2nd Battalion would drop around Canea town. Two platoons of the Assault regiment would take out the anti-aircraft guns south of Canea, while another Company was to carry out a similar task in the Akrotiri peninsula.

The second wave of Battle Group Centre was to be flown in during the afternoon of D-Day. The 1st Battalion of Sturm's 2nd Regiment was to jump over and around the airfield at Retimo while 3rd Battalion would drop east of the town.

Brauer's Battle Group East, consisting of 1st Regiment and elements from Corps troops, would drop in two waves around Heraklion – the 1st Battalion to the east of the objective, the 3rd Battalion to the west and the bulk of 2nd Battalion of 2nd Regiment to the south. Burkhardt's 2nd Battalion would jump over the airfield. A Company of the anti-aircraft machine-gun battalion would reinforce and support Burckhardt's group.

The 3rd Regiment's orders, issued at 01.00 hours on 18 May, made the objectives of 'Mercury' very clear. 'XI Flieger Corps, supported by 8th Luftflotte, will capture the island of Crete by seizing the principal airfields and important areas by air and sea landings. These will be held until relieved by Army troops (5th Mountain Division).' The code-message which would set the operation in train was 'Mercury' followed by X-Day and X-hour. Zero or X-Hour was calculated as the time when the first wave flew over the target.

Throughout the night of 19/20 May, the men prepared themselves. Machine-gun belts were filled, grenades primed, the final clothing parades held to ensure that each man's equipment, uniform and weapons were in first class order. There was little time to sleep. The Jus had to be loaded with the weapons containers, and into some machines the artillery was manhandled and parachutes fitted. Then it was time for the departure parade, the final exhortations from the unit commanders and at last the order 'To the aircraft, march!' Each man holds in his mouth the metal clip end of the long static cord, leaving his hands free to pull himself up into the aircraft. The metal clip will fasten onto a jump-wire running inside the aircraft. The other end of the 20ft-long static line fastens on to the flap of the parachute pack. The parachutists carry no personal

Below: Preparation for the flight to Crete included donning lifejackets. (Brian L. Davis)

weapons other than a pistol. The four weapons containers in the aircraft's bomb-bay will be dropped together with the unarmed Paras. The Jaeger who will land in gliders carry their arms with them.

Adolf Strauch, who served in 2nd Battalion of 2nd Regiment, kept a diary and part of the entry for 19 May, reads: 'It is evening and darkness lies over our tents. A group belonging to the Company lying next to ours is singing. We were told today that our next objective is Crete.... Part of 2nd Regiment is to drive a wedge at Retimo between the western and eastern parts of the island and to take the town. ... Our Company will form part of a battle group whose task is to protect the western flank of 1st Regiment. According to the briefing the invasion will be easy. Our recce planes have brought only comforting details back with them. It is expected that at the end of the first day of battle we shall have achieved a favourable decision. Those of us with experience have other thoughts.

While it is still dark, on airfields at Megara, Corinth and a great number of other places, the radial engines of the Jus are roaring, flares are fired; white lights which curve up into the night sky. At that signal, shuddering and quivering with the throbbing power of their engines the first of the five hundred aircraft which have been collected for 'Mercury', roll along the runway, gather speed and take off. The wing lights are soon lost to sight in the dust storm which every departing aircraft has thrown up and only then does the realization come that each machine taking off creates a thick, opaque, blinding cloud of sand. This fact causes consternation among the Luftwaffe dispatching officers for they had planned for the aircraft to take off in rapid succession. But this is not possible. The pilot's vision is obscured and visibility is only a matter of a few yards. No pilot can be expected to risk his machine and the soldiers he is carrying in such conditions. On all those airfields with only narrow, untarmacked runways, the same picture is presented of Luftwaffe Staff Officers seeing their carefully worked-out time tables rendered useless by the slow dispersing dust clouds.

Meanwhile, rising out of that ground murk the Jus fly into clear air and take course for Crete. The sights and sounds and experiences of that day are clear in the minds of all who made the flight and from the recollections of several men who took part the following compiled report has been made. 'Dawn came and went. We flew on until below us we could see the dun-coloured, inhospitable-looking terrain with mountains blinding white in the sunlight. These peaks ran along the length of the island like a spine. Pillars of black smoke rose still and straight into the blue sky. The Luftwaffe had been softening up the enemy and destroying his opposition.

Above: Adolf Strauch, seen here wearing the Iron Cross he had been awarded.

There was little flak. The Stukas had been most effective as had the men of the Assault Regiment whose task it had been to attack the anti-aircraft guns. But even without the disturbance of flak fire the machines bucketed about in the air turbulence. The engines changed note. The pilot was throttling back. It would not be long now. The light on the bulkhead showed red. It was the signal "make ready!" Two minutes to go. The dispatcher walked along the body of the machine checking that each man's static line hook was firmly fixed to the jump wire. By the time he had completed his task the bulkhead light had changed to green. "Ready to jump!" and we moved forward to the exit door on the port side of the aircraft. Two of the Ju crew had already removed the door and we could feel the air blowing in. Our sergeant would be the first to jump. He stood braced in the doorway looking slightly upwards as per the drill book. He would not have seen that the light on the bulkhead had changed to white, but at the sound of the klaxon horn he flung himself forward and out of the machine to be followed by the rest of us in quick succession. When each man jumped the Ju bounced upwards a little in the air as the aircraft load was lightened.

There did not seem to be much firing from the enemy on the ground and we landed quickly on to a fairly rocky field. It was surprisingly quiet – well except for the sound of aircraft engines. No small arms fire. No artillery. We doubled forward to the canisters, rolled them over to get at the locking pins, opened the flaps and collected our weapons. It was comforting to have a firearm again. It really is a terrible feeling to fall unarmed through the air knowing that you are unable to fire back at anybody on the ground who is firing up at you. By the time that we had armed ourselves and were grouped into Sections and Platoons, runners had arrived ordering us to join the remainder of the Company. At that concentration point the officers and NCOs were given their orders and we then set off towards our objective. We were in Crete for the loss of only one man who had broken a thigh bone.'

Despite the seeming ease with which these men had landed it must be said that for the greatest number of paratroops and gliderborne troops the landings had been frightening and the losses suffered had been disastrous. There had been casualties suffered even before the landings took place. The glider which was carrying General Suessman broke loose from its tug aircraft and crashed on the island of Aegina. There were no survivors. Only the first landings around Maleme were made against limited opposition. The initial objectives – anti-aircraft guns – were soon knocked out, the Maleme–Sphakia road cut and the river bridge captured intact, but the most important objective of Battle Group West – Point 107 dominating the airfield – could not be taken by so small a force as No 4 Company. Until Point 107 was taken New Zealand artillery observers could direct fire upon the transport aircraft bringing in the follow-up troops and these would have to make their landing run-in under shellfire. Losses might prove to be unacceptably high. Therefore, it was imperative that Point 107 be taken. One of the early casualties – and one of the most serious to Battle Group West – was the severe wounding of its commander, Major General Meindl. There was, as a

Left: The German aerial armada sets out for Crete, flying at low altitude in order to attain maximum surprise, 20 May 1941. (M. Klein)

Above: Flying to Heraklion, 1530 hours 20 May 1941; an aircraft of the second wave. (Adolf Strauch)

Right: Descent at the drop zone to the west of Heraklion on 20 May. (Adolf Strauch)

Left: The Gotha glider.

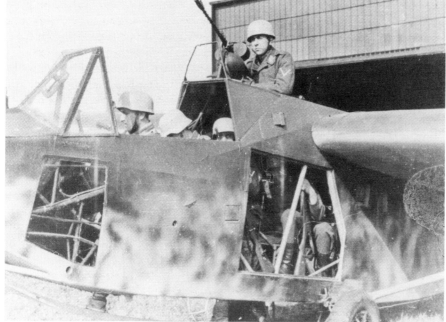

Left: Experience showed that gliders were very vulnerable to ground fire on their approach to land, so a dorsal machine-gun position was later fitted to give covering fire. This picture shows one such glider; the cockpit hood and side have been removed to show the interior. (M. Klein)

Left: The DFS glider.

consequence, no firm central direction to the battle for Maleme and the struggle for Point 107 lacked that flexibility and power that Meindl would have shown. The New Zealand battalion grouped round the hill, soon recovered from the surprise of the initial German attack and, together with the other battalions, carried out counter attacks along the length of the Brigade front. In bitter, often hand to hand fighting, the 3rd Battalion of the Assault Regiment was almost totally destroyed.

The units of Battle Group Centre, both para-dropped and glider-borne, met disaster as their machines made the approach runs. The anti-aircraft guns had not been knocked out by the bombing and opened fire at the waves of Jus flying slowly and steadily towards Canea and the Akrotiri peninsula. To avoid the AA fire the aircraft broke formation before they reached the landing zones. The consequence was that the para units were dispersed over a wide area, some of them coming down over an Australian unit bivouacked under canvas north-west of Galatos. Australian stories of hundreds of German parachutists being shot during their descent are not substantiated by German accounts. A post-battle report by Medical officers of 7th Flieger Division showed that very few of the Jaeger dead were found still in harness. Tests carried out later in the war showed that even first class marksmen could only score one hit out of 340 shots fired at a dummy figure from a range of 160 yards (150 metres). At twice that distance a total of 1708 rounds needed to be fired before a hit was scored. It is one thing to fire at a man descending swiftly through the air and quite another to hit him.

The greatest number of casualties to Heidrich's 3rd Regiment were suffered as the three battalions struggled to group and advance upon their objectives. The 3rd Battalion took such heavy losses that for the first days its scattered men fought as little islands of resistance barely able to hold out until relief came. They were quite unable to undertake offensive operations.

By contrast the Engineer Battalion and support groups which were landed at Alikanou suffered few losses in landing but were under constant pressure from British and Dominion forces seeking to drive them from the position which they had occupied and which dominated the two roads. The battalion's given task, of destroying a British encampment just over a kilometre to the south of Alikanou was not realized and the British units in the area reacted vigorously against the Para Engineers. Alikanou had been named as the sector in which divisional TAC Headquarters and the Advanced Dressing Station for the Medical detachments were to be set up.

'Our objectives were detailed in briefings given to us in the days before the mission was flown. Not only the task of the Division but that of our battle group, our battalion's

target and also the Company objective. We were told that there was little water on Crete, so that our water-bottles would have to last us two days. We were issued with the usual thirst-quenching sweets but I found these to have little effect. The area was said to be featureless and once on the ground we were told to orientate ourselves by using certain distinctive artificial landmarks. Among those were the masts of Canea radio station, but I never saw them. The main roads were much better reference points; those and our compasses were much more reliable.

Briefings warned us of the need to avoid becoming involved in house to house fighting in the villages. Such actions would be a heavy drain on the limited stocks of ammunition and grenades which we carried. We were to commandeer all means of transport and bring the vehicles to a central collecting point where they would be distributed as required. We had all been taught to drive captured British Army trucks and these were to be used in those stages of the battle after we had consolidated; namely, those of exploitation and pursuit of the defeated British.' As a contrast to the post-battle reports which spoke of the island being garrisoned by crack units of the British and Dominion armies the Jaeger were told to expect to meet, 'An enemy demoralized by defeat in Greece and one who was war-weary. How wrong the planners were. The Colonial troops were excellent soldiers of high morale and expert in fieldcraft. They were all marksmen. It was obvious to us, very soon after landing, that the British had garrisoned Crete with the best units of their Colonial forces.'

Of the five hundred Ju 52s that were employed to carry the first wave, only seven were lost, although many returned showing the marks of bullets and shellfire. The British anti-aircraft guns had not all been knocked out and had given a good account of themselves. So, too, had the British and Dominion infantry who had been trained to fire at low-flying aircraft, and the wings of many transport planes showed evidence of their skill in musketry.

The euphoria of the first run-in, the limited anti-aircraft fire and the low losses in transport machines combined to give Student and his officers a false picture of what was happening in Crete. Headquarters was unaware that Suessmann, the divisional commander, had been killed or that Meindl had been wounded at Maleme. Lacking precise information on the progress of the ground fighting, Student still saw Canea as the principal assault area and prepared his second wave detachments. These were to take off in the afternoon and would consist of the second contingent of Battle Group Centre together with the whole of Battle Group East. The official history of the Para Engineer Association records the obstructions that prevented a punctual departure. The chief problem, that of dust clouds raised by aircraft taking off, had still not been resolved. Delays built up and the transport machines carrying the Jaeger detachments arrived over their objectives either singly or in only small groups.

The British and Dominion troops on the ground were waiting for them – had been waiting for some time. It had been planned that the transports would follow close behind the Stuka dive-bombing raids. The Para Engineers' history goes on to record that it was not possible to contact other airfields and postpone the bombing because sabotage had destroyed all telephone links in XI Flieger Corps Area. It had, therefore, not been possible to abort the Stuka raids which went in on schedule at 15.15 hours. That raid which should have been followed immediately by a Para drop, served only as a warning signal to the defenders' ground forces that an airborne assault was imminent. But the minutes passed without the Jus appearing and as the day drew on tension relaxed in the Retimo and Heraklion areas. Then, late in the afternoon, the air raid alarms sounded and some minutes later a gaggle of aircraft came into view. It was the second wave – hours late and up against a defence ready to receive it.

The remainder of Battle Group Centre, consisting of Sturm's 2nd Para Regiment, dropped around Retimo, the 1st Battalion of Sturm's regiment was with Brauer's Battle Group East and as a substitute Sturm was reinforced by a Para Artillery Company and two Companies of the Para Machine-gun Battalion.

Adolf Strauch's diary gives us his impressions of that first day of combat. '20th May. Midday and it is boiling hot. Impenetrable clouds of dust lie above the airfield. The Ju 52s have come back from the mission; but not all of them. Our impressions were right. Before we load the weapons containers we have to remove the first dead from the damaged machines. The aircraft crew do not say much. It is 14.00 hrs. We take off. At 16.00 hrs we shall jump. The heat is unbearable. We do not have tropical uniforms and weigh a ton with all our equipment. We fly over the sea. The fighter planes which should be escorting us and which should beat down the enemy opposition when we drop, pass us – flying back from Crete. Bad organization somewhere.

At about 16.00 hrs "Get ready!" In front of us is the coast of Crete. "Ready to jump!" Our height at which we shall drop is 500 feet (150 metres). The siren sounds. We jump. I

Below: The Fallschirmjaeger move to their concentration area while more of their comrades fall from the sky. This photograph dramatically illustrates the low-altitude of the drop. (Brian L. Davis)

Right: Two Para NCOs remove the contents of a medical container after it has landed in Crete. The container held 16 flapped cases. Distributed among them were muslin bandages, field dressings, soap, calicil acid ointment, formaldehyde ointment, alkaline eye ointment and Losantin (anti-gas tablets), safety pins, adhesive zinc plaster, tourniquets, chloroform-ammonia-ether mixture. acetylosalicil, opium and cardiazol tablets. There were bottles of iodine and bismuth bandages for burns. In some there were also hypodermic syringes, scalpels, scissors, forceps, needles, sutures and powdered blood. Each Jaeger carried on his person one large and two small field dressings. (M. Klein)

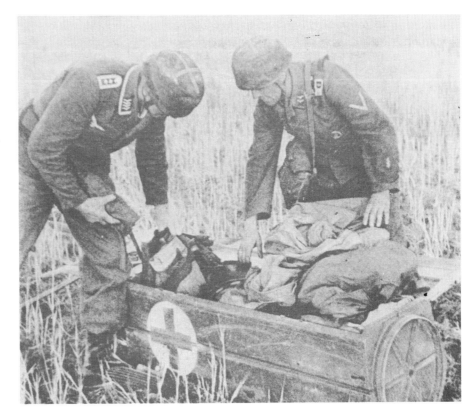

Right: The sentry in a standing patrol keeps a lookout. (Brian L. Davis)

hang in the air and try to orientate myself. I make a good landing in a vineyard. I reach my weapons container. We assemble and take up formation. Enemy reaction is weak. The heat unbearable.

'The 1st Regiment flies in in close waves. They, too, jump at 150 metres at a speed of 75 mph (120 kms). There are no German fighter aircraft to be seen. The British anti-aircraft artillery and field guns fire continually. Burning machines drop out of the sky. We can see individual Jaeger jumping out of the exits. The pilots hold their machines on course until they crash. A whole battalion has been destroyed. The night is cool. We have dug in ready to face the enemy who will come from the West.'

Battle Group East, which formed the mass of the second wave, was made up principally, of Brauer's 1st Para Regiment. Its task was to take out the town of Heraklion and the airfield there. Burkhardt's 2nd Battalion, together with supporting groups from the machine-gun battalion, was to jump over the field, with Walther's 3rd Battalion to the west and with the 2nd Battalion of 2nd Regiment to seal off the airfield on its western side.

The British and Dominion forces were waiting for this opportunity to avenge the losses which the Stuka raid had caused them. There was little point in firing at the Jaeger as they descended but once on the ground they were shot

at, harried and hunted before they could reach their weapons canisters. The losses to both 1st and 2nd Regiments were very heavy. The landings by Battle Group Centre at Retimo and at Heraklion failed to gain their objectives and the attackers, unable to group and to go over to the offensive, could only form small perimeters, hoping either to be relieved by their own forces or expecting to be attacked and overrun by the British. For them to hold out, isolated as they were, was a sort of victory. The units which had dropped over the Retimo airfield were driven back and Sturm, Commander of 2nd Regiment, was taken prisoner for a short while.

Worse was to befall Battle Group East. Most of Burkhardt's 2nd Battalion was lost in the drop and Walther's 1st Battalion was too weak to do more than fight its way to the eastern edge of the airfield. Schulz's 3rd Battalion could not get into Heraklion but was held at the western edge of the town.

By late in the evening of the 20th, the situation on Crete was that the landings in the east of the island had failed. In the centre, around Canea, there was limited success with some small Para perimeters joining up in the 'drops of oil' technique, but none of these perimeters were able to mount offensive operations. In the West around Maleme, the aggressive attacks of the Assault Regiment had cleared

Below: Fallschirmjaeger pass the debris of their delivery. Trees have always proved dangerous to parachutists. Crete, 1941. (Brian L. Davis)

Right: Having concentrated after landing, the Fallschirmjaeger deploy for the attack. Those in the foreground are carrying ammunition canisters for 81mm mortars. (Brian L. Davis)

part of the airfield, but Point 107 had still not been taken.

When wireless communication was finally made between the troops in the island and General Student's HQ he became aware at last of the true situation on the ground and realized that the key to victory was no longer Canea but Maleme. It would be on Maleme airfield that the Alpine Division's regiments would have to be airlanded and from where he would open the assault which would capture the island. Aware, also, that Maleme needed a strong commander and a reinforcement of fresh troops, Student gathered together a group of 550 Jaeger and placed them under the command of Colonel Ramcke. This reinforcement group dropped during the afternoon of the 21st, to the west of Maleme. The energetic Ramcke asked for a report. He was told, in an otherwise gloomy briefing, that the Assault Regiment's 1st and 2nd Battalions had gone in at first light and had conquered the crest of Point 107. The New Zealand defenders of the airfield could not hold out for long, dominated as they were by the Para battalions on the hill. The airstrip fell and the signal was sent that the first transports could be dispatched. In the period between the capture of the airstrip and the arrival of the aircraft the Jaeger worked hard, using a captured British tank as a bulldozer, to drag wrecked aircraft and other obstructions from the runway. The first Jus landed under shellfire. Some were hit and again the runway was littered with wrecked aircraft. Locally commandeered vehicles supported the tank in its effort to clear a path for the aircraft. As these touched down they were braked hard – the runway was a short one – and out of them spilled the mountain troops. Then the machine was away again and another was coming in to land. The mountaineers doubled forward to thicken the Para line. A firm foothold now existed around the Maleme airfield.

The other Para units scattered along the northern side of the island continued to hold out against British counter-attacks, with the Jaeger unaware that the battle was now swinging in their favour. Adolf Strauch's unit waited in the heat of the 21st for a British attack, but none came. His diary reports, 'Heavy fighting in the town. We have contact with the enemy – partisans.' His diary entry for the 22nd says, 'We have beaten off the attack of an enemy battalion. One of our battalions drops as reinforcement into the battle area. A 3.7cm anti-tank gun lands near me. It came down supported by 5 parachutes. A little further off a motor cycle combination crashes to the ground and is totally wrecked. The 'chutes did not open'. With the arrival during the 22nd, of General Ringel, General Officer Commanding 5th Alpine Division, control of the battle passed out of the hands of Luftwaffe General Student and his Jaeger. There were still patrols to be undertaken and on 23 May contact was made with survivors of 3rd

Above: A number of the second wave troops, who flew in by Junkers, were injured as the aircraft crash-landed at Malmes. These machines are from No. 1 Squadron of No. 1 Special Services Group. (M. Klein)

Regiment. With the link-up made, the Para regiments prepared to take, at long last, the objectives which they had been ordered to gain on the first day. This was to be no easy task. Adolf Strauch reports that on the 23rd an attack by his unit upon the town was beaten back. 'We had to defend ourselves. We are without water or food. Our losses are growing.' On the 24th, 3rd Regiment seized the village of Galatas and the heights dominating it. A reinforcement battalion of paratroops dropped on the 25th to support Battle Group East and other detachments came in on the same day as 2nd Regiment. Fighting was still bitter on the 24th, a day during which Adolf Strauch recorded an air drop of food and ammunition. His unit lay waiting and ready to receive a British attack from the west but none came in.

On the 25th, a quick thrust by his battalion broke the British encirclement and as a result contact was gained with other Jaeger units. The 'drops of oil' tactic was beginning to work. A British counter-attack to drive back the groups that had escaped encirclement, was repulsed by swift action on the part of Strauch's battalion. He recorded that the unit was without water and that the water points and wells were covered by British fire. 'It is 45 degrees in the shade and we are frying on the lava rocks.'

Contact between the Jaeger and the Alpine troops during the 26th, led to a local British resistance being beaten down as well as to the capture of the town and harbour of Canea and of Suda Bay. Although this was considered to be a mopping-up operation, Strauch records that the British were still fighting with confidence and obviously did not consider that they were losing. 'Over the radio our opponents offer to take our wounded. We accept that offer and the badly wounded are handed over. But those Jaeger who can still walk do not go over, but stay with the unit.'

During the 27th fighting ended in the western part of Crete but there were still some Para drops undertaken. One on the 28th, was made to take out the airfield at Heraklion, but one arranged for the 29th, was no longer needed. The British had begun to evacuate their forces from the southern side of the island. The pursuit stage of the operation could now be left to the Alpine Division to whom command of the battle had already passed.

There remains to be told only how the sea-borne troops fared. These were to have formed the follow-up to the original assault troops. The convoys of ships, carrying two battalions of a regiment of 5th Alpine, as well as Jaeger from 7th Flieger Division and the heavy weapons of both Divisions together with some Panzer, were intercepted and either sunk or dispersed by the Royal Navy. So great were the losses suffered in that disaster that only 52 men of the two battalions of the Alpine Regiment went into action on Crete.

The participation of 7th Flieger Division and the Corps troops in the battle had come to an end. It was time for resting and regrouping and for assessing the losses which had been suffered. The 7th Division had put into battle 22,000 men of whom 3,250 were killed or missing with a further 3,400 wounded. The Assault Regiment alone lost 700 in killed or missing. Adolf Strauch concluded his story of the battle for Crete with the words. 'We paid dearly for our victory. Every third man had been killed, every second man wounded. Our victory was no victory. Now that the strain of fighting was over the illnesses and sicknesses that we had fought down came out and malaria, dysentery and jaundice struck. We awaited new orders and expected

Right: Allied troops surrender. (M. Klein)

Right: For some, transport was available in the form of captured vehicles, in this case a British 15cwt truck, still bearing its Arabic markings from Egypt. (M. Klein)

Right: While the aerial assault went in, the Germans also attempted to send troops to Crete by boat, but they were destroyed or turned back by the Royal Navy. This is a caique, a commandeered local boat, to which the Germans have added a 2cm Flak gun. (M. Klein)

Above: Heraklion surrenders to the conquerors from the north.
(Brian L. Davis)

that the next operation would be against either Cyprus or Suez. I spent some time as guard on the British prisoners and exchanged addresses with two Australians. We made arrangements to meet after the war. Our orders have arrived. We are not to go into a new battle but have been ordered home where new intakes of men will bring us up to strength.'

It has been suggested that Hitler, shocked at the casualties that had been suffered in the Crete operation, ordered that the airborne regiments were to be broken down into battalions and that the Jaeger should be employed only in ground fighting. This suggestion is invalid for orders to raise new divisions were issued and air operations were planned against both Malta and Cyprus. In addition there were other airborne missions carried out during the war, which would refute the idea. The reasons for the few airborne operations that were carried out after Crete is perhaps due to Hitler's realization that the element of surprise had been lost as a result of that campaign, and the growing shortage of suitable aircraft. It must be admitted, however, that the battles which the Jaeger were to fight in the final years of the war were almost exclusively ground operations.

Crete was a hard-won victory for the Jaeger and for General Student who planned and executed, for the first time in the history of warfare, the capture of an island from the air.

In the first weeks after the end of the campaign the Jaeger were employed in that necessary but sad task of recovering and burying their fallen. The several regimental cemeteries which had been laid out and the memorial stones which had been dedicated were removed at the end of the Second World War. The Cretan authorities exhumed the bodies from each of the unit cemeteries and buried them all in one single area. A huge cross of sacrifice stands now in the garden of remembrance in which they lie.

For those post-battle months most units were under canvas using the tents which had been left behind in the British evacuation and living on British Army rations. 'These we thought excellent, at first, but we soon became bored with corned beef and meat and vegetable stew. We were intrigued by some items of food; there was a peculiar pale jam manufactured in Haifa which was quite tasteless. We also thought the English meat puddings an odd choice of food to be included in an almost tropical diet, but we liked the South African tinned fruit which we found delicious.'

By the last week of July a large German garrison was in Crete and had taken over control of the island. The last Jaeger units could be taken home for leave and regrouping in a Germany which was now obsessed with the new war against Russia, one in which, at that time, the 7th Flieger Division was not involved.

6. In the East dark clouds are gathering'
THE EASTERN FRONT, AUTUMN 1941

It was, perhaps, the terrible losses suffered by 7th Flieger Division in Crete, that caused it to be left out of the first operations in the war against Russia during the summer of 1941.

While on the Eastern Front German armies thundered towards Moscow, Leningrad and Kiev, the Jaeger regiments and battalions of 7th Division, back in their several depots, were busy taking in recruits fresh from training school and distributing them to those Companies that had suffered the most severe losses in the Balkan operations.

By such infusion unit strengths were built up and the individual recruits were strengthened physically and were taught the Para ethos, so that in a short time they were rock hard and battleworthy. For these new men, grouped round a cadre of experienced Jaeger, the baptism of fire was not too distant. On 24 September, divisional headquarters received a movement order. The 7th was to be flown, by battalions, to the Leningrad sector of Army Group North, which had flung a ring around most of the city and the surrounding area.

It had not been Hitler's intention to storm Leningrad. The Fuehrer saw little point in committing first class units to fight at a disadvantage in street battles against Voroshilov's twenty divisions of militia backed by the Red Army garrison and the Baltic Fleet. Far better to starve the city into surrender. He was to change that policy a year later when he realized that its citizens would sooner die than give in. The Russians, to whom Leningrad, formerly St. Petersburg, had an older, more emotional appeal than Moscow, fought with desperate fury to smash the encirclement. They were helped by Hitler's bewildering decisions. At one time he halted the Panzer advance upon the city until the infantry armies could reach the halted armour. That pause gave the Red Army the chance to regroup and to undertake the construction of defences. Then he removed from Army Group North most of its armoured formations in order to strengthen the drive on Moscow. With the Panzers now gone the Russians sent in mass assaults against numerically inferior German forces and seized the military initiative. It was to bolster the wavering German battle line against the massed assaults of the Red Army that 7th Flieger Division was ordered to the Leningrad Front. We must, at this point anticipate the actions in which they would be engaged and say that whenever the battle line was ruptured, a Jaeger unit, sometimes a regiment, more usually a battalion but often only a Company in strength, would be taken from the sector on which it was already fighting and sent to the new crisis point. These dramatic and immediate missions caused the Jaeger to name themselves 'The Fuehrer's Firemen'. Because its units arrived only piecemeal to the Eastern Front and because they were used in these small fire brigade actions, 7th Flieger was never able to fight as a single formation in the first actions which it undertook in that first winter of the war in Russia.

The first units of 7th Flieger Division were flown out to airfields in the operational area of German Eighteenth Army during the last days of September 1941. These were 1st and 3rd Battalions of 1st Para Regiment, together with 2nd Battalion of the divisional assault regiment. The 2nd battalion of the Assault Regiment was selected because 2nd Battalion of 1st Regiment was being converted to become the Training Battalion.

The military situation in the area of Eighteenth Army, one of the two armies of Army Group North which were investing the Leningrad area, was that the advances made by the German and Finnish armies had almost totally encircled the city. From the south-western suburbs the German line ran south east to Sluszk, then ascended and ran north-eastward along the western bank of the River Neva to Schlusselburg on the south-eastern shore of Lake Ladoga. On the western shore of the lake the Soviets held an area of territory extending northwards for 75 miles (120 kilometres). The Finnish section of the encircling line, to the north of the city, dipped southwards through the Karelian peninsula to a point on the Gulf of Finland about seven miles (twelve kilometres) north-west of the city. The battle line of Army Group North was not continuous but was broken by two salients: one to the south-west of Leningrad and one to the east of the city. It

was to pinch out that eastern salient that the Russians were making their most determined attacks. It was only twelve miles (twenty kilometres) wide and had on its eastern side the several armies of the Russian Volkhov Front. If they could break through the salient wall from the east and link up with the Leningrad forces which were hammering against the salient's west wall, Leningrad would be relieved and a vital rail link would have been restored. The Red Army made almost ceaseless attacks to force a breakthrough and to gain the River Neva.

It was to deal with a crisis that the first Jaeger units were plunged during the night of 29/30 September, when 1st Regiment's battalions took over 1st Infantry Division's sector running southwards along the Neva from the Schlusselburg to Viborogskaya. The Assault Regiment's battalion was first into action when it was sent direct from the troop transports into action to reduce a Soviet bridgehead at Petroschkino into which Red Army engineers had managed to bring a number of armoured fighting vehicles. Supported by the fire of No. 2 Company of the Para anti-aircraft machine-gun battalion, the Assault Battalion swung into the attack and drove the Soviets back to the river. But this had been no easy action and the Jaeger learned there on the Neva of the tenacity with which the Russian soldiers fought. Losses to the battalion were heavy as the Companies fought off one Soviet attack after another, but the Jaeger held the line, their determination and battle skill forcing the Red Army units to reduce the scale of their attacks. On 7 October, a crisis on another sector, that at Viborgskaya, caused the Assault Battalion to be pulled out of the Petroschkino sector and put in to stem the thrusts in the new area.

When 3rd Para Regiment reached the line on 1 October, some of its officers were posted to those detachments which had lost theirs in the recent savage fighting. The Regiment went immediately into action and 3rd Battalion, which was on the left flank of the Assault Battalion, opened a series of assaults which reduced the Red Army's bridgeheads on the Viborgskaya sector of the Neva to a few isolated but strongly defended perimeters. The 2nd Battalion of 3rd Regiment then came into the area and took post on the right flank of 1st Regiment.

By the middle of October the Headquarters of 7th Division had arrived and, although only one Jaeger regiment was in position, formally took over command of that Divisional sector of the River Neva area. Other Fallschirmjaeger units began to come in, the last being the divisional Engineer Battalion whose No. 3 Company was soon involved in battle against a Red Army regiment in the woods around Ssinyavino. The other Engineer companies were sent in individually to reinforce 3rd Regiment's ring around the Russians at Viborgskaya.

In Para circles the Ssinyavino woods earned for themselves the reputation of a terrible killing-ground. Supreme Stavka, the highest military body controlled by Stalin, in a fresh effort to raise the siege of Leningrad by sweeping the German forces from the southern shore of Lake Ladoga, concentrated a massive force. The 55th Red Army and an *ad hoc* collection of units, the Neva Operations Group, had orders to fight westwards and to link up with 54th Red Army of the Volkov Front which was to strike from the east. The place where the Soviet formations were to link was Ssinyavino.

Fighting in the woods and along the Neva continued through the short winter days and the long, dark, freezing nights. The first winter in Russia is remembered by many Jaeger as a time of privation and utter misery, but they held their line until mid December when the Division was relieved and posted back to Germany. The efforts of the individual battalions had held the front, but the fact that the Division had not been committed as a whole and in offensive operations had had an effect upon the morale of the Jaeger.

An example of the small-unit operations which the Paras had fought is that of No. 3 Company of the Engineer Battalion which was put into the sector held by 328th Infantry Regiment. The Engineer Company had orders to launch a silent attack in the nearby woods against the enemy who had pushed his trench lines forward until they were only a couple of hundred metres from the headquarters of one of 328th's battalions. How strong and how alert the enemy was, the infantry officers could not say, but they did suspect that the Soviet troops were supported by armour. Moving slowly and silently the men of No. 3 Company crept towards the enemy. Ten minutes after crossing the start-line the sound of rapid rifle fire, the detonation of grenades and cries of 'Hurrah!' told the infantry officers that the attack was going in and was succeeding. This short fire-fight did not end there. The Russian soldiers rallied at a strong point which was only taken after the bayonet had done its work. Eighty prisoners were taken. The advance was carried forward until strong resistance was met; the Soviet infantry were backed by armour. One of the Engineer's tank-busting teams was called forward. A Jaeger charged at the vehicle. His arm came back to lob a grenade into the open hatch but the Russian tank commandant realizing the danger slammed it shut. The tank's heavy gun was then fired, but undeterred the Jaeger stuffed a second grenade up the barrel and pulled the detonating cord. He then moved to the side of the T34 and at close range fired a succession of rifle grenades into the side armour. The grenade inside the barrel then exploded and confident that he had stunned the crew the Jaeger very calmly placed a 3kg hollow-

Above: Through the devastated forests and swampland of Volkov, in a scene reminiscent of the Western Front during the First World War, Fallschirmjaeger make their way along a makeshift causeway, their balance aided by their personal 'Volkov sticks'. Ahead is a 20mm Flakvierling gun position. (Brian L. Davis)

charge behind the turret. The resulting explosion caused the tank ammunition to be set off in a sympathetic detonation. The T34 blew up.

It must not be thought that that Jaeger's attack had been carried out in isolation. All round him his comrades were fighting down Soviet soldiers using rifle fire, bayonets and entrenching tools. A mass of Red Army men stormed forward, their advance covered by the fire of heavy machine-guns. The Engineers flung back that assault and destroyed a second Red tank which had come forward to support the infantry. The Company's task did not end there. New Russian threats caused it to be put in at a number of threatened places along the front of the Army infantry regiment. The 110-man Engineer Company had fought all day and during these hours of combat had destroyed two tanks at close quarters, had killed 250 of the enemy and had taken 200 prisoners.

From the War Diary it can be seen how the Company's strength melted away in the fierce, almost unceasing Soviet attacks. By 7 November, the Company, which two weeks earlier had begun the campaign with 143 Jaeger, was down to 24 and had had to be heavily reinforced by men from other Companies. They, too, had been hard hit. No. 4 Company had been reduced to one NCO and ten other ranks, while No. 1 could muster only seven NCOs and thirty men.

On 16 November, No. 3 Company, whose battle we have followed, was relieved from the line by 1st Infantry Regiment. The Para Engineer Battalion then returned to Germany.

On the Eastern Front, as we have seen, 7th Flieger Division was not deployed as a single formation. The 1st and 3rd Regiments had been involved in bitter fighting in the north, near Leningrad, while 2nd Regiment was held in reserve in Germany. That regiment was not to remain inactive for long.

The advances of Army Group South into the Ukraine had been a succession of brilliant triumphs. The Ukraine, Russia's bread-basket, had been overrun, the Don basin, a major source of Soviet industrial power, was under threat, and in the course of these spectacular advances during the summer and autumn of 1941, a great many Red armies had been destroyed and hundreds of thousands of Soviet soldiers taken prisoner. Then, as the first signs of winter made their appearance, the Russian hosts went into a general counter-attack which had, by the end of November, forced Army Group South on to the defensive. A serious situation developed, with that overstretched major formation having insufficient forces to master the crisis. A check by Army Group South of formations which could be used to bolster the defence indicated that 2nd Para Regiment and certain Para Corps troops were available. Movement orders were issued. Two battalions of 2nd Para Regiment, together with the 4th Battalion of the Assault Regiment, detachments from the Para Anti-tank Battalion and a Company of the Para Machine-gun battalion, were soon *en route* to the Eastern Front. 'The train journey seemed endless,' recalled one Jaeger. 'We were held up for long periods while other units were rushed through. We thought that our orders would have given us the the highest priority, but this was not the case.'

'That journey made me realize for the first time the enormous vastness of Russia. We went via the General Gouvernment of Poland and into Belorussia. Once through that region, which was more or less Westernised, we entered one which was the Russia of our imagination. Of fields so vast that they stretched to all the horizons. Imagine a field of sunflowers 30 kilometres long. Truthfully said, the terrain was a sort of prairie, a land sea on which the occasional little village seen far away was the only sign of human life. It was, at once a depressing and an exciting country. Depressing in its monotonous vastness; exciting because it was so obviously fertile.'

The journey for the Para Battle Group, commanded by Colonel Sturm, ended east of Stalino and the units defended a sector along the River Mius around the little town of Charzysk. Battle Group Sturm held its positions throughout the winter of 1941–42, and if the climatic and battle conditions in Army Group South were not as bitter as they were in the Leningrad sector where 1st and 3rd Regiments were embattled, they were still abnormally hard. Losses incurred in beating off the Red Army's attacks, losses from one's own attacks and the sickness of troops inadequately clothed and fed, took more off to the hospital than did bullets, and more limbs were lost to frostbite and gangrene than to shellfire. It was a time of trial and tribulation.

The worldly hopes upon which Adolph Hitler had set his every endeavour in the high summer of 1941, had turned to ashes by the winter of that same year.

The *Blitzkrieg* victories in Yugoslavia and Greece, the capture of Crete, the early success of the Afrika Korps in the desert and the fast, triumphant assaults in the territory of the Soviet Union had seemed to be milestones on an unobstructed road to military glory. Winter and Germany's unpreparedness to meet its brutal severity, halted that progress along the victory road. The fearful experiences of that first winter in Russia brought home to the Nazi leaders, perhaps for the first time, the magnitude of the war in which they had involved their country. The losses in men had been horrendous and never again was the Third Reich to reach the high peak of strength that had been hers in the summer of 1941.

By Midsummer Day Germany was involved in a two-front war and by December this had expanded to become a world war. She was now confronted by three main enemies whose productive potential outstripped her own and whose manpower resources were, if not inexhaustible, undisputedly infinitely greater than those of Germany.

By the end of 1941, the full potential of the Allies had not been brought against the Reich so that she was still, as she had been since the summer of 1940, the strongest power in Europe. Although her armies had suffered a reverse in Russia, Germany would be certain to reopen operations in the East once campaigning weather had returned. But the campaigns of the coming year would not be the confident, joyous blaze of conquest that had highlighted the year 1941. Future battles would be hard fought and won, even harder.

1942

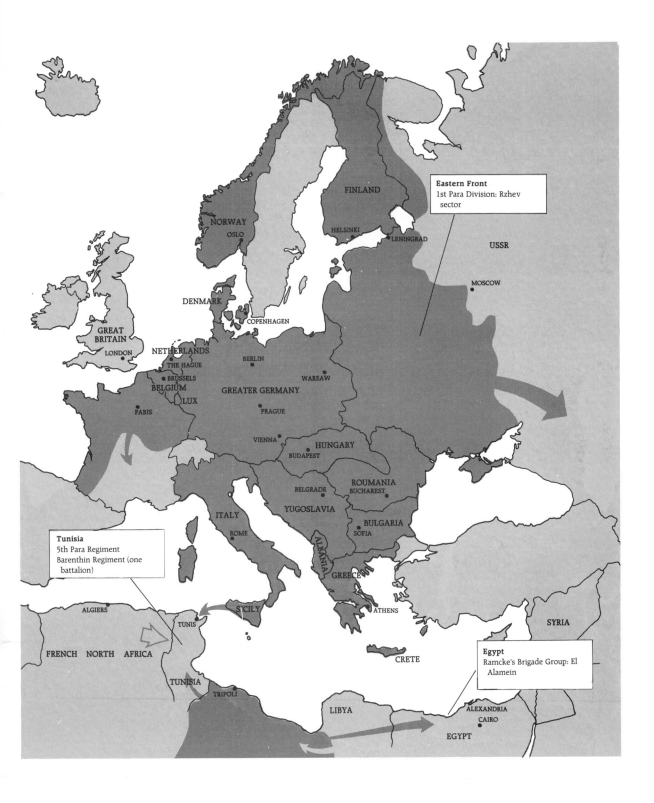

Eastern Front
1st Para Division: Rzhev sector

Tunisia
5th Para Regiment
Barenthin Regiment (one battalion)

Egypt
Ramcke's Brigade Group: El Alamein

7. 'The banners are flying in the east wind'

THE EASTERN FRONT, JANUARY-DECEMBER 1942

The winter of 1941–42, was one of the hardest of the twentieth century and its cruelty was one for which the German Army on the Eastern Front was unprepared. The leaders of OKW were convinced by Hitler's political obsession that the Soviet Union was a rotten, ramshackle edifice doomed to collapse with a firm kick of the door. In that conviction they had accepted that the war against Russia would be a short one and had planned accordingly. They agreed totally with Hitler's thesis that the war with Russia would be begun and completed before the onset of winter. As a result, they made no provision to supply the armies in the field with adequate winter clothing. The belief of the OKW in the Fuehrer's military forecasts proved to be naïve and the plans they produced based upon those forecasts were unworkable.

The war with Russia was not concluded within a matter a months. The long, hot days of summer and early autumn, with their swift advances and incredible gains in territory and prisoners, were succeeded by the rains of late autumn. Torrential, day-long downpours falling upon the unsurfaced roads of the Soviet Union, turned them

Below: A heavy machine-gun position of 8 Company, 2nd Regiment, on the River Mius in January 1942. (Adolf Strauch)

into mud slicks which held all wheeled vehicles fast. Even the Panzers, lacking the very broad tracks with which the Red Army's tanks were fitted, could not easily escape from the thick slime of the *rasputisa* – the clinging mud of autumn and spring. In October the first frosts hardened the ground sufficiently for Panzer operations to begin again. Released from the mud the Panzers roared forward towards the declared final objectives. But before victory could be gained the deep and bitter winter arrived, bringing with it the horrors of frost-bite and gangrene to those who were unprepared to meet it. And the German Army was unprepared.

When it became clear that the soldiers on the Eastern Front were suffering unbelievable hardships, Josef Goebbels offered the services of the Nazi Party's organizations to conduct a nation-wide appeal for the Home Front to donate warm clothing to the Fighting Front. This offer was rejected by the military authorities who feared that so public an acknowledgement of their lack of foresight would lead to a loss of national confidence in the Army leadership. The soldiers of the German Army on active service during the cruellest winter of the century were condemned to suffer to save the face of their most senior commanders.

Lacking the sort of clothing capable of withstanding the biting cold, most of the men of the German Army fought wearing their standard uniforms. The hard winter froze the breech-blocks of the artillery pieces; truck and tank engines had to be started up and run for long periods in order that their radiators would not freeze and, indeed, all things mechanical had to be specially protected by such *ad hoc* means. Only the fighting men lacked protection and suffered accordingly. 'To commemorate that first winter in Russia, those of us who survived it were given a medal whose ribbon tucked into the same button hole as that of the Iron Cross 2nd Class. Because the ribbon of that winter campaign medal had a predominantly red colour, we survivors called it either the "Mincemeat Medal" or the "Order of the Frozen Meat".'

For as long as the winter lasted so did the misery of infantry warfare; of fighting off attacks by warmly clad Siberian riflemen acclimatized to the weather. Of assaults by Soviet tanks whose engines did not freeze up and of barrages by Russian guns which suffered from neither mechanical defect due to freezing nor a shortage of ammunition. The cruel weather was not allowed to halt German military operations. The Army had to adapt or die. It adapted.

In the River Mius sector the Jaeger of 2nd Regiment and of 4th Battalion of the Assault Regiment, were in action fighting off waves of Red Army men who stormed in furious attack against the Fallschirmjaeger defensive positions. Battle Group Sturm held its line against all assaults, but to the north of its positions a situation which had been serious had deteriorated and had become a crisis. An élite formation was needed and quickly to master the crisis. The call was for units of Fallschirmjaeger and the turn of the year Battle Group Meindl was created out of the last uncommitted units of the 7th Flieger Division. That group consisted of 1st Battalion of the Assault Regiment, the Jaeger regimental headquarters and a battalion of the Artillery Regiment. Compared with the numbers which had been committed to the vast summer campaigns it was little in the way of reinforcement, but each unit however small was some support to the under-manned battle line.

In early February 1942, Meindl's group arrived on the Eastern Front and took up positions around Vyasma, a town to the east of Smolensk, where the Russians had made the most determined efforts to smash through. Losses on both sides had been heavy and the German formations had been reduced by casualties to miscellaneous collections of SS and Luftwaffe fragments, the remnants of first class formations destroyed in battle but still fighting fiercely. These little groups, weakened by losses but high in morale, were embodied into Meindl's Battle Group.

Switching the Red Army's main thrust from point to point, Stalin and Supreme Stavka then resumed the attack in that sector of the line at Yuknov which 2nd Regiment was holding. The Red Army's blows struck heavily and damagingly, threatening a breakthrough. To meet this new challenge Battle Group Meindl was rushed from its positions at Vyasma and thrust into the line at Yuknov. Its arrival was opportune and its units, put immediately into action, were instrumental in holding the fiercest Soviet attempts to breakthrough.

Weeks of bitter fighting in sub-zero temperatures and the fearful casualties inflicted upon the Red Army by Fallschirmjaeger who were fighting for their very existence against a skilled enemy and a climate which was that enemy's closest ally, brought a halt to operations around Yuknov. With the sector now considered secure, Meindl's group was available for action on any other threatened sector. He was sent to the River Volkhov area. There Fallschirmjaeger units were embattled not only with the Red Army in the marshes of the river, fighting to smash the ring around Leningrad, but also against the assaults of the city's garrison, striking south-easterly to seize the important rail and road junction of Mga and thus to break the encirclement.

The battles for Volkhov were among the most bitter fought on the Eastern Front in the early part of 1942. It was from the River Volkhov sector that the Red Army

made its westward attacks to smash through the German salient and gain touch with the defenders of Leningrad. So bitter was the struggle in that area and so deeply was the memory of it etched in the minds of many who fought there that, as a memento of their sufferings, they carried so-called 'Volkhov' walking-sticks which they had carved during the long and freezing nights spent on the northern sector of the Russian front.

The first missions carried out by the Jaeger of 7th Division, were not those of a single major formation. In every case the Para unit, irrespective of size, had been put into the line to close a breach, to hold the position abandoned by other troops or to lead the assault in some desperate enterprise.

When 2nd Regiment was posted to Russia the situation in which Jaeger units were used as fire brigades still obtained. In was an action of that type which brought 2nd Regiment, in March 1942, from its positions in southern Russia to the swamps and forests of Volkhov, near that northern sector where 1st Regiment had fought at the end of 1941.

The Soviets were still making the most violent efforts to smash the eastern salient and with one major offensive smashed had pulled back to regroup before making another attempt. For this new assault several Red Armies of the North-western and Volkhov fronts were to be employed. Stavka's plan was for these to make a concerted effort which would surround German Sixteenth Army whose Divisions were holding the salient. Included in the units which Stavka had assembled for the new operation were Morozov's Eleventh Red Army and Vlassov's Second Shock Army, both élite units and both under orders not to fail in their endeavour. Their dedicated and veteran

Communist commanders could be expected to use the utmost severity to achieve Stalin's orders that the siege of Leningrad be raised. Stavka's plan was for Eleventh Army to turn the flank of German Sixteenth Army. The Russian High Command knew that this would be a hard task, but Morozov's highly trained and specialist units were expected to fight and win. Once the flank of Sixteenth Army had been turned the other formations of Volkhov Front would fall upon the Germans and begin to tear the Divisions to pieces. Under cover of these assaults the units of Vlassov's Second Shock Army would rise out of the swamps and dense forests in which they had been hidden and in an all-out drive would carve out a corridor between Leningrad and the River Neva.

The tenacious defence by the German Divisions of Army Group North frustrated that plan and what had been envisaged by Stavka as a fast operation using ski troops, motorized sledges and waves of infantry advancing under furious barrages, collapsed in the fire of the German defenders who knew that they were literally fighting for survival. Stavka, undaunted by the losses which these first attacks had incurred and ignoring the terrible conditions under which the Russian soldiers were fighting, ordered the hopeless assaults to be continued. In an effort to revive the dying offensive Vlassov was ordered not to wait for the situation that had been planned but to bring his troops into action without delay. They were to make an all-out effort, and it was the violent struggles of Second Shock Army that brought 2nd Jaeger Regiment northwards from Stalino.

Reinhard Hoffmann, the author of the following account, served with No. 5 Company of the anti-aircraft machine-gun battalion, a Corps unit which gave support to

Left: Spring 1942 in a forest clearing amid the swampy woodlands of the Mius area. Visibility was limited severely by the densely packed trees, making ambush a constant threat. (Adolf Strauch)

Right: The high water table meant that digging slit trenches was impossible, so the wood – in plentiful supply – had to be used to make defensive positions. Here Corporal Gallenkamp keeps watch by his MG34. He was one of many who were never to return home. (Adolf Strauch)

Right: Rations on the Mius front, April 1942. They had to be brought forward by hand for the last five miles because of the difficult terrain. At this point, rations per man per day were down to one cup of soup and a slice of bread. (Adolf Strauch)

2nd Jaeger Regiment. He had volunteered for the paratroops in April 1941 and his first missions had been with 2nd Regiment around Stalino in the southern area of Russia.

'In April 1942, we were relieved from the line by Italian Alpini and brought back to a suburb of Stalino. We all believed that we were being pulled out in order to be trained for new Para drops. According to rumour we would be attacking either Malta or Gibraltar. After a couple of weeks' rest we were suddenly ordered to entrain. Thus began a journey into the unknown and we rode backwards and forwards across Russia. The rumours flew thick and fast. We were being posted back to Germany, said one rumour. No we aren't, said another, we are being prepared for a drop on a group of islands in Lake Ladoga. When we reached Lithuania and the German-Polish frontier we were all convinced that we were going home. Those hopes collapsed like a pack of cards when, towards the end of April, we were billeted in Tosno (in

northern Russia) and so near to the Front that we could hear the rumble of gunfire. Now and again Iron Gustav, an old Russian aircraft, flew over dropping the queerest collection of explosive devices upon us. . . .'

From Tosno we were taken to the Volkhov sector which was being held by 21st Infantry Division under whose command we were now placed. It was on that sector that Ivan was making the strongest efforts to break through between Tosno and Schuydova. It was our task to frustrate the Russian efforts to break through and also to launch counter-attacks at those places where he did succeed. The mention of the village of Lipovka will revive terrible memories for all those of 2nd Regiment who fought there. In the middle of the village General Sturm set up the regimental TAC HQ. Our Company lay in reserve positions in a wood south-west of the village with Company TAC HQ in Lipovka, in the cellar of a house. Two platoons of our Company were on duty at any one time as local defence.

Left: 13 May 1942: a patrol returns, Strauch, from whose album these pictures are taken, is the man indicated on the right.

During the 8th and 9th May 1942, the Ivans around Lipovka tried to smash through to seize and to cut a main road. Their attack was preceded by a furious barrage during which a direct hit on our Company HQ killed twelve men. While we were burying our dead comrades the following morning the barrage began again and behind it stormed the Red Army infantry. The force of the follow-up attack was such that the Russians achieved small penetrations of our line. We local defence platoons were ordered forward to support Major Pietzonka's 2nd Battalion which was under extreme pressure. Before we moved off twenty Red Air Force machines attacked Lipovka and their bombs, crashing into the houses, buried some of the two platoons. We had to dig out our comrades before the mission could be undertaken. When we finally did set out to strengthen the line we were only twenty in number and were escorted by a tank because the whole area was infested with partisans. The Panzer was of little use for it was soon stuck fast in the thick mud of the forest path.

At about 17.00 hours we reached the battle area and reported to the Jaeger Company commander whose Company had been all but destroyed and had only six men left. There were snipers everywhere and even before we had taken up our positions we had one of our group badly wounded. During the night the battalion was surrounded and throughout the following two days we fought a battle that swayed first one way and then the other. We machine-gunners were then ordered to fight our way back to Lipovka and to gain touch with the regiment. Outside the village we found the men of the Supply Echelon manning the line. They had been taken from their ordinary jobs and were serving as Jaeger. We reported to the regimental commander and were then ordered to return to the battalion with new instructions for Major Pietzonka. As we made our way back through the woods we were attacked by Ivans and forced to withdraw to the outskirts of Lipovka. Barely had we shaken off these Russians when more of their infantry, supported this time by low-flying aircraft, flung in a strong attack. We beat it

Left: In the middle of an attack. The Russian bunker is but a few yards away, behind the dense screen of trees. (Adolf Strauch)

off. A second attack was launched. We beat it off. At last light the Ivans pulled back and we made a quick thrust through the woods and rejoined the battalion in the front line.

On 13th May, some Panzers and SP guns came up and with their help we not only sealed off the penetrations which Ivan had made but also drove him back to his original lines. His attempt to reach the main road had failed once again. The regiment had lost heavily in this battle. Our Company alone lost 50 killed in action and 120 wounded. But that was not the final account. The 14th May, was the hardest and bloodiest day of battle. The commander of 21st Infantry Division ordered the remnants of 2nd Regiment to attack through shattered woods and swamps against the enemy. Our commander's objections, on the grounds of the losses his regiment had suffered and the tiredness of his men, were rejected contemptuously by the commander of 21st Division. General Sturm then flew off to Berlin to carry a complaint to a higher authority in Berlin. We still had to carry out the attack which would be led by Major Pietzonka. We were to cross the start-line at 06.00 hours behind an artillery barrage and covered by Stukas.

We had closed up to the start-line by 05.30 hours so that as soon as the barrage and Stuka attacks opened we would be ready to move off. Let me add at this point that a great many of our comrades were suffering from swamp fever. One of them with a temperature of over 39 degrees collapsed but would not allow himself to be taken back to the first aid post in Lipovka. He was afraid that he might be considered a coward if he left his men. Before we began the attack a patrol was sent out with orders to bring back a prisoner. Back came the patrol with a captured Ivan. . . . The minutes ticked toward 6 o'clock, but there was no sound of either artillery fire or of aircraft engines. We all thought that the attack must have been called off but then five shells passed over our heads and exploded into the enemy lines. We were given the order to advance. Our Company was 40 men strong. No. 1 Platoon was led by Sergeant Kalwan. The second platoon, about eighteen men, I led. Because of the swamp to our right we had no contact with the unit on that flank and there was a gap of about a kilometre in our front between our neightbours and ourselves. The Company Commander took post centrally, between the two platoons. His second in command was with my platoon, on the right flank, covering the gap. We sloshed forward through swamp, mud, vegetation and the decaying bodies of the Russian dead moving as quietly as possible so as not to alert the Ivans to our presence. After an advance of about 700 metres we hit the Russian unit from which our patrol had taken its prisoner. They opened fire. We dropped to the ground and fired at them from behind the shelter of tree trunks. I noticed that one of Ivans had fired all his rounds and was busy trying to reload his machine-gun. A thought struck me – this is our chance. I shouted out, "Come on lads!" and with hand-grenades, machine-pistols and a loud cheer we stormed their positions. It was a hard battle. From each slit trench, from behind every tree, between the roots of the trees, camouflaged with leaves they lie there firing at us. They fight to the last. When there are no more left to fight we carry on with our advance but do not get far. About 300 metres ahead of us there are two knocked out T34s with another, a double turret tank. We reach them and then from Ivan's main positions he launches a strong counter-attack. Their attacking cry is "Hooray!" not "Hurrah!" which is what we shout. We fire as fast as we can and in our defensive fire their attack stumbles and dies.

They have been hit hard, but it has been hard for us. Less than three hours have passed and half our men are either dead or wounded. The sergeant who led the patrol which took the prisoner lies badly wounded. My runner who tries to reach him is shot through the carotid artery and dies almost immediately. I try to bandage the sergeant but he waves me away, "Don't bother. This is it. I've fired off 1,200 rounds and Ivan has had no easy victory in killing me. The main thing is that we have won." He died on the way back to the Dressing Station. I checked and found that we had only eight men left. The Company Commander's runner races towards me, but before he can reach me he collapses, shot through the stomach. While I bind him up he gives the officer's message. "Pull back. The enemy is outflanking you." The tireless stretcher-bearers try to bring out all the wounded and I put the badly wounded runner behind a tree while I try to work out a plan for the withdrawal. The Ivans have worked their way forward. The situation is serious, but I must not cause a panic among the men by ordering a hasty retreat. The wounded man can guess what I have in mind. He passes me his ammunition. I tell him that if the stretcher-bearers don't take him then I will carry him on my back. He tells me his father fell in the First World War and one of his brothers in this one. I comfort him. He will not be left behind. The Company commander works his way forward to us. He has seen what has happened and has brought the stretcher-bearers with him. We place the wounded man on a shelter half and pull him yard by yard and from tree to tree out of immediate danger.

Eventually we join the rest of the Company. By 17.00 hours we have fought off three more Russian infantry assaults and finally take up defensive positions in the place from which we started our attack. The Russians have also lost heavily, but the gaps in our ranks are men who are irreplaceable. Platoon strength is now only eight men. Some of the other Companies have had even heavier casualties. After that terrible day we enjoy a quiet period during which we carry out only reconnaissance or battle patrols. In the middle weeks of June an infantry unit relieves us and we are taken to billets in Shudova, a transit stage on the journey home to Germany and a well-deserved leave.

After our leave had expired we returned to Depot and met there those who had been wounded and who had now returned to us after convalescence. It was at this time that our Company finally became accepted as part of the battalion. When the Company went to Russia we had been a young group with no battle experience but we had proved, in those never-ending battles, that we were as good as the other Companies. The decorations that had been awarded proved that. Nearly every man had won the Iron Cross Second Class, most wore the wounded badge and the Company had won four Iron Crosses First Class during the fighting for Volkhov.'

Another man whose war-time recollections are coloured by the fighting for Volkhov was Adolf Strauch, a veteran of Corinth and of Crete. The hardships and dangers of war were not unknown to him, yet it is the memory of what happened at Volkhov which is the most vivid in his mind. He wrote the following account because, and he stresses this, the part played by the Fallschirmjaeger in the Volkhov battles has been ignored. Strauch appreciates that these omissions on the part of other authors have not been deliberate. They have occurred because the Jaeger had been put in small detachments and their actions have been absorbed into the history of the unit to which they were subordinate. Strauch served in No. 8 Company of 2nd Regiment and this is the story of that unit's actions in just a few of the 70 days he spent in the fighting for Volkhov.

Strauch begins by claiming that this is no battle report. 'Battle reports are like files in which an event is discussed, judged and evaluated. The individual soldiers; the little group is of small account in the recording of great events. This is, therefore, a report from the viewpoint of a simple soldier who, together with his comrades spent seventy long days and nights seeing nothing but trees, living in a swamp, without shelter, without even a slit trench. One who was often poorly fed and who stilled his thirst with melted snow and from puddle water. Who was infested with lice, was plagued by mosquitoes and riddled with fever. Who had to be constantly alert and whose time was spent either in attack or in defence. This is a report without heroes or heroics, which describes the suffering that all soldiers undergo and a report which commemorates my own comrades and those of the Russian Army.'

It is the middle of April. In an hour we attack. In the woods there is still deep snow. To our front a few machine-guns are firing. We have a recce patrol out in the woods. That is their machine-gun fire. Yesterday my mate Karl was killed. He fell beside me, shot by a sniper. It was just like the situation in the song, *I had a good comrade!* When you are charging into the attack you have no time to say goodbye to those who fall, and when we shout our battle-cry there is no feeling any more. The fighting machine which was once a man runs like clockwork until it is exhausted – then fear sweeps in. The Russian soldiers fought with heroism and incredible bravery. They stayed up in their trees or lay on the ground pretending to be dead and when we passed over them they attacked us. It was our fire power that finally crushed them.

In the broken terrain we do not get very far forward. Our losses are mounting. The Russians defend their positions in the high woods supported by snipers. We have to cross open country. I took over Karl's machine-gun so as to work my way up towards the high woods. My cover is good, but another of my comrades falls near me. Shot through the stomach. The enemy fire concentrates on me. I cannot move to help him. His cries, "Stretcher-bearer!, Stretcher-bearer!" are terrible. He must be suffering agonies. I give covering fire as he is dragged back through the snow. As the light begins to fade it becomes quieter. We take up all-round defence for the night. Branches from the fir trees are our camp. But who can think of sleep? My jackboots are full of holes. Snow water has got into them and has begun to freeze. The nights are still very cold. Dawn is peaceful and quiet. Our enemy has pulled back. The wounded are safe. We go out looking for our fallen comrades and lay them side by side in the snow to say our farewells. Our Company commander, Lieutenant Jacob, is among the fallen. Lieutenant Kirsten, my platoon commander, takes over command of the Company. The Supply Echelon sends up hard tack and some overcoats. In my water-bottle are the remains of some rum which I got at Christmas. I share it out and we drink it as a toast to my promotion to sergeant. What we had endured is recorded in the history of 21st Division as follows. "To overcome the danger of being outflanked the 2nd Para Regiment and 1st Battalion of 151 Infantry Regiment were seconded to the Division. On successive days other troops joined the Division. On 15th April, 2nd Para Regiment and 3rd Battalion of 151 Regiment succeeded in gaining touch in the Tigoda swamp."

It is the first week of May. We expected an attack on May Day but none came. I led a recce patrol to find out what new tricks our enemy had been up to. We thought that the Russians might be in positions in good ground in the high woods. I went out with two others into the swamp. We worked our way forward until we were close enough for me to confirm our suspicions. Suddenly there was a Russian in front of us. He was terrified and raised his arms. We had captured a Russian Ensign. Then came the morning of 8th May. In the poor light of dawn our outposts reported that they had seen movement in the enemy positions. Quietly we took post. Then we could see the first earth-brown shapes. They were looking for cover behind the trees and were not yet clearly visible in the half-light. The tension was unbearable but our fire discipline held. When they were twenty metres away we opened fire. It was hell. The machine-gun barrels became overheated with the firing, but still the Russians poured towards us. They would not turn back. A Russian FOO must have been near my position, lying behind a tree. I could only see his arm movements. The mortar fire which he directed crashed down on us. Sergeant Kabisch was wounded near me. The platoon commander Haehnel was knocked out. Corporal Maus took a direct hit. Corporal Drusche was bleeding to death from the artery in his neck that had been torn open by a bullet. I took out an armour-piercing grenade and fired it. It burst against the tree trunk where the Russian FOO was hidden. Suddenly there was no movement. Then the Russians fired smoke so they could regroup under its cover and then attack again. But our Airborne artillery pieces carried on firing through the smoke. We had to keep changing the barrels on our machine-guns. That was the first day. During the next day the Ivans came back again and the killing went on. And again on the following day they tried to smash their way through our line. Then they gave up and pulled back.

We have just returned from a battle patrol. We have lost men killed and wounded. Our group is getting smaller in number. I bandaged a wounded comrade and my overalls and hands are covered with blood. I can't wash them. We have no water and can only quench our thirst with melting snow that drips from the birch trees. . . . Today, the 13th May, we have orders to attack the Russian positions. Our No. 6 Company will make the attack with us. We have no contact with the other Companies.

We are in the middle of the attack. The Russian positions are only a few metres in front of us. A piece of shell casing has torn open Corporal Zimmermann's leg. I fire the machine-gun from the hip and as I charge forward I trip over a tree root and fall only inches away from the firing slit in a Russian bunker. Dazed I lie there, press my face into the earth and wait. But they do not fire. Instead they come out. "Germanski!, Germansk! Do not shoot!" I am still alive.

We have no contact with the infantry. Our Company is a remnant. No. 6 Company furnishes a recce group to go out and to gain touch with the infantry. The patrol does not come back. We hear the sound of firing in the woods. I am ordered to take out the next patrol. We take compass bearings. Three men go out with me. We march through the high woods. I can only hope and silently pray. Suddenly there is a red wire in front of us; a telephone wire. We follow it hoping that it is one of our lines. We emerge from the wood and can hardly believe our eyes; there is a road ahead of us, a corduroy road peppered with shell holes. At the end of the red wire there is the TAC HQ of an infantry regiment. A Major is commanding the remnants of the regiment. Wounded come out of the woods. I report and am told that our battalion will be taking over this sector. Two other Jaeger come into the TAC HQ. I do not know them. I hear the words of their

Right: Regrouping in the Russian positions after the attack. The Germans made careful search of such positions seeking food; ammunition was plentiful, but the troops were almost starving. (Adolf Strauch)

report, "No. 7 Company, Para Regiment 2. One sergeant and one man reporting." The Jaeger are at the end of their tether but the Major comforts them. He turns to me and tells me to return with my men along the wire and lead the battalion in. There is firing in the woods ahead of us; machine-gun fire and then mortar bombs exploding. Our battalion has come forward and is meeting stiff enemy resistance. Then there is quiet. The battalion has gained touch with the infantry.

Extract from the 21st Division history. "On 13th May, a major German counter-offensive went in. After days of bitter fighting and suffering heavy losses a firm front was established running from Dubovik in a south-westerly direction to the Tigoda swamp. In those nine days the German troops gave their all and proved to the enemy that all his efforts were in vain. From that time on this was a quiet sector."

It is June in the green hell. We took over the infantry regiment's sector with our remnants. We do not have Companies and Platoons any longer, only small groups. I am sent out with seven men to hold an advanced post which we call the "outsider". It is a hundred metres to the next machine-gun post. In the thick undergrowth of this primaeval forest we have fitted up trip wires fastened to explosive charges, so that we shall not be surprised. The nights are light except for one hour between midnight and one o'clock in the morning. It was during that dark period that a Russian assault group tried to break through our line. Thanks to our alarm system we were warned. In the cross-fire of our two machine-guns the Ivans do not get through. They bombard us with mortar bombs. My machine-gun receives a direct hit on the barrel. By some miracle I am unwounded. We cover the Russian dead with branches because the weather is very warm. It is quiet along the line today. We know that some of our regiment have been back in Germany for some time now, resting and refitting. We wait every day for our relief. In the summer heat we are plagued by swarms of mosquitoes. We cannot stay in the trenches unless we are protected by gloves and a veil. These insects are so blood-thirsty that even a trip into the bushes means that certain delicate parts are under immediate attack. We scratch ourselves madly. The lice, too, are more active in this hot weather. I have fever and shivering fits.

Last night a Russian group got through the positions held by our neighbouring group. We have to keep a good watch out because some of the Ivans are behind our lines. We had visitors today. Two of the Russians who broke through come in and ask for cigarettes and chocolate. We can give them what they ask for because our supply system is working well at the moment. A General came up to see us the other day. Engineers are building dug-outs.

We are to be relieved but only to be put in on another sector. There is no joy in that. A Russian gunner must have been playing with his anti-tank gun for there is a sudden shell burst. A fragment of the casing tears through my jackboot and sticks out of my calf. It isn't a Blighty one. A bandage and a tetanus shot are all I get. I am very tired. All I want to do is to lie down and sleep. To sleep for whole nights through, but before all that to take a bath. It is a lovely day. The MO comes in and has a look at my wound and I am sent to a Field hospital. It is 23rd June, 1942. After 70 days I have finally got out of the woods but I am not alone. The battalion is also leaving to go back Home.'

In July 2nd Regiment reached Germany but when its period of leave was expired it did not rejoin the other units of 7th Flieger. By that time the decision had been taken to raise a second airborne Division and the regiment was placed directly under XI Flieger Corps command until work could begin on creating the new Division.

During the early summer of 1942, OKW ordered that a Brigade-sized group of Para units be formed and sent as an assault unit for Rommel's offensive to capture the Suez Canal. Among the Jaeger units selected for that Brigade was 1st Battalion of 2nd Regiment which was moved, together with the other units, via Greece, Crete and Tobruk into the desert battle line at El Alamein.

Among the plans worked on but not carried out was an airborne attack to cut Eighth Army's water pipeline. Talking through the plan showed that the air-landed units could not be evacuated by German aircraft and would be too few in number to fight their way back through the British lines. An earlier plan had been to capture Malta by an airborne operation carried out by a joint German/Italian force. The Luftwaffe Research Establishment produced two pieces of equipment which would be used for the

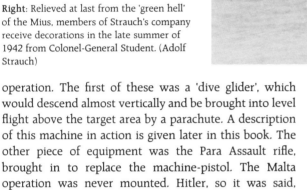

Left: June 1942. Not content with inflicting the miseries of wet and cold upon the opposing troops, the Russian climate provided a summer hazard in the form of swarms of mosquitoes. By this time, German formal unit organization had practically broken down; the survivors of the fighting battled on in small groups, the thick undergrowth making this very irregular warfare. Ambushes were common, so trip-wires were necessary to avoid surprise. (Adolf Strauch)

Right: Relieved at last from the 'green hell' of the Mius, members of Strauch's company receive decorations in the late summer of 1942 from Colonel-General Student. (Adolf Strauch)

operation. The first of these was a 'dive glider', which would descend almost vertically and be brought into level flight above the target area by a parachute. A description of this machine in action is given later in this book. The other piece of equipment was the Para Assault rifle, brought in to replace the machine-pistol. The Malta operation was never mounted. Hitler, so it was said, cancelled it because he could place no reliance upon the Italian Navy which was to escort the follow-up troops.

The detaching of 2nd Regiment required that a new regiment replace it on the War Establishment of 7th Flieger Division, and the 4th was raised during the time that the 7th was in Normandy, resting, regrouping and training the men who had come in to make good the losses suffered on the Eastern Front. This is, perhaps, the appropriate place to recall that several Para units were raised in France. This is not as surprising as it might seem. France, although occupied was a country in which the soldiers of the Occupation Army found it possible to live extremely well. In the rich agricultural regions of Normandy and Brittany there was good food, excellent wine and a sense of peace. There were, of course, training and exercises to undergo, as well as manoeuvres and battle drills through which recruit soldiers become proficient in their trade or veterans regain certain skills which they may have lost.

Late in 1942, an airborne mission was planned as part of Operation 'Blau', the German summer offensive of that year. Operation 'Blau' was a two-pronged thrust with one arm striking for Stalingrad and the other for the Caucasus. It had been intended that a Jaeger would support the German Alpine troops whose attacks were to take the northern side of the Caucasian mountain range while the Paras would be dropped around Tuapse, on the southern

side. With the mountain barrier overcome and in German hands, the Paras and the Gebirgsjaeger would move down into the oil field region of southern Russia.

By the middle of September planning had been completed and preparations for the jump were nearing conclusion. The Jus were assembled on their departure airfields; the Jaeger units, now fully equipped and up to war establishment, were ready to undertake the mission – even though they had not been told the objective. Many who would have flown on that operation have said that it would be a relief, after the terrible experiences of the past winter to be used once again in the role for which they had been trained. Then came the order to stand down. The planned operation had been cancelled. Instead the Division was to prepare for another spell in the Line fighting an infantry-style battle. The news was sobering for the year was already far advanced and the prospect facing the men was of a second winter in Russia.

The Division did not return to its former operational area and to Army Group North but took post around Smolensk, under the command of Army Group Centre. Its task was to defend a 56-mile (90 kilometres) sector of front to the north of the Smolensk–Vitebsk highway, extending from Demidov, via Dukovschchina to Jarchevo. It was an important area; one in which High Command expected the main weight of a Russian winter offensive to fall. It had been in the sector which 7th Flieger took over that the deepest Red Army penetrations had been made during the Russian operations of 1941–42. Stavka's intention in that winter battle had been to remove the danger to Moscow by sweeping Army Group Centre from the approaches to the capital. The fighting throughout that first terrible winter had been hard and when at last the Soviet attacks had been halted by the deep and clinging

Left: 'O' group on the Eastern Front. (Brian L. Davis)

Above: Anti-aircraft lookout: An MG 42 emplacement on the Eastern Front. (Brian L. Davis)

mud, a vast salient had been driven into the German line. It was High Command's appreciation of the situation that that salient would be a springboard for a Soviet offensive.

Those High Command fears were relayed to Major-General Petersen, the General Officer Commanding 7th Flieger Division, an officer who believed that aggressive operations unsettled the enemy. He issued orders that all battalions would carry out intensive patrolling and local attacks. When Major-General Heidrich took over command of the Division during October, he maintained the same high level of aggression and many patrols ranged deep behind the Russian front line and into the rear areas, before returning with important and detailed reports on the Red Army's build-up.

One interesting feature of those deep penetration patrols was the fact that on many of them local Russians either participated actively or else acted as guides. In the village in which No. 3 Company of the Engineer Battalion was billeted there was a Russian Home Guard unit. This detachment had been raised by the Germans to defend the village against partisan attacks and it was commanded by a former subaltern officer of the Red Army. It was he who led many of the more successful patrols that penetrated deep behind the Red Army lines.

Thanks to the offensive behaviour of the Jaeger regiments during their spells of duty in the line, Red Army activities were seldom made against 7th Division's sector but went in against those held by less aggressive German units.

Throughout the winter months patrolling and local attacks were the standard operation carried out by the Jaeger on the southern side of the Russian salient. There was no major winter offensive on that central sector of the Eastern Front because, at this time, the great battle at Stalingrad was reaching its climax and even Russia's vast resources of manpower were insufficient to allow the Red Army to conduct a major battle on more than one sector at a time. But Stavka was preparing for a major offensive that would follow on from Stalingrad and which was intended to crush the German armies in southern Russia. The time for that had not yet come, and December 1942 passed in a series of small but costly engagements to clear the Russians from tactically important high ground and to straighten out the regimental and the divisional front.

An example of that was the attack by one of the battalions of the Assault Regiment to capture the ridge which connected two hills, 'Russian Hill' and 'Green Hill'. It was known that the ground was held by a reinforced Red Army battalion. It was the plan of the Assault Battalion's commander to infiltrate his Companies through the Russian lines and then to carry out an attack from behind those positions. In addition to the Assault Battalion an Engineer group, mine-clearing teams and flame-thrower detachments were detailed for the patrol. A surprise attack from an unexpected direction and supported by flame-throwers should enable the battalion to achieve its given task with speed and few casualties.

Silently the Companies moved forward behind the mine-clearing teams. Then the tactical situation changed dramatically. In one column two mines exploded in quick succession. It was clear that there could now be no question of surprising the enemy. Speed of attack was now the most important factor. There could be no question of penetrating the Russian trench line and attacking it from the rear. The battalion would have to make a frontal assault against an entrenched enemy that had not as yet reacted to the mine explosions.

The Engineers with their flame-throwers and explosive charges move forward to spearhead the assault. When they are in position the quiet order is given and the Jaeger, in tactical formation, storm up the slope toward the Soviet outpost line. The Engineer group leader orders 'Flame!' and a sheet of fire envelopes the first Russian strong-point in the outpost line. Machine-pistol fire pours into the bunker which erupts in a loud explosion. In addition to the sentries on duty it must have held explosive charges or mines. That's one strong point dealt with and all along the battalion front other bunkers fall to the Para's swift advance. The charge moves across the unmanned first trench line and into a shallow wadi where the Ivans are sleeping in their dug-outs. Red Army men awakened by the sound of firing start to pour out of the dug-outs but before they can grasp what is happening bullets from the machine-pistols cut them down. Flame-throwers are in action all along the line and then the heavy detonations of satchel charges as these blow up one bunker after another. The Jaeger work their way along the second line of Russian trenches, bombing and machine-pistolling their way forward, rolling up the enemy line. Suddenly, there are no Ivans left. Those that have not been killed or taken prisoner have fled. The objective has been taken. Soon the first groups from the Jaeger battalions come up to relieve the assault battalion and to consolidate the area. The attack has been a success.

We who live in temperate climates can have little idea of how terrible life on the Eastern Front in winter could be. That of 1942–43 may not have been as brutal as the exceptional one of 1941–42, but it was still hard for those who had to spend it in trenches cut into frozen soil. The snowstorms, the low temperature which froze machinery and then the thaw which filled the trenches with slush are phenomena rarely experienced by us. Trench foot succeeded frost-bite and the hospitals were filled with more men suffering from sickness than had been wounded in action. But the Germans had learned many lessons from the first winter campaign of 1941 and were able to avoid the terrible losses of that first year. Activity on the Jaeger front was restricted to minor operations until late in March, when, following a heavy and prolonged barrage, the Red Army infantry attacked with massive tank support.

This furious assault, after five months of relative inactivity, gave the Soviets an initial advantage, but this period without major operations had also allowed the Jaeger commanders to build up reserve forces ready to meet such an eventuality. The waves of Russian assaults were met by Jaeger counter-attacks; at places where the Para positions were lost to an overwhelming Red Army thrust it became a matter of honour for the Jaeger to recover them by an immediate counter-stroke.

The Red Army's offensive against 7th Flieger Division – now 1st Fallschirmjaeger Division – was no accident. Soviet Intelligence had learned that the formation was to be relieved from the line on a home posting, and the Russians reckoned that the Jaeger, anxious to get away safely, would be unwilling to take unnecessary risks. They had reckoned without the Para ethos. General Heidrich gave orders that the relief operation was to be immediately halted. The Jaeger regiments would stay and hold their positions until the units taking over had had a chance to accustom themselves to the conditions and were familiar with the terrain. Shortly after that, the Soviet attacks lessened in weight. The losses to the Red Army units fighting against the Paras had been so high that Stavka had been forced to cancel the offensive. The fighting died down, the new units learned quickly and at long last the Jaeger, exhausted after more than half a year's combat in terrible conditions, returned to Germany and then were sent to France to retrain, to rest and to recover, first in fruitful Normandy and then deep in southern France in the area of Avignon where, together with 2nd Fallschirmjaeger Division, it formed, as XI Flieger Corps, the OKW strategic reserve for the southern theatres of operation.

8. 'Forward; across the graves; forward'

NORTH AFRICA, NOVEMBER-DECEMBER 1942

The African theatre of operations was one in which no Fallschirmjaeger units served until the late summer of 1942, when a Brigade group was sent to the desert and smaller detachments to Tunisia in November of that year. Space does not permit me to describe in detail the reasons that caused the Germans to become involved in fighting a war in Africa. An outline must suffice. When France signed an armistice with Germany in June 1940, it had seemed to many that the war was over and that peace had returned. It was a vain belief; Britain still unconquered, resolute and defiant, was at war with the Italians in their Libyan empire. Following the Italian declaration of war against Britain, the Italian Army advanced into Egypt during the late summer of 1940. In December they were flung back in total disarray by the outnumbered but skilfully led British Imperial Force commanded by General Sir Archibald Wavell. Hitler, fearing that the British would seize Italian Libya and thereby drive his ally out of the war, ordered that a German Panzer force be sent to support the Italians.

The Deutsches Afrika Korps, under Erwin Rommel, reached Tripoli in February 1941. Its initial operations held and then drove back Wavell's army. This defeat was brought about as a result of Churchill's order for Wavell to use part of the desert Army as an expeditionary force to Greece. A disastrous campaign led to the evacuation of the bulk of the British/Dominion force to Crete where it was attacked by 7th Flieger Division in Operation 'Mercury', during May. A fresh evacuation was the result.

In the African desert a series of inconclusive offensives by both sides marked the course of 1941 and the early part of 1942. In May of that year Rommel determined upon a major operation which would destroy the British Eighth Army. He would breach the British line at Gazala and his Panzers would sweep through the gap to Cairo, Alexandria and the Suez Canal. Britain would not only have lost her main base in the eastern Mediterranean, but the short sea route to the Far East would have been cut. The war in Africa would be won. Rommel's optimistic offensive was halted in front of a British defensive

complex known as the El Alamein Line, which had been constructed between the Mediterranean in the north and the impassable Qattara Depression in the south. The German commander called upon his soldiers for one final effort, but they had fought themselves to a point of total exhaustion and could not meet his demands.

Rommel knew that he must go over to the defensive until the arrival of reinforcements allowed him to resume the failed assault. British Eighth Army. already numerically superior, would grow stronger with every passing week, and must soon go over to the offensive. Rommel intended to dissipate that attack by the use of minefields. The width of the area in which the desert battles were fought was narrow, at places less than 60 miles (96 kilometres), and the German commander intended to reduce that narrow width still farther by laying not just 'fields' but whole 'marshes' of mines which would cover the greatest part of the front line and be several miles deep. With the British offensive halted Rommel could then counter-attack and resume his own halted offensive.

OKW decided to send an élite force to support the offensive and ordered General Student to organize a Brigade-sized Battle Group of Fallschirmjaeger detachments. Student chose units which would create an all-arms unit and invested command of it in General Ramcke, a legendary figure whose reputation was to be enhanced as the result of the fighting during the El Alamein offensive of October 1942.

Ramcke was given a number of separate battalions, some of which were veteran units from the Eastern Front, others made up of men who had just completed basic training and who were, therefore, not experienced in battle. Each battalion was a self-contained battle group and was named after its commanding officer. Kroh's battle group was 1st Battalion of 2nd Regiment. This had recently returned from Russia. Huebner's was 2nd battalion of 5th Para Regiment. Battle Group Burkhardt had been a Training Battalion, which had been reformed after a short period of active service, while von der Heydte's battle group was a newly established Training Battalion

which had recently completed its drills and jumps. To give muscle to the Jaeger battalions, 2nd Battalion of 7th Para Artillery Regiment, a Para anti-tank Company and one Company each of Pioneers and Signallers were attached.

Following the dispatch of an Advance Party the main body of 'Para Brigade Ramcke', moved by battalions from Greece to Tobruk and was then brought by truck into position in the centre of the German line. Its task would be to exploit the anticipated breakthrough of the British El Alamein Line. Rommel's attacks did not achieve that aim and by the beginning of October the Axis forces were back on the defensive. Ramcke Brigade and the Italian Folgore Division then occupied positions in the south between the Deir el Mreir and the Munassib Depression. Months earlier the whole of that geological fault had been occupied by the British as a fortified area of their defence lines, but it had been captured during the German summer offensive. The new garrison, Ramcke's men and those of the Italian Division, improved and extended the earlier British defences. By the time that Rommel's mine 'marshes' had been laid, the expertly sited and constructed Munassib Depression, garrisoned by tough and determined Jaeger, lay surrounded by the strong defences of those 'silent soldiers'.

The British offensive Operation 'Lightfoot', the battle of El Alamein, opened on 23 October. Facing Ramcke's Brigade were units from 50th Tyne/Tees Division whose role in the opening stages of the offensive was one of support. In view of the reputation of the German Paras and the known strength of the Munassib defences, the first actions of 50th Division, on the opening night of 'Lightfoot' were limited to patrol activity. On subsequent days its units made probing attacks against the Axis positions, but the main battle was being fought to the north of Ramcke's positions and his battalions were not engaged in heavy fighting. In that northern sector, following days of bitter struggle, the British assaults threatened to break the German line. If that happened Ramcke's Brigade would face the propect of being outflanked and cut off. To avoid this, on 2 November 1942, his Brigade was ordered to leave the positions which it had held for months and to move into newer ones fifteen miles to the west; but not for long. A massive British penetration in the north, this time through Italian-held positions, once again threatened to cut off the Paras. New orders from Panzer Army Africa for the Brigade to retreat westwards to the area of Bir Fuka were unrealistic in that Fuka was nearly 100 miles away across areas of desert already occupied by Eighth Army. To reach Fuka Ramcke's Brigade would have to march the entire distance; there was no unit transport and only the artillery pieces were motorized.

For two days the Brigade force trekked across the desert heading in a general westerly direction, parallel to the British advance and often under attack. Then the line of march was changed northwards. Ramcke intended to reach the Via Balbia, the only surfaced road in Tripolitania and therefore the principal supply route for Eighth Army. He planned to capture British trucks to carry his men back to the new positions at Fuka. Shortly before dawn on 6 November, a Para attack overran a large convoy of trucks whose drivers were asleep in their cabs. Ramcke Brigade had had incredible good luck. The trucks were loaded not only with food, drink and petrol, but also with cigarettes, whisky, chocolate and all the canteen supplies for an entire Armoured Brigade. With full stomachs and smoking like chimneys, the Brigade reported in that same day. The 'old man' feared nobody and certainly not the Staff Officers – German or Italian – who had not, in his opinion, done enough to help his unit and had, in fact, written it off.

Right: Sentry with an MG 34. (Brian L. Davis)

There is an ending to the story of Ramcke Brigade in Africa which demonstrates the strength of unit loyalty. No. 2 Para Engineer Company, which had formed part of Huebner's Battle Group, had by the middle of November been so reduced in number that 90 per cent of its men were in hospital. They were ordered to return home to Germany on sick leave. At that time news was received that the parent unit – the Para Corps Engineer Battalion – had landed in North Africa with the contingents that had been sent to counter the Allied thrust into Tunisia. Not one of the Para Engineer Company who could have gone home on sick leave took advantage of that posting. All of them – the fit, the sick and the convalescents – rejoined the battalion which was fighting in the mountains. The survivors passed into prisoner-of-war camps, as did those of Ramcke's Brigade when the campaign in Africa closed during May 1943. But the time of their fate is not yet come. The campaign in Tunisia and the part played in it by the Fallschirmjaeger of 5th Regiment has yet to be described.

In the first week of November 1942, German agents in Spain reported to Berlin that a large convoy of Allied ships, escorted by powerful naval forces had passed Gibraltar. It was believed by many in the highest circles in Germany, including Hitler and Goering, that this indicated an invasion of either southern France or the island of Corsica. It was a logical deduction to have made. It was obvious that the Anglo-Americans would choose to attack a vulnerable area of southern Europe or a French island neither of which could be properly defended by the weak military forces of the French Vichy Government.

That deduction was not shared by either Mussolini or Kesselring, the German Commander-in-Chief, South, both of whom considered that this operation was directed at the French colonies in North Africa, probably Tunisia. If the Allies were to invade that country Rommel would be trapped between the Anglo-American invasion force to the north and Eighth Army to the south. The Italian Empire would be lost and, as a consequence, Germany would lose the strategic initiative in the Mediterranean theatre.

At 04.00 hours on 8 November 1942, the objectives of the Allied armada were made known when the troops invaded Morocco and Algeria. Once the Eastern Task Force was firmly ashore in Algiers, General Anderson, commanding the newly formed British First Army, was to lead it in an advance to capture Tunis. The advance guard of First Army would be 'Blade Force', two Brigades of British 78th Division and an American armoured group.

Only a few hours after news of the first landings had been reported, the German Special Envoy to the Vichy Government met Marshal Pétain. He told the French Head of State that it was not sufficient for Vichy merely to break off diplomatic relations with the United States as a mark of displeasure at the invasion. The Reich expected the Vichy regime to declare war on the Allies. Neither Pétain nor his Prime Minister, Pierre Laval, was prepared to take that step, just as they had rejected the demand from the American Special Envoy that Vichy France declare herself for the Allies.

The news that an Allied force was about to invade North Africa and not southern France, was given to Hitler when his special train was halted at a small railway station in Thuringen. He was *en route* from his Field Head-quarters on the Eastern Front to Munich where each year, on the anniversary of the failed *putsch* of 1923, he gave his Party comrades a commemorative speech. On receiving the news of Allied intentions he called an emergency conference. He rejected out of hand the proposal that the German forces in Africa be brought back to the mainland of Europe to be used in the defence of that continent. He determined to hold Africa and spoke to Field Marshal Kesselring in Rome. The telephone conversation was brief.

'Kesselring, what can you put into Africa?'

'The only units immediately available, mein Fuehrer, are two battalions of 5th Para Regiment and the Defence Company of my own Headquarters.'

'Send whatever is available. We do not intend to lose Africa. You are to prevent that happening.'

The Fuehrer's demand that Kesselring oppose a huge Allied invasion force with two battalions of Paratroops and a Headquarters Defence Company was bitter to the Field Marshal. For months he had been anticipating an Allied move in the western Mediterranean and had asked OKW for at least one Division from its reserve to be stationed in Sicily ready for immediate deployment. His proposal had been rejected time and again. Now a crisis had developed and there was no major formation that could be put in to meet it. Kesselring had always been aware of the strategic importance of the Mediterranean theatre, an awareness not shared either by Hitler or by the General Staff, both so obsessed with the Russian Front that they had consistently starved Rommel of men and supplies. Now the time of reckoning which Kesselring had forecast was at hand. This was, however, no time for recrimination or condemnation. It was a time for swift and positive action.

Moving with his customary efficiency and thoroughness Kesselring alerted the units which he would send immediately to North Africa and looked about for officers upon whom he knew he could rely. Luftwaffe Colonel Harlinghausen was named as Air Officer

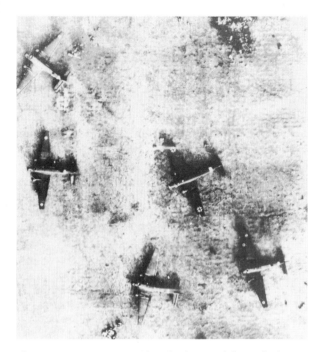

Above: Tunis airport came under relentless attack from Allied aircraft, now becoming dominant in the Mediterranean theatre. In this picture can be seen the wrecks of burned-out aircraft; November 1942. (M. Klein)

Commanding Tunisia, with orders to use his squadrons to seize bridgeheads around Tunis and Bizerta and to hold these open until the follow-up troops arrived. Among the first senior commanders to land at Tunis airport was General Nehring who had served with Rommel. Although *en route* to the desert he was ordered to report to Kesselring who gave him the task of expanding the German bridgeheads as far to the west as possible; to the Algerian/Tunisian border if that could be achieved. Kesselring could give Nehring no Staff to assist him, no transport and no signals facilities and although that officer was named as commander of XC Corps he had no troops to command. In an expression of sardonic wit Kesselring demanded that an officer be sent to Tunisia; one with the thick red stripes of the General Staff down the side of his trousers. The Allies, through their spies, would soon learn of that high-ranking officer's presence and would conclude that major German military units had already arrived for the Anglo-Americans would not believe that there could be a high officer who had no troops to command.

Meanwhile, a slow but steady stream of individuals and fragments of units had been reaching Tunisia. All was grist to the mill. As early as 8 November, the day of the Allied invasion, a stream of Junkers aircraft had been bringing these in. One *ad hoc* Company was created out of the men of Ramcke's Para Brigade who were waiting in Athens to

be air transported back to the desert. These splinter groups were formed into Para Company Sauer, named after its commander. The Company arrived on Tunis airfield where it was immediately commandeered by Colonel Harlinghausen and given the task of helping the Luftwaffe defend the airfield. By 13 November, Sauer had set up an outer and inner defence line and then, together with other detachments which had been flown in, constructed Battle Group Sauer, which formed a complete defensive perimeter around the city of Tunis. The city was now firmly in German hands.

It will be recalled that Kesselring had told Hitler that there were two battalions of 5th Para Regiment which could be sent to Africa. That regiment had been created in May 1942, to be one of the components of 3rd Fallschirmjaeger Division. The regiment's cadre were the remnants of the three battalions of the Assault Regiment which had been brought back to Germany after fighting in Russia. Around this nucleus of battle-hardened veterans other units were grouped. In July 1942, with the 5th regiment almost completely raised, Captain Huebner's 2nd Battalion was posted to Ramcke's Brigade in the desert, while Jungwirth's 1st Battalion and Knoche's 3rd Battalion were sent to Reims to train for Operation 'Hercules', the airborne assault upon Malta. That operation was aborted and the two battalions of 5th Regiment thus became available for service in Tunisia.

All combat units, at some time in their lives, receive orders committing them to battle at short notice. Such units, aware of that possibility, discipline themselves for speedy departure. The order from Kesselring's headquarters putting the two battalions on full alert was received only hours after Hitler and the Field Marshal had spoken on the telephone. The 3rd Battalion marched that same night, entrained and within two days had arrived in Caserta. A hastily formed advance party roared through the sleeping countryside of southern Italy, reached the airfield at Naples and with only a brief refuelling halt in Sicily set off again for Tunisia. The pilot was forced to fly the Ju at wave top height to avoid the RAF fighters which dominated the skies. The RAF's command of the air was demonstrated again when Spitfires attacked the airfield upon which the Junkers bearing the 3rd Battalion's advance party, was making its landing.

That advance guard was ordered to pass through Tunis and block the western road leading to the town. For lack of unit transport, runners carrying messages between units, for as yet no wireless sets had arrived in the bridgehead, used the Tunis tram system to travel between one headquarters and another. The situation of individual soldiers, isolated fragments of units and splinter groups being air lifted to a theatre of war where they were to be

Left: Advance elements of 5th Regiment pass through Tunis about 11–12 November 1942 on their way to the battle front. They sing as they march. (Rudi Hambuch)

Left: Twentieth-century war comes to Tunisia: Arabs watch as the Ju 52s begin to fly-in troops to revive the flagging German war effort in North Africa. (Rudi Hambuch)

used to plug holes in a flimsy defence line, was typical of conditions on the German side during the first weeks in Tunisia and of the situation which met the follow-up Para units when they arrived in the bridgehead.

General Nehring, commanding a Corps which had no Staff Officers, no supplies, transport or formally established units, was expected to hold a vast area inhabited by the French, whose allegiance was only nominally for Vichy, and a native population whose loyalty was suspect. At Troop level the confidence which Para training bred in the Jaeger enabled them to hold isolat:d outposts on the empty roads and to overcome the difficulties which faced them in those early chaotic days.

At dawn on 12 November, a fleet of Ju 52s, escorted by Luftwaffe fighter aircraft, brought in the first elements of 3rd Battalion. These were unloaded, the planes refuelled and then flown back to the Italian mainland where new groups were emplaned. This shuttle continued throughout the 12th and lasted until 16 November, by which time both Fallschirmjaeger battalions were at Tunis and had taken up defensive positions around the town. Using

tourist maps bought in shops, for no maps of the operational area had yet arrived from Germany, the Para formations of Schirmer, Knoche and Sauer, took positions in the perimeter. Schirmer held the west side of the city and Sauer the southern defence sector. Knoche's battalion was ordered to thicken Schirmer's battle line as soon as the Rear Party arrived. The 1st Battalion began to arrive on the 15th and was put into the line.

The position of the French authorities began to cause problems for the small German garrison whose commanders had had impressed upon them that the perimeter must be extended westwards towards the Algerian frontier. Any attempt by the Paras to do this was immediately countered by the French who brought up tanks. The Paras had, as yet, no heavy weapons to counter the French threat nor could they run the risk of provoking the Vichy forces who might attack the airfields and halt the shuttle bringing in fresh troops. Diplomacy, not force of arms had to be, for the foreseeable future, the policy which the Paras would be compelled to follow. Diplomacy would be the weapon that would allow the perimeter to

Right: Part of the advance guard of 5th Regiment *en route* for Medjez-el-Bab early in November 1942; they are about to begin operations to extend the defensive perimeter westwards into the mountains. (Hans Teske)

be expanded until contact was made with Allied troops. Thereafter, it would be weapons that would talk.

It was not until 16 November that the daily communiqué issued by OKW announced that 'German and Italian troops had landed in Tunisia with the full agreement of the French Head of State and of the military authorities in Tunisia.' Those Axis forces were still few in number. In addition to the two battalions of Major Koch's 5th Fallschirmjaeger Regiment, there was the Para Engineer Battalion under the command of Major Witzig, an Army replacement battalion which had been *en route* to Rommel's Army, a battery of four 88mm guns and an armoured car Company. That formed the German contingent. The Italians furnished two battalions of the élite San Marco marine infantry and two battalions from the 'Superga' Division.

On that morning of 16 November, Captain Knoche and two other officers were arrested while carrying out a reconnaissance of the French units facing them on the western road. It was there and then that diplomacy – perhaps bluff would be a better word – gained a victory. Using his aide-de-camp, Quedenow, as an interpreter, Knoche, requested that the local French commander pull back his troops as far as Medjez el Bab. In addition he must allow the German paras to set up three bridgeheads on the western bank of the River Medjerda at Medjez el Bab, at Tebourba and at Jedeida.

Through the chance of being taken captive, the three German officers were put into touch with General Barre, the local senior commander and the man who could open the way for the German perimter to be extended. His Division held the area around the town of Medjez el Bab. The English translation of that name is 'Key to the Gate' and the side which held Medjez el Bab could control the course of military operations. General Barre, believing Knoche to be the delegated representative of General Nehring's Corps – a false impression which Knoche took no trouble to correct – agreed to bridgeheads being set up by the Paras at Jedeida and Tebourba, as well as to the

evacuation of territory up to Medjez itself – but no farther westwards would the French withdraw, nor would they permit the Germans to establish a bridgehead on the west bank of the river in that sector. As the French pulled back in the other sectors, No. 9 Para Company moved forward, crossed the River Medjerda and established bridgeheads at Jedeida and Tebourba. At senior level it was decided to take Medjez – either by direct assault or by bluff. Acting on Nehring's orders, Knoche formed a small battle group. One and a half Companies of Paras and a half Company of a regiment made up the infantry contingent. Two 88mm guns, five anti-tank guns and some Flak formed the support group. Another and even smaller battle group, made up of a platoon of 5th Regiment's Heavy Weapons Company, was ordered to race ahead of Captain Knoche's group and to announce itself as the 'Advance Guard of a newly landed Fallschirmjaeger Regiment'.

At Medjez Knoche was able to convince the local French commander to let his groups move towards Beja, where General Barre had his headquarters. Before they entered the town they were met by officers of the General's Chief of Staff. The attitude of the French officers was suspicious. They seemed to be intent on delaying Knoche's detachments. That attitude was understandable for British troops from 'Blade Force', men of the 6th Battalion, The Queen's Own Royal West Kent Regiment, had already entered Beja and had sent out a battle patrol to seize the small hamlet of Jebel Abiod which stands on the crossroads Bône–Bizerta–Beja.

The two columns of 'Blade Force' were spreading a thin film of troops across Tunisia, occupying towns and villages which dominated road and rail junctions. While 36th Brigade, the left-hand column, was in northern Tunisia, moving in the general direction of Bizerta, 11th Brigade was striking for Medjez. A clash between the Axis and Allied armies on that sector could not now be long delayed.

That clash came about in the Jebel Abiod sector. While Knoche had been negotiating with the French at Medjez, up in the north a battle group under Major Witzig of the Para Engineer Battalion, was advancing to seize Tabarka. The route to that small town was via Jebel Abiod towards which three Companies of 6th Battalion of the West Kents, a troop of armoured cars, a machine-gun group of the Northamptonshire Regiment and a battery of 25pdrs was also heading.

In the early afternoon of 17 November, the British recce unit, saw, identified and reported the presence of a column of enemy tanks and motorized infantry moving from Mateur towards the crossroads and the village. There was little time for the British to dig in although the German Para Engineer history described the defensive system as well constructed. The West Kent's fire discipline was excellent and not until the first Mk IV tank was 200 yards distant did the battalion's anti-tank guns open up.

Commanding the anti-tank gun platoon was the famous Kent cricketer, B. H. Valentine, and his order to open fire was also the signal for the 25pdrs to begin firing and for the Northampton machine-gunners to join the battle. In the first few minutes, eight of Witzig's tanks were knocked out and his column was immobile in an area devoid of all cover. The confusion did not last long. At the sound of the first shots the Para Engineers leaped from their trucks and went into the drill which months of combat on the Russian front had taught them. From small patches of dead ground they opened fire upon the West Kent positions on the eastern side of the village. Behind the thin line of Paras the heavy weapons were deployed and a fierce fire-fight developed. In an effort to give close support to the Engineers, one of the 2cm Flak guns was brought right forward and used with great effect until the fire of the 25pdrs was concentrated upon it and a direct hit killed the crew and smashed the gun.

Neither the Germans nor the British were strong enough to destroy the opposition. Both were only small battle groups with limited strength and both needed to be resupplied with ammunition. By last light the fighting had died away. The British still held the village and, therefore, the crossroads at Jebel Abiod, but Witzig held the high ground which dominated the area. His positions were concentrated around 'Cactus Wood', where his Companies dug in.

During the night the heavy weapons were withdrawn. A formal structure was being established in Tunis, within which all the fragments of units were to be concentrated and formed into the 'von Broich' Division. The wholesale commandeering of vehicles and weapons for the newly formed Division affected the Witzig Battle Group, as we have seen, by the removal of its heavy weapons. At troop level, too, the confiscation had its effect. The transport to hospital of Witzig's wounded men was delayed when the

vehicles in the Para Engineer Battalion's rear headquarters were all requisitioned by von Broich's officers. These men refused to release the trucks so that the wounded could be evacuated, justifying their stand on the grounds that this was now a divisional and not a Para regiment responsibility. In the event Division took its time and not until the following morning were the Jaeger wounded evacuated.

On a happier note, the Para Engineer Signals officer, using improvised methods, established a telephone link with divisional headquarters which then connected Witzig, in the front line, with Kesselring in Rome. By this *ad hoc* means the battalion commander was able to advise Supreme Commander, South of the extent of his battalion's westward thrust and also that at Jebel Abiod his battle group had halted the allied drive in the north.

On the Jebel Abiod sector, although neither side was on the ground in sufficient strength to force a decision, both fought hard – the Germans to expand and the British to reduce the perimeter. Intense patrol activity marked the passage of the bitterly cold nights. In the matter of patrols the Germans were superior; they were seasoned campaigners. The British were still new to battle conditions and for the greatest number of the men of 78th Division, the past fortnight had been a brutal initiation into the warrior's trade and that against the finest combat troops in Africa – Witzig's Para Engineer Battalion.

At midnight on 21 November, a fighting patrol from his No. 1 Company went out to raid a group of houses near the village of Jebel Abiod. Moving slowly and wide in order to pass the main British positions, it was not until 03.00 hours that the Paras reached the attack area. Quietly they grouped round their young commander. Machine-gun groups were left behind to cover the withdrawal once the main body had done its work and two platoons moved silently through the darkness of the night. There was a sudden challenge from a British sentry. The patrol had been discovered. The two platoons went in at a run. Before the British troops in the houses could react the Paras were in the village. Front doors were kicked open and charges of high-explosive flung inside. The crashing detonations wrecked the little houses. From positions deeper within the village the slow-firing Vickers machine-guns opened up and lines of tracers lanced into the hills firing on fixed lines, hoping to hit something. A little later flashes to the west of Abiod and then the soft whirring of shells in flight, showed that the British artillery was firing a defensive curtain. On their way through these barrages of shell and machine-gun fire to their own positions, the Para Engineers took casualties, but it had been a most successful raid demonstrating to the British the combat efficiency of Witzig's men.

For the time being the northern arm was secure. Farther to the south, around Medjez el Bab, the French were still prevaricating – their delaying tactics frustrating the 5th Para Regiment while allowing the Anglo-Americans to occupy tactically important ground in the western areas of Tunisia.

As a result of Allied military initiative and French delaying tactics, British airborne troops had captured the ports of Bougie and Bône. With these in their hands the Allies were now only 120 miles (190 kilometres) from Bizerta. Soon reinforcements would come in through the ports to exert pressure upon Witzig's Para Engineer Battalion and the battalions of 5th Regiment, which still constituted the main German defence forces in the west of Tunisia.

On the 17th, Captain Knoche persuaded the local French military commander of the Medjez sector, to pull back his infantry, armour and guns to the west bank of the River Mejerda. The French colonel was still adamant that Germans might not set up a bridgehead on the western bank or hold the bridge. It remained, therefore, a sort of no man's land between the German and the French.

Nehring, who had now formally assumed command over all the forces in Tunisia, anticipated that a major Allied thrust could be expected on the 18th. He knew that the few formations under his command were not an homogeneous force holding a firm perimeter and supported by heavy weapons. Rather were they small groups often having no particular unit allegiance but formed into *ad hoc* detachments. Nor was the battle line they held continuous and firm. It was more a string of unconnected strong points; usually, tactically important hills or road crossings in the west of Tunisia.

No Allied assault came in that day and utilizing every minute to its full advantage, Nehring decided to secure a perimeter in the deep south of the country. He would seize Gabes which had both a port and an airfield. Through that town Rommel's desert army, retreating in front of British Eighth Army, would have to pass to reach the safety of the bridgehead in northern Tunisia. Nehring had only a few troops which he could commit to that enterprise. Those he selected would have to be hard and resourceful soldiers. Such men were to hand; Para engineers who had been *en route* to Ramcke but who had been commandeered and grouped as part of Battle Group Sauer. To the Para Engineer detachment was added a Company of 5th Para, a cyclist Group and another Company from Kesselring's Headquarters Defence Battalion.

Twelve Jus carrying the battle group set off, but as the first of the aircraft made its landing run at Gabes, it was met with anti-aircraft and machine-gun fire. The group turned back towards Tunis but *en route* a new battle plan was worked out and six of the aircraft diverted to land on flat ground about 25 miles (40 kilometres) from the airfield. Immediately on landing two patrols went out and a little later a third was dispatched. That group, seven paratroops commanded by a lance-corporal, was captured and taken to Gabes airfield for interrogation. The confidence of the Jaeger impressed the French who believed the story that unless the patrol was released and the airfield surrendered, German dive-bombers would attack and destroy it. The group was held overnight on the airfield and shortly after dawn the sound of aircraft engines was heard. The French believed the noise to herald a Stuka attack, but they were mistaken. These machines were Jus bringing in another airborne group. The French fled and the jubilant patrol talked down the transports. Gabes was then occupied and with the subsequent capture of nearby Gafsa, the two most important

Right: Men of a rifle company, well loaded with equipment, on their way to the battle front in central Tunisia in December 1942. These are 'second generation' Fallschirmjaeger, young recruits filling the places of those who have already fallen in Crete and Russia. (Rudi Hambuch)

towns in southern Tunisia were in German hands. The capture of Gabes pre-empted an American thrust by only a few days. On 20 November, the first tank detachments of US II Corps struck towards the town but were held and flung back. Southern Tunisia was now a firm part of Nehring's perimeter.

The whole area of the Tunisian battlefield saw many scenes similar to that, but as Allied strength grew pressure mounted on the scattered units which constituted the, as yet unconnected, German perimeter. In Witzig's area British paratroops began to push forward in the Sidi Nsir sector while 78th Division resumed infantry attacks at Abiod. Under this double pressure Witzig's group was forced to pull back in a methodical, rearguard action until they had reached prepared positions at Jefna. There the withdrawal stopped. It was the point where the battalion had to stand if the northern flank were to be held. From Jefna there could be no retreat. Aggressive defence by Witzig's battalion strengthened by the arrival of the vehicles and other battalions of the Engineer Regiment secured the northern flank. Farther to the south the situation around Medjez el Bab was still fluid, but thanks to the audacious Para bluff at Gabes the deep southern sector was securely in German hands. Slowly, as more Axis troops arrived in the country they were sent out to occupy strategic sectors of Tunisia; towns and high ground. A real perimeter would soon be established in place of the wide-flung and unconnected strong points.

Baulked by the firm defence of 21st Para Engineer Battalion in the Jefna position, the mass of British 78th Division turned south-eastwards to force a crossing of the River Medjerda at Medjez. Even as the first British units drove towards the town, Koch, 5th Para Regiment commander, was planning to seize it. This was to be a Jaeger assault preceded by dive-bombing. His orders to Knoche were that if the planned Stuka attack weakened French resistance the Paras were to attack and cross the river. If the aerial bombardment failed to have the desired effect and the French showed that they were prepared to offer determined resistance, no Jaeger attack should be undertaken.

At 11.30 hours twelve Stukas, with fighter escort, began the bombardment of the French troops around the Medjerda bridge. While the Jus were screaming down Knoche's three columns dashed forward. The first cleared most of the houses on the eastern bank, and while fighting was being waged by the second group for some fortified houses near the police station, the third column waded across trying to capture the bridge by all-out assault. That first German attack failed. Fighting swayed backwards and forwards as the French launched counter-attacks to drive the Paras from the eastern end of the bridge. With the element of surprise lost and fearful that the French would outflank his group, Knoche broke off the unsuccessful attack.

Late in the afternoon the regimental commander reached the battlefield area, discussed a new battle plan with Knoche and organized the delivery of a truck filled with high-explosives. Knoche's new plan was for ten small patrols of ten men each to filter through the eastern half of Medjez el Bab, wade or swim across the river and, having grouped on the western bank, for each to attack an allocated sector and destroy the enemy positions in their areas.

An hour before midnight the groups reached their form-up lines and punctually at 23.59 hours, the first of them moved away into the dark night. At intervals the other patrols crossed their start-lines. Moving cautiously and without sound the groups slipped past French and Allied units to reach the west bank where they waited for Zero-hour. At 01.00 hours came the first of a chain of explosions. A hollow-charge grenade attached to the outside of a parked tank smashed the vehicle completely. It caught fire and flames spread to the soft-skinned fuel trucks.

To the Allied troops the noise of the explosions and the confusion all indicated a strong German attempt to cross the river. The French and American defenders, unaware that the enemy was among them, opened fire and betrayed their defensive positions. The Paras attacked and destroyed them. The fire-fight rose to a crescendo, died away and then broke out with renewed fury as both sides, having taken stock of the situation resumed the battle. The Paras fought their way forward from the outskirts of Medjez into the town itself, concentrated there and took up all-round defence. The Allies, determined to break this island of resistance, used armour in a dawn attack, but the Para experience on the Eastern Front, in close combat against tanks, allowed them to destroy two vehicles. The French, American and British troops who had been holding Medjez withdrew from the town in some con-fusion, leaving a mass of supplies, fuel and other *matériel* in the hands of the jubilant Paras.

There was no time to rest. The perimeter had to be extended westwards, Schirmer's battle group, which included artillery, pursued the retreating enemy forces up the Oued Zarga road and reached the high hills of that name, during the afternoon of the 20th. A night attack to bypass the village and to outflank it was held up by heavy and accurate artillery fire, until an 88mm of Schirmer's command, opened up and smashed the British battery with long-range fire. The Jaeger had reached the start-line of their assault when the order came for them to pull back and to concentrate around Medjez. Throughout the

Above: Men of 5th Regiment, with the short-barrelled version of the 81mm mortar, in position in the hills of Tunisia. (Rudi Hambuch)

units to be concentrated for a major offensive operation. Although their patrols were always aggressive and well conducted, there was a feeling that more might have been accomplished had 5th Regiment had the chance to fight as a single body and in the most important sector, Medjez el Bab, and not in penny packets over a wider area.

The importance of collecting the dispersed elements of the regiment were shown when a major Allied assault struck the defensive line around Medjez. This attack, spearheaded by American armour, came in first at El Aroussa, captured that place and threatened to develop into an operation that would strike the Medjez garrison in the back. To deflect the blow at El Aroussa Koch formed a battle group and sent this racing towards the threatened sector. The 88s attached to the group found the American tank men cruising about at the eastern exit of El Aroussa. The guns opened up and under this furious bombardment the Americans were driven back. Then the battle group raced back to Medjez where a second Allied tank attack had opened. During this major offensive the Paras were forced back from their bridgeheads and from the western bank of the River Medjerda. A rearguard from No. 10 Company covered the withdrawal out of Medjez and blew up the bridge. A new battle line was centred to the west of Massicault and the slowness of the Allied pursuit gave 5th Regiment a day or two to recover from the weeks of unending strain. Only patrols needed to be sent out and on one of those, on 30 November, the German Jaeger clashed with British paratroops, the men of Frost's 2nd Battalion, who had been dropped near Pont du Fahs with orders to destroy the German aircraft on the airfield there.

The Jaeger were grateful for the short respite from battle, but were too experienced as soldiers not to realize that they were being rested before being given a new and major task. By the end of November, General Nehring controlled a force at last capable of effective offensive operations. In addition to infantry and artillery a detachment of Tiger tanks had reached the Tunisian theatre, the Luftwaffe had gained air superiority and for the moment there were no difficulties in the matter of supplies. Nehring decided to mount an encircling operation in the Tebourba area, a scheme to which Kesselring gave only reluctant assent. It was to be the task of the Jaeger to strike out of their positions, drive through El Bathan and close the ring which would have been thrown around the Allied forces in that area. Nehring knew that his attack was a gamble, but his orders had been to extend the German perimeter. In pursuit of those orders, as well as to pre-empt the Allies, he considered that an offensive was necessary. In order that his attack be mounted at full strength, every fighting soldier in northern Tunisia was

following days waves of Allied attacks were made against the Para positions outside the town, of which a night charge by French Spahi horsemen was the most impressive.

By the end of 22 November, it could be claimed that the Paras had established three principal points upon which the defence of Tunisia depended. In the north, in the south and now in the centre of the country, they were the keystones of the German defence around which the battle line was being constructed. Protected by the Jaeger shield more and more German units flooded into Tunisia.

Despite the additions to their strength, the military tasks which were set, the need to act as firemen and to rush from one threatened sector to another, changed the role of the Paras. They had been trained to fight an attack type of warfare. Here, in Tunisia, the dispersal of their strength along the extended perimeter did not allow their put into the operation, leaving only a handful of men and a pair of 88mm guns to guard the western approaches to the capital.

The attack in the Para sector opened with a feint thrust up the road towards Medjez by a battle group made up of elements from 3rd Battalion of 5th Regiment. Armoured cars led the assault and the men of 3rd Battalion advanced through the open country on each side of the vehicles, with the anti-tank and anti-aircraft guns bringing up the rear of the column. This was no uncontested advance and much of the opposition was both violent and heavy. But where British infantry threatened to halt the advance, the Battle Group's heavy weapons were brought forward to crush the resistance.

The 5th Regiment's 1st and 2nd Battalions, with their flank covered by 3rd Battalion's battle group, made the principal assault upon El Bathan supported by Panzer and led in by Stuka dive-bombers. The Allied troops, faced with this concentration of force, evacuated the small town and when the pursuing Paras reached the crest of the road leading down into the Medjerda valley, they saw the battlefield; columns of smoke rising from burning vehicles and farm buildings, a scene of desolation which extended for miles into the far distance.

During the afternoon of 4 December, the units regrouped and with Panzers spearheading their advance opened an assault to tackle Jebel Lanserine, a high peak to the west of the Tebourba road. The German offensive closed on 5 December, and when it did the position on the north-western side of the perimeter, which had been driven in during the middle weeks of November, had been restored. The success at Tebourba ended the first phase of the campaign in Tunisia and ensured that when Rommel's Panzer Army Afrika came up out of the deserts of Libya into the Tunisian bridgehead, it would not find the Allied armies at its back. That threat had been annulled.

An incident during this battle is recalled by Hans Teske, a runner in 5th Regiment, to whom I am indebted for allowing me to include this account from his unpublished memoirs.

'Early in the morning of 2 December, an elderly Arab, having an air of great authority, came into our positions and told Lieutenant Schuster that some 35 British paratroops had occupied a nearby farm. A battle group of motor-cycle combinations and two Volkswagen cars fitted with machine-guns for anti-aircraft defence, was soon created. I travelled on the pillion of the motor cycle carrying Lieutenant Schuster. He rode in the side-car manning the on-board machine-gun. Our elderly Arab guided us across some rough terrain and past a large Bedouin encampment, near which there was a dead camel whose decomposing body poisoned the air. Our cross-country journey ended when we reached a good road along which we made fair speed. At a crossroads we halted and Schuster sent the two cars out on reconnaissance. The terrain had changed again. As we drove along, large boulders loomed up suddenly out of the fog or mist patches. It was an eerie landscape.

Near the Abbaci farm our Arab guide left us and we first drove past the farm and then turned round to come back towards it. Schuster swung the machine into the farm-yard. The other motor-cycle combinations and crews stayed outside, but remained ready to give us covering fire if we needed it.

The French owner of the farm, a M. Rebourg, accompanied by his daughter Geneviève, came out to meet us. Lieutenant Schuster introduced himself and explained the purpose of our visit. Geneviève told us that British paratroops had been in the farm but had left after refreshing themselves with water.

As a result of the bitter cold of the previous nights I had caught a chill. At the farm I needed to "spend a penny" and left the group to go to a haystack only a short distance from a barn. Stopping only to put my rifle in the side-car I hurried to the haystack. A little later, with a feeling of great relief I was about to rejoin Schuster and the French couple when I heard children's voices. Youngsters had come up to look at this stranger, who was something new and exciting. Then, something made me raise my head and look at the barn. I was shocked to see a British paratroop officer standing inside it with his rifle covering me. Another paratrooper was lying flat on his back, at the officer's feet – either wounded or dead.

At that time I did not know, of course, that there were some 70 British paratroops on the farm. They had been given orders not to shoot unless it was absolutely unavoidable, in order to protect the civilians. A single false move by me would have resulted in a fire-fight which would have caught the Arab children, the farmer and his daughter as well as a number of farmhands. Behind the British officer (Lieutenant Peter Stainforth) I also saw several Bren guns pointed at me. One of them was manned by Lieutenant Dennis Rendell (who has since become another good friend).

In a split second I knew that Peter Stainforth had the safety of his wounded men as well as that of the children, at heart. I pretended not to have seen him and he, in turn, ignored me. I returned to Lieutenant Schuster who had now finished talking with the French couple. We climbed back on to the combination and drove out to rejoin our waiting comrades. It was hard for me to sling my rifle on my shoulder and to act naturally, knowing than an armed enemy was behind me. The next minutes were an eternity. Peter Stainforth and I have talked about the incident since, and agree that had I acted otherwise and reported his presence, German tanks from a nearby unit would have attacked and in that way the civilians, the British soldiers and the farm would have been destroyed, for there was no way in which Stainforth and his men could have defended it.'

During the final weeks of December and the first weeks of January 1943, while 5th Regiment was fighting in the south of the perimeter, No. 3 Company of the Corps Engineer Battalion received orders to undertake Para drops and glider landings behind British lines. The object was to destroy bridges and railway lines. Poor weather, the inability of the Ju 52 pilots to find and identity the targets as well as strong enemy defence led to the failure of all the missions. From some of those operations the Jaeger reached their own lines only after long and fatiguing marches, but there were some groups, those from No. 3 Company in particular, which were captured. The Jaeger were accused of espionage, tried by summary court martial, found guilty and shot. When Field Marshal Kesselring learned what had occurred he forbad all future air drops. It was a tragedy which haunted the Jaeger for a long time.

From a position of strength in the summer of 1942, Germany passed to the threshold of defeat by the end of that year.

The war in Africa, in which German armies had produced such victories in May and June, saw those same armies in retreat by November and in danger of being cut off by an Allied force which had landed behind them in the French North African colonies. Only the swift deployment of 5th Para Regiment and the Para Engineer Battalion had prevented the total collapse of the Tunisian bridgehead at that time.

In Russia, the German Army's storming drive towards Stalingrad and the Caucasus had met fanatical resistance from the Red Army and had suffered such losses that the objectives of the summer campaign would not be achieved. In view of the deteriorating military situation, German High Command was forced to cancel a planned paracute operation in the Caucasus, one which would have had wide-ranging strategic consequences. It no longer had any relevance. In Stalingrad itself German Sixth Army was bleeding and dying.

The 5th Para Regiment, which as stated above had been sent to Tunisia, had been raised to form one of the components of a planned 3rd Para Division. The nucleus around which the 5th was raised was the former Assault Regiment. To keep that name alive it was borne by 5th Regiment, until the end of the campaign in Africa when the Axis forces surrendered. The title of 'Assault

Regiment', was then inherited and carried to the end of the war, by 12th Para Regiment of 4th Fallschirmjaeger Division.

By the end of 1942, the strategic military initiative was passing from Germany to her enemies. Within six months she would be no longer capable of conducting an aggressive war but would be forced on to the defensive. The defeats suffered by the Third Reich in the year 1942 were harbingers of things to come.

When, at then end of December 1942, the fighting in French North Africa died down, it was followed by a period of relative calm; neither side was yet strong enough to strike the decisive blow but there was constant patrol activity and local attacks to seize some tactically important hill or strategic crossroads.

An example of those small battles in Tunisia early in 1943, and the type of men who fought them, is the story of Erich Schaefer, the officer mentioned in Hans Teske's account. Schaefer, one of the Para 'originals' had risen through the ranks and during the bitter fighting on the Eastern Front had been commissioned to the rank of Second-Lieutenant.

His No. 1 Company of 5th Para Regiment, acting as the advance party of the regiment, landed at Le Marsa airfield and was ordered to Pont du Fahs, at that time considered to be a quieter sector than either Bizerta in the north or Gabes in the south, where the fighting was more intense. Central Tunisia was one of the relatively quiet sectors until Schuster arrived. Nehring, the commanding General, needed accurate Intelligence on Allied movements. It was vital for him to know how far into Tunisia the Anglo-American forces had penetrated and in what strength. Schuster's Company went out night after night on reconnaissance and battle patrols to gain the information Nehring demanded. As a result Schuster's Company became the unofficial assault group of the Pont du Fahs sector, ready at a moment's notice to move out on a mission.

During the second week of January 1943, the Company was given the task of carrying out a reconnaissance in force up the road between Bou Arada and Medjez el Bab. At the base of a hill, Point 311, Schuster held two platoons back while he went forward with the leading sections of the first platoon to put out piquets on the nearby hills. Possession of the high ground was vital in that type of reconnaissance operation. He positioned the first platoon and left them, then went on to deploy his other two platoon commanders. The Company, in trucks and on motor-cycle combinations, made a swift advance. One of his platoons occupied Point 306, and another began to move to take up positions on Point 305. Schuster, on that hill, saw that British infantry had already taken the neighbouring Jebel Rihane. Then the sound of heavy engines was heard on the cold morning air. Eighteen British tanks were moving forward, attacking Schuster's men before they could dig in and consolidate the hill which they had just occupied. If the Jaeger were driven from it the British advance could continue towards Tunis. Schuster moved downhill to bring his other platoon forward and to organize a defence against the tanks. Some time after the Churchills were first seen Schuster was missed. Anxiety about the Company commander's fate became less important as the British tanks rolled down the road towards Medjez el Bab and struck No. 3 Platoon which was waiting for the Company commander to come back and to lead it forward to its position on the hill.

Word that Schuster was missing spread quickly and when no news of the officer was received Koch, commanding 5th Regiment, had leaflets printed and dropped over the British positions. These read that the regimental commander was prepared to hand over a captured British officer in exchange for Schuster and indicated the esteem in which he was held throughout the regiment. Koch warned the British in his leaflet that if Schuster were not handed over, their positions on the Bou Arada would be destroyed by Stuka attack.

Meanwhile fighting went on around the hills and it was at the end of a short but furious fire-fight that Schuster was found. British tanks, supported by fire from 25pdr batteries had struck No. 1 Company, but were forced to pull back. The infantry of 78th Division flooded back with them. No. 1 Company had also suffered heavy loss and after the stretcher-bearers from both sides had carried away the wounded one of the Jaeger in a forward slit trench noticed a man lying almost hidden from sight among the rocks. He crawled forward and rolled the body over. It was that of Schuster.

The corpse of the Company commander – he had been killed not knowing that he had just been promoted to full Lieutenant – together with those of thirteen of his comrades who had died in the battle for Point 311, were brought down from the cold, bare mountain and buried on 13 January, at La Mornagha cemetery. Schuster, one of the originals of 5th Regiment – a soldier who had survived the fighting in Belgium in 1940, in Crete in 1941, and Russia fell in Tunisia.

The continual rain and the bitter winter of 1942–43 halted all major operations in north Tunisia. But behind the front lines, in which the shivering Jaeger and their equally frozen opponents kept watch, a build-up of troops and *matériel* had begun. Only in the far south of that country were there any major operations as British Eighth Army drove out of Tripolitania. The lines in Central and Northern Tunisia, fixed by the winter weather, ran from Mateur to a point east of Medjez el Bab, down to Pont du Fahs, Djebel Daboussa and Pichon.

On the Allied side new Divisions, more tanks and more aircraft had come in. On the German side of the line a steady flow of units from Rommel's desert Army had thickened the line and allowed, at long last, the exhausted paratroop units to be rotated. One welcome reinforcement to Witzig's Para Engineer Battalion was Tiemen's No. 2 Company which returned from its service with the Ramcke Brigade in the desert Army. Among the units which arrived from Europe were elements of the Hermann Goering Division. To flesh out these elements the 5th Para Regiment was posted to and absorbed by, the Division in March 1943, and was thereafter known as Jaeger Regiment Hermann Goering.

The first major operation in which the new Jaeger regiment was involved was 'Ochsenkopf' in March, a successor to two earlier actions, 'Eilbote 1 and 2', in neither of which had Koch's regiment had any part to play. The two southernmost of the four German battle groups in the battle was made up of the mass of the Goering Jaeger Regiment serving with Kampfgruppe Schmid and 2nd Battalion with Kampfgruppe Audorff. At first light on 26 February, the four battle groups, after a night spent moving forward in pouring rain, moved into the attack. In addition to Koch's regiment in the south, Witzig's battalion in the north was also taking part in the offensive with orders to seize and hold Jebel Abiod.

Koch's two battalions moved off at last light on the 25th. Jungwirth's unit moved briskly forward; the Companies crossed the Bou Arada–Goubellat road and then turned westwards through terrain covered with thick shrubbery. In the growing daylight the battalion, now clearly visible, came under heavy British defensive fire and suffered heavy loss forcing it to be pulled back. Schirmer's 3rd Battalion was mounted, for the attack, on the armoured fighting vehicles of 10th Panzer Division. Outside El Aroussa British tank and artillery fire forced the battalion to halt. At dawn on the 27th a British counter-attack came in but was repulsed. A second was broken up by Stuka attack. A third assault, this one supported by Allied bombers, was flung back, as was a fourth and then a fifth.

Hans Teske, who took part in the offensive, recalls the operation: 'At dawn on 28th February, a warm, spring-like day, I took some wireless equipment to forward positions north of El Aroussa. At some Arab huts I took the

equipment out of the side-car of my motor cycle, strapped it to my back and began to walk towards the front line area, hoping not to be spotted by British positions on the Jebel.

On the road from Tally Ho corner to El Aroussa, a German paratrooper appeared from behind a haystack. By a stroke of luck he was the man who needed the equipment. A bullet had put his group's radio out of action. Just up the road, only 200 yards away, there were several stationary enemy tanks. Further to the right lay "Steamroller Farm", an area where our 3rd Battalion, mounted in trucks, would meet our 1st Battalion, which was attacking along the Jebel.

Just after I arrived the battle opened and the enemy's armoured thrust was directed against the farm and 3rd Battalion. I returned to the Arab huts to pick up my motor cycle and found several wounded comrades waiting to be transported to the rear. One had had his nose shot off, one was shot through the chest and the others were less seriously wounded. My motor-cycle combination had only two seats; one pillion and one in the side-car. Just then someone pointed out a badly wounded British soldier lying in a ditch which was swept by the fire of British machine-guns. He lay some 60 feet or so from a wadi which I knew I could reach. Although I was not protected by the Red Cross I decided to try and bring him in.

This would not be easy for first I had to cross a mined area. Luckily, when I did it there was no British machine-gun fire. I moved along the wadi and heard a faint moan. Looking over the wadi's edge I saw the wounded soldier,

Above: An awards ceremony of Witzig's Para Engineer Battalion, winter 1942/3. The commanding officer is here seen congratulating Corporal Becker on the award of the Iron Cross. (Hans Teske)

leaped out of the protection of the wadi and sprinted across to him. Immediately fire opened on me and a bullet hit me in the right foot. The man was too heavy to be lifted so I pulled him back to the wadi. The British machine-gunners stopped firing while I did this. In the wadi I put him into a sitting position and gently shook him. After a little while he recovered enough to become lucid. He had been shot through the chest and may have been lying out there for a complete day. I asked him to put his arm around me and we tried walking but he had great difficulty in moving his legs. His grip around my shoulders, however, was very firm. We crossed the minefield and I put him into the side-car. By seriously overloading the machine I took him and six others to the RAP. While driving along the main road machine-gun bullets came whistling over our heads. At the RAP I was given permission to return and pick up other wounded. A Volkswagen accompanied me on this trip. Before I set out again I saw the man whom I had rescued, a soldier of the London Irish Rifles. He was transferred to a Tunis hospital and our MO, Scheiffele, was confident that he would survive his wound.

As a result of my action I was recommended for an award. At the beginning of March my unit was withdrawn from the line for a few days rest and on 16 March, in front of the whole battalion my Commander, Captain Hans

Jungwirth, decorated me with the Iron Cross 2nd Class.'

While Hans Teske was rescuing the wounded, other British assaults were being made against the Para battalion holding the road. Tiger tank support had been promised to the Jaeger but none came. Instead a new British tank advance was made. In close-quarter attacks the lead tank was knocked out and as more and more British machines rolled across the Jaeger's slit trenches the order was given to pull back and to reform in a nearby wadi. Only 50 men reported and it was not until 4 March, that that small group was able to rejoin the rest of the battalion at Goubellat. The losses to 3rd and 2nd Battalions had been disastrous and those suffered by No. 11 Company had all but destroyed it as a fighting force. Operation 'Ochsenkopf' was broken off.

It was clear to Kesselring and to the OKW that the war in Africa was ending in a German defeat. Hitler might reassure Mussolini that the campaign would continue, but such promises had no value. Even an Axis bridgehead could not be held indefinitely without reinforcements of men and a flow of supplies and *matériel*. At troop level there was an awareness that Allied strength was being built up but there was among the Jaeger the conviction than man for man they were better soldiers than their opponents.

Before he returned home to Germany Koch attended the ceremony when the 5th Regiment received its new title of 'Jaeger Regiment Hermann Goering' and all ranks were issued with the cuff band of that Division. By this stage of the campaign the individual Para companies and battalions which had formed and held the original perimeter had been regrouped into other units. Witzig's battle group, now part of von Manteuffel's Division, took part in an attack around Jebel Abiod and gained initial successes. But the 78th Division's counter-attacks flung back Manteuffel's Division beyond Sedjenane. The perimter was being forced in.

One incident in the fighting around Sedjenane during March 1943, the fighting for Point 283, is recalled by Reinhard Hoffmann who was serving with the Para Engineer Regiment 'Barenthin'. It is a small unit action, typical of the many which made up the whole mosaic of the war, but it demonstrates the determination and durability of the Jaeger. It does more than that. In this account we shall see how the German forces in Tunisia were under such strain that a group of men who had been specially selected for promotion had to be put into action and were almost destroyed. Those men would have been the future leaders of Jaeger units. Their knowledge and experience would have been invaluable. Instead they were used to plug a gap and were lost. If this had been an isolated instance of such waste it might have been

excusable. It was not. Particularly in the middle and final years of the war similar small, specialist groups were flung into action to hold a position or to regain one that had been lost. And in those attempts were nearly always destroyed. The loss of potential leaders in such a way was incredibly high.

The scale of fighting on the northern sector of the Tunisian front which had reduced as the year closed continued into the first months of the new year and in that stalemate situation the Barenthin battalions were able to run courses. One of these was to train junior NCOs for promotion. Hoffmann, who was ordered to run such a course, realized that he was also being tested as a candidate for a commission and applied himself to the task with a great deal of energy and pleasure. Pleasure because many of those with him on the course were men who had been his comrades during the bitter winter campaign in Russia.

That course was never completed. The British 2nd Para Battalion was one of the élite Allied units battling to break through on the Sedjenane/Beja front. The bitter fighting by the Jaeger to hold Point 283 and the Red Berets to capture it had all but destroyed the 2nd and 3rd Platoons of Hoffmann's Company. Reinforcements were needed to hold the line and he was ordered to take the men of his course. 'Within an hour we were mounted on motor-cycle combinations heading down the road towards Sedjenane. At about 15.00 hours on 16 March, we reached the Company area where orders were issued that we were to relieve the unit on the hill. The survivors there could not hold the positions much longer. An enemy artillery barrage falling all round the hill scored a direct hit killing two men, one of whom, Sergeant Sommer, had been married by proxy, only days earlier.

We passed quickly through the shellfire and began to relieve the forward troops, but the enemy realized what we were doing and aware that a relief is a period of confusion, made an attack. Unluckily for him, we were not only old soldiers but we knew these positions well from earlier days. We settled ourselves into the shallow slit trenches and waited for the Red Berets to come on. Although the trenches were shallow they were well sited and we had excellent fields of fire. The attack was defeated. Then down came an artillery and mortar barrage. My immediate group was lying forward of the other two so we were the first to be attacked when the British Paras came back in a second assault. They stormed uphill towards us and were soon within grenade-throwing range of our trenches. They flung their bombs, took cover until these had exploded, got up and rushed forward at the charge. We were waiting for them and in close-quarter fighting managed to beat them back for a second time. All around us there were cries for stretcher-bearers. There were so many wounded. It was clear that the hill could not be held for long against such furious artillery barrages and determined enemy infantry attacks.

A runner brought orders that when the enemy attacked again we were to pull back a hundred metres to a new defensive position and that we were to hold this until 18.30 hours. Then we were to withdraw to a mining position. 'Mine F', which lay about three kilometres behind us and where a new battle line was being set up.

Above: Reinhard Hoffman, anti-tank platoon commander in the Barenthin Regiment, poses for a photograph by the side of a dugout at, Jefna, January 1943. (R. Hoffman)

Below: Schuster, another veteran, here seen as an NCO. He rose through the ranks and became immensely popular – so much so that when he went missing Koch printed and distributed leaflets in English demanding his return. Schuster was killed in action in Tunisia. In this picture, Reichsmarschall Goering is presenting Schuster with the Knight's Cross. (Rudi Hambuch)

The next British attack was not long in coming and while we were leap-frogging back 100 metres as ordered we lost more men. My runner was missing, a sergeant and a corporal wounded. But our enemy had had enough too, and the fighting died away with only now and again single shots ringing out.

The lightly wounded men were detailed to carry the more seriously wounded back to 'Mine F'. We gave them an hour's start before we ourselves started to move back at 18.30 hours. Before leaving we fired off a few bursts to convince the enemy that we were still in position. I felt uneasy about 'Mine F' and just short of it halted the march to check the position. There was a lot of movement there, particularly of the little British tank known as the Bren gun carrier. This was not unusual because we had captured a number of these useful little vehicles but I was still not convinced and a silent approach showed that my fears had been correct. The mine was now held by the British who were settling in for the night.

In the oncoming darkness there was no way we could work our way around the mine and so we rested for the night in the thick undergrowth of a cork forest intending to continue our march on the next morning. As you can imagine we were all hungry and not just tired but completely exhausted from the events of the day. Sentries were posted, we ate what scraps of food there were in our pockets and lay down to sleep. The night passed quietly and at first light we set out again with me leading the group and carving a way through the forest undergrowth with a house knife.'

This has been the story of a small action fought by only a few men and described almost laconically by one who took part in it. We must imagine the feeling of seeing the British attack storm uphill, then the Red Berets coming within grenade range and the hand-to-hand fighting. Hoffmann does not describe those feelings – they were a part of everyday life and as such so familiar as to need no elaboration. In his lines it is clear that the dead are not mourned when they fall – there was no time. Only later when the attack has been beaten off and a quick check carried out does the realization come that some more of the pupils of his NCO Class, a few more friends and veterans of the Eastern Front have been killed. To write about a battle in such understated, matter of fact terms is, perhaps, the best way of describing the horror of noise, violence and death which was war at the lowest military level.

By the middle of April British Eighth Army in the south of Tunisia and the Anglo-American forces in the north had linked up. The end in Africa could not be far off. Still, von Arnim sought to delay the inevitable by launching attacks, including Operations 'Fliederblute' in 5th Para sector. This

1. Sergeant-Major Peter Arend, a veteran Fallschirmjaeger who fell in Tunisia. One of the original members of the Para Engineer Detachment, he had fought in all the unit's campaigns thus far. (Rudi Hambuch)

2. Major Gericke of Assault Battalion Koch. One of the first volunteers for the Fallschirmjaeger arm, he survived the war and became a general in the army of West Germany. (Author's Collection)

1. 2.

was only a spoiling attack and did little to delay the series of assaults which the Allied armies now undertook to end Axis resistance in Africa. The key to Tunis was still the little town of Medjez el Bab and although the place itself was in Allied hands the Hermann Goering (5th Regiment) Jaeger held the high ground dominating the Medjez–Tunis road. Before the general assault could begin those Jaeger companies and battalions would have to be driven back or destroyed.

Casualties had so weakened the Regiment's strength that individual Companies held sectors which in other theatres would have been the responsibility of a battalion. The regiment's front extended from north of the Medjez–Tunis road to Goubellat. It was out of these positions that the Jaeger attacked during Operation 'Fliederblute' and to which they returned when the offensive ended.

Even while they were engaged in that attack, on other sectors of the Tunisian front the Allies had opened the first of their major offensives. On the Hermann Goering Jaeger sector the pressure was applied by 4th British Division, newly arrived in Africa. It was against veteran warriors in well-sited and excellently constructed defensive positions that the British battalions of 12th Brigade were 'blooded' and they lost heavily. The key point in the German line was a house surrounded by a high, thick, impenetrable cactus fence. This hilltop farmhouse was known to both sides as 'Cactus Farm' and the battles for it dominated the fighting in the Medjez sector. The Jaeger defenders in 'Cactus Farm', a single platoon of 48 men under the command of a sergeant, Schaefer, had good observation looking towards Tunis and along the road. Attacks on 28 April by a Company of 1st Royal West Kent Regiment, on the 29th by companies of the 2nd Royal Fusiliers and on the 30th by three Companies of the 1st

West Kents were all driven back by Schaefer's determined men. In the night attack on the 30th, some of the West Kent soldiers managed to force their way in to one or two of the ruined farm buildings but were driven out in hand-to-hand fighting.

In another attack upon the farm Schaefer saw a squadron of twelve Churchill tanks climbing up the hill towards him. He ordered the German artillery to fire on the farm area. The tanks smashed through into the farmyard, but the Jaeger, firing from their concreted positions, forced the supporting British infantry Companies to ground. Then a troop of Tigers entered the battle. Four of the Churchills went up in flames. Two Tigers were knocked out and the other Panzers pulled back. The remaining British tanks smashed through the thick cactus hedge into the farm. Schaefer leapt from his slit trench. Ignoring the shells that were falling around him he ran alongside the first vehicle and fixed a hollow-charge grenade to its flank. A sideways leap took him into another slit trench which sheltered him from the blast as the British tank blew up. Impressed by their platoon commander's example other Jaeger went out and attacked the Churchills. Only five of these reached their own lines.

US bombers then attacked the area and behind that bombing attack another British infantry/tank assault came in. It was beaten off. Only hours later another combined attack was made and that too was driven back. Fourteen British tanks were destroyed during the day. In the night an officer from 1st Battalion reached the farm and told Schaefer that he must hold out for only one more day. During the final day of resistance in 'Cactus Farm' a Brigade attack came in, but once again Schaefer's orders to the German artillery to fire on his own positions held off the British armour and infantry. Later that evening the

3.

4.

3. Hans Teske, who joined the Fallschirmjaeger in 1942. He was taken prisoner in Tunisia, and today plays a very active role in the old comrades' association. He now lives in England. (Hans Teske)

4. Reinhold Hoffman, a Para Engineer who received the German Cross in Gold. He was taken prisoner in Tunisia. (R. Hoffman)

sergeant and the survivors of his platoon pulled out of the farm and marched up the road towards Massicault where the new battle line had been set up.

All along the Jaeger perimeter the losses of the past days had been high, but perhaps nowhere greater than among the men of Witzig's battalion which, by the end of April, had been reduced to two officers (one of whom was Witzig), four NCOs and 27 men.

The final Allied attack went in on 6 May and its weight smashed through the German perimeter. Local counter-attacks, some of them spearheaded by the last Panzers of the Army Group, slowed the Anglo-American advance but could not halt it. By the early afternoon of 7 May the armoured cars of 11th Hussars and the Derbyshire Yeomanry had entered Tunis followed by the infantry of the Queen's Brigade. Tunis fell to the Eight Army and only hours later the Americans had entered and seized Bizerta.

The British advance up the Medjez–Tunis road had rolled over the small groups of Jaeger fighting desperately to hold back the armoured and infantry assaults. Those Paras who survived passed into captivity where they were soon joined by the remnants of Rommel's Panzer Army which had surrendered in Cap Bon. The war in Africa had ended and the greatest number of the Axis soldiers who fought there were taken prisoner. Some, notably the Jaeger of 2nd Battalion of 5th Regiment, managed to board a ship heading for Italy and thus escaped. Other officers and Jaeger, among them Major Witzig, also determined to avoid the final capitulation. He and a number of men from the Engineer Battalion found a motor boat o 1 which they sailed across the Mediterranean and reached Italian waters.

Another example of the determination of the Jaeger to avoid capture and to fight on is the story of Reinhard Hoffmann and four of his comrades who found a 10-foot rowing-boat on the coast and decided to sail it home. In the darkness of the night they carried it to a small harbour near Bizerta, launched it and then rowed round the harbour looking for an outlet to the sea. Finding none they waited for the morning.

'At about 06.00 hours on 9th May, we were back on the open sea. We had some rations, a couple of oars fashioned out of bits of a truck and ration boxes and a compass. None of us had any idea of seamanship, but undeterred we began our journey across the Mediterranean. We intended to make for the island of Zembra, near Tunis, which we could see on the horizon and which we hoped to reach by nightfall.

We had been rowing for about two hours when we saw an American air attack go in against our troops who were still fighting. Otherwise the day passed quietly. The sea was as flat as a billiard table, the sun was pleasant and we were glad that our rowing had brought us a couple of hours nearer to Germany. During the course of the day motor boats passed us and we thought sadly of how quickly these would reach Sicily. At about 15.00 hours, as we neared Zembra, three destroyers appeared. We thought these would be Italian and looked forward to being rescued. Then we saw that they were intercepting the motor boats a id sinking them. Through binoculars I could see that the flag which was flying was the British one and we all prepared to be taken prisoner. But the ships turned away and opened fire on our Army's positions in Cap Bon.

At 16.00 hours a storm blew up and we did not know how we would cope with the water that came pouring into the boat and threatened to swamp it. We all baled with whatever was to hand and as our little boat danced on the crest of the waves we saw again the three British destroyers. We were now quite ready to surrender and flew a white flag but they passed us by with shouts of "Germans ahoy!" The storm increased in fury and we had no hope of maintaining course as we were all busy baling out. To make speed we made a primitive mast and used a cut-up tent half as a sail. We finally reached Zembra at about twilight and saw that it had no beach on which we could land but only high steep rocks against which the waves were pounding and towards which we were being drawn by the waves. I told my comrades that when we struck the rocks we should try and climb them so as to reach the summit where we would be safe. We had unbelievable luck. A giant wave crashed us on to a rock which holed our boat but held it fast. In between the pounding of the waves we scrambled to safety and found a small cave where we spent a freezing night soaked through and hungry, for all our food and equipment had been swept away in the storm.

Next morning, the 10th May, the sea was calm again. We retrieved our boat from the rocks on which it was impaled and hid it. They we set off to investigate the island. Our main concern was to find water for we were all thirsty from the exertions of the previous day and the salt air. On a plateau on top of the cliffs we found a small stream. Thank God we had found water. Two Messerschmitt planes passed overhead but ignored our signals and then an Italian hospital ship passed quite close, but also did not see – or would not see – our waving.

In a collection of small huts at one end of the 4 kilometre long island we came across a large group of sailors, part of the crew of the sunken German destroyer *Hermes*. I reported to an officer and we were fed. During the following day British destroyers bombarded our island and when the sailors hoisted a white flag the fire ceased and the ships turned away. Captivity could not be far off now but we Paras decided to repair our ship and to set sail. We were determined to reach Germany or to die in the attempt. We had no intention of becoming prisoners.

The Naval Lieutenant, to whom we told our plan, thought we were mad trying to cross 120 kilometres (75 miles) of sea in so small a vessel, but convinced of our determination he gave us all the help he could. The boat was repaired and made ready for sea. An emergency sail was fitted and by afternoon our nutshell was ready. I hoped to crew her with some sailors as replacements for our wounded comrades but only one would take the risk. That man had had a telegram announcing the birth of his first child and, despite his misgivings, decided to take a chance with the Paras. It was as well that he came with us for he saved our lives. As we sailed along I saw a floating mine and decided to blow it up with a shot from my rifle.

Our naval comrade told us what would happen if I did.

We had set sail again at about 20.00 hours and soon the silhouette of the island had vanished from our sight. The calmness of the night was suddenly disturbed by the sound of Ju aircraft engines and three of them flew low over us heading homewards. We had food enough, proper oars which the Navy had given us, life-jackets and a list of the 150 men on the island. This latter, together with the ship's log-book were handed to me with orders that if were taken prisoner I should hand over the list of names but should destroy the log-book.

Daylight on the 12th showed us a completely empty sea, but at about 6 in the morning a sailing-boat passed on a parallel course and then at midday a destroyer appeared. It intercepted the sailing-boat and took off the crew. An hour later and it was closing in on us. A warning shot ordered us to heave to and through a megaphone we were told to hurry. We flung all our equipment into the sea before climbing a rope ladder on to the deck of HMS *Hurley* which brought us to Valletta in Malta. Prisoners we may have been, but faithful to our oath as Jaeger our small unit fought to the last.'

Two permanently established Jaeger units, 5th Regiment and the Para Engineer Battalion, were lost in Tunisia and needed to be reformed for the German Army organization did not allow a break in unit numbering. Those men of 5th Regiment who were in Germany on convalescence or on leave, together with those of 2nd Battalion who had escaped from Africa by ship, were regrouped into a new 2nd Battalion of 5th Regiment, under the command of the convalescent Major Schirmer. That battalion was then posted to 2nd Para Division but the new 5th Regiment was not raised completely until March 1944, when it was posted to 3rd Para Division.

The loss of the Corps Engineer battalion was also one that had to be made good. But OKW senior officers, viewing the situation of the Para organization, had already decided to raise an Airborne Army for which the Engineer establishment was not just a battalion but a Regiment. Plans were laid. A few men of the original unit who had escaped from Africa returned to the depot where they were reunited with other former members who had been in Germany when the campaign ended. To this cadre of veterans were added companies of new men so that by the middle months of 1944, the Engineer Battalion was fully raised. This then became 1st Battalion of the planned regiment with Witzig serving as both regimental commander and officer commanding 1st Battalion. A 2nd Battalion was then raised around a cadre of the Training battalion and was followed by a third.

1943

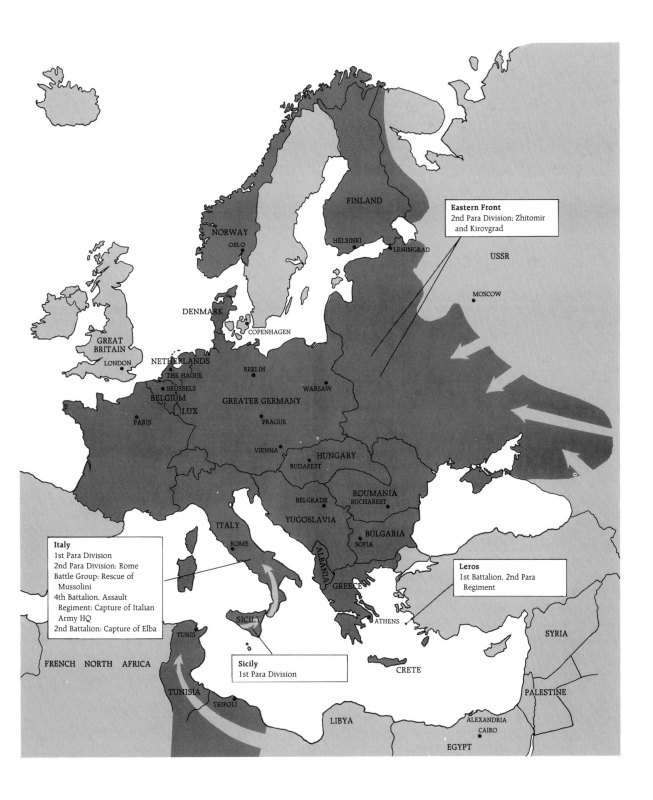

Eastern Front
2nd Para Division; Zhitomir and Kirovgrad

Italy
1st Para Division
2nd Para Division: Rome
Battle Group: Rescue of Mussolini
4th Battalion, Assault Regiment: Capture of Italian Army HQ
2nd Battalion: Capture of Elba

Leros
1st Battalion, 2nd Para Regiment

Sicily
1st Para Division

ICELAND

NORWAY
OSLO

FINLAND

HELSINKI

LENINGRAD

USSR

MOSCOW

DENMARK

COPENHAGEN

GREAT BRITAIN
LONDON

NETHERLANDS
THE HAGUE
BRUSSELS
BELGIUM
LUX
PARIS

BERLIN

WARSAW

GREATER GERMANY

PRAGUE

VIENNA

HUNGARY
BUDAPEST

ROUMANIA
BUCHAREST

BELGRADE

YUGOSLAVIA

BULGARIA
SOFIA

ITALY
ROME

ALBANIA

GREECE

ATHENS

SICILY

CRETE

SYRIA

PALESTINE

TUNIS

FRENCH NORTH AFRICA

TUNISIA
TRIPOLI

LIBYA

EGYPT

ALEXANDRIA
CAIRO

9. The fall of the Fascist eagle
ITALY, JULY-DECEMBER 1943

When the war in Africa ended it was obvious that the Western Allies would follow up this major blow to the Axis, by a swift military operation in the Mediterranean. Although the Germans had lost Panzer Army Africa, their Italian allies had suffered far more. Their overseas imperial possesions had been captured and that forfeiture caused repercussions in the highest circles of government – in the Fascist Grand Council.

The rumblings of discontent with Mussolini's rule, coupled with the war weariness of the Italian soldiers were made manifest during the period following the end of the war in Africa. During June and July a number of small, Italian islands were invaded by Anglo-American forces in almost unopposed operations and then, on 9 July, Montgomery's Eighth Army and Patton's US Seventh Army, landed in Sicily. Many Italian military units surrendered immediately and others after only token resistance. In the opinion of the soldiers and of the Sicilian people, who welcomed the British and the Americans, the war was lost and there was no sense in dying for a lost cause. There were, however, some formations which stayed loyal to their German allies, but even that faithful minority reduced in number with every fresh Allied advance towards the island's capital. On the Italian mainland, discontent in the Grand Council resulted in the deposing of the Duce, his arrest and his imprisonment by the Badoglio Government. He would be held until such time as the new Italian Government could hand him over to the Allies. Soon after Mussolini's overthrow came the invasion of the Italian mainland and the opening of a campaign during which one town, Cassino, came to signify the heroism of the ordinary soldier of both sides.

In both the Sicilian and the Italian campaigns Fall-schirmjaeger played a distinctive part. They held Rome, helped disarm the disloyal Italian Army, rescued Mussolini from a mountain-top prison and undertook a Para drop to recapture the island of Leros. More than that; during the offensives for Cassino as well as in the fighting

around the Anzio beachhead, they covered themselves with imperishable glory.

The story of the war in Italy begins with Operation 'Husky', the Allied invasion of Sicily. During the night of 9/10 July, two aerial fleets set out from airfields in French North Africa. Near the coast of Sicily the waves of aircraft transporting the British and American paratroops overflew the naval armada carrying the Allied assault landing troops. A Second Front was about to open.

The Axis garrison on Sicily which was deployed to meet the anticipated Allied attack, was predominantly Italian and was commanded by General Guzzoni. Lieutenant-General Hube, led the German troops on the island; XIV Panzer Corps. This comprised the Hermann Goering Panzer Division and 15th Panzer Grenadier Division.

The Allied assault by sea and air shattered the Italian coastal defence Divisions and brought to naught the Axis battle plan which had been prepared to meet it. A new one had to be made; one which, in the light of prevailing conditions, would have to be based upon the Germans bearing the full weight of the battle. It was obvious that just the Divisions of Hube's Corps could not hold the island. The best that they could do would be to delay the Allied advance until reinforcements arrived to thicken a strong defensive line in the mountainous east of the island and which would be centred around the volcano of Etna.

Until that defence could be established XIV Panzer Corps must launch immediate counter-attacks against the weaker of two Allied armies and drive it back into the sea. The remaining and isolated enemy force would then be destroyed by an all-out German assault. It was considered that Patton's Seventh was the less experienced of the two Allied armies and should, therefore, be the easier one to defeat. The Hermann Goering Division was ordered to attack. Its task was to fling Patton's Army off the beaches on the island's southern coast and back into the sea.

British Eighth Army had landed at Augusta on the eastern coast of Sicily, intending to carry out a swift advance into the Catania Plain and to follow that with the seizure of Messina. It was the task of the Axis forces in eastern Sicily to prevent this, but they were too weak to accomplish it. Reinforcements would have to be sent without delay. Speed of action was the most important consideration.

Among the formations held in OKW reserve was XI Flieger Corps, at Avignon, in southern France resting after a long period of bitter fighting on the Eastern Front. During the night of 10/11 July, a warning order was issued which alerted the units of 1st Para Division. The movement order followed only an hour or two later. Some detachments were air transported to Rome and over the following three days were flown to Sicily. Para Regiment 3 and the 1st and 3rd Battalions of Para Regiment 4, together with the Para Machine-gun Battalion and detachments from other Corps troops, dropped by parachute or were airlanded around Catania. Para Regiment 1 moved by rail to Naples and there awaited orders to move to the Sicilian battle front. In the course of the following days Army Divisions were ferried into the island to strengthen the defence.

The terrain on the eastern side of Sicily was good defensive country and the Jaeger were veteran soldiers who used their considerable knowledge to set up first class positions. The disposition of the units of Para Regiment 3 were excellent examples of the use of ground.

Major Rau's 2nd Battalion took up position near Franco-fonte while Boehmler's and Kratzert's battalions were echeloned northwards around Lentini and Carlentini. The battalion at Lentini was reinforced on 13 July, when the Machine-gun Battalion and other groups reached it. Later, the 1st and 3rd Battalions of 4th Regiment and Para anti-tank and artillery sub-units also reached the battle area and much later two Companies of the divisional Engineer Battalion moved into the 4th Regiment's perimeter around the bridge at Simeto.

The fighting for eastern Sicily is really the story of that bridge across the River Simeto. The shortest distance between the beaches at Augusta, where the British had landed, and Messina was along the eastern side, but that short route was restricted to one main road which threaded its way through mountains and across rivers. It was on Sicily's eastern side that the Fallschirmjaeger were deployed to contest Eighth Army's advance.

The commanders of the Para Division knew that if Montgomery and his veteran divisions forced the mountain barrier and reached the Plain of Catania, they would have good going, and the armour could speed northwards to the capital. To prevent this happening the British must be held south of the Catanian plain – and the Simeto bridge was the key. It was there that the Jaeger must stop Montgomery, for behind the Paras were no

Right: The regimental aid post of a Fallschirmjaeger unit on the Anzio beachhead. (Brian L. Davis)

other units capable of offering determined resistance.

As we have seen, the first elements of the Paras had begun to land on and around Catania airfield during the night of 12/13 July. Their arrival pre-empted that of British forces by only a matter of hours for during that same night British paratroops jumped over the airfield at Catania in the first of a two-part operation intended to take Catania at a run. The second part of that operation was sea-borne assault at Agnone by British commandos who came in that night.

Catania airfield was the scene of intense activity during the 13th and for several succeeding days. Following the British Para drop, which was quickly mopped up by units of the Hermann Goering Division garrisoning the area, the 3rd Para Regiment jumped there on the 14th, their descent following that of the Para MG Battalion. The area was under almost constant bomber and fighter attack by the Allied Air Forces and at intervals heavy units of the Royal Navy fired large calibre shells on to the airfield area. Catania, in the words of one Jaeger who passed through it was, 'a very lively spot'.

During the night of 13/14 July, a second British airborne assault was made to the north of the Simeto bridge with their landing zone being directly in the area held by the Para MG battalion. The MG battalion had been told that the Para Engineers would be making a night drop to strengthen the River Simeto positions, but they had not expected their comrades to drop so far forward. Thus, there was no alarm, '... when we heard aircraft fly low overhead. We guessed that these were transports and were then aware that gliders were swooping down and that men were falling from the sky. That these were the expected Para Engineers was the first thought of all of us. Even after the troops had landed their identity was still not clear. The error was excusable. Both we and the Tommies wore the same style of overalls and our helmets were almost identical. It was the whistles and the shouted orders that first alerted us....' The British reacted more quickly. They had an objective to gain and their units struck south-eastwards from the German MG Battalion positions, reached and captured the bridge. They were not to hold it for long. A Jaeger counter-attack mounted by fragments of units and led by a Staff officer from Division, recaptured it; these operations ushered in days and nights of bitter fighting, the brunt of which was borne by 4th Regiment.

There was, indeed, a drop by the Para Engineers at last light on the 14th, but over Catania airfield. When the first men to jump stood in the doorway of the Jus and looked down on to their drop zone they must have wondered into what hell they would soon land. Fires were burning across the whole area and so many anti-aircraft shells were exploding in the sky that the pilots, concerned for the safety of the aircraft, failed to throttle back to jump speed but roared across the airfield at maximum speed. The consequence was that the battalion was scattered over a very wide area.

It was not until the early hours of the morning that the Engineer Battalion had concentrated and was *en route* down the arrow-straight Roman road from Catania to the River Simeto. The battalion's arrival was warmly welcomed by the fragments of units of 4th Regiment, whose last survivors were still defending the sector against a series of attacks by 50th Tyne/Tees Division. The Engineers' No. 1 Company took over the sector and in a quick thrust across the bridge, seized it and formed a perimeter on the river's southern side.

On the 15th, a Brigade attack, supported by Churchill tanks, was repulsed. The men of No. 1 Company moved out of the thick, almost jungle-like cover of the river bank and attacked the armoured fighting vehicles at close range. A second attack, this one led by armour and supported by British paratroops, reached as far as the bridge but did not have the strength to cross it. The reason for this was that in the final stages of the assault the British Paras were without tank support. In the heat of the battle an 88mm gun had been brought forward and it opened fire at a range of only 900 yards (800 metres), knocking out eight of the Churchills. The rest of the squadrons broke off the attack and called for artillery support. Guns of the Royal Artillery then opened a furious barrage during which a direct hit on the 88 smashed it and killed the crew. There had been such severe casualties to the Engineer Company that it was feared a new British assault might overrun it. Men needed to be found quickly. As reinforcements, those Jaeger not normally found in the battle line; Company clerks, cooks, and wireless-operators were put into the fight, their action helping to stem the advance by Eighth Army's finest infantry Division. The loss of the 88mm gun made any defence by the unsupported Jaeger, however staunch, only a matter of time and the bridge passed into British hands, although attempts by 50th Division to cross it were beaten back by the fire of an SP gun of the Hermann Goering Division.

Two days later and the bridge was once again in German hands. By that time every officer of the Engineer Battalion had been killed or was missing in action and a sergeant-major was acting as commanding officer until the remnants were taken under command of 4th Regiment. On the 17th, the bridge again fell into British hands and this time, under Eighth Army's relentless pressure, both 4th Regiment and the Engineer Battalion were pulled back. The Simeto bridge had been lost. The way to the Plain of Catania seemed to be open to Montgomery's men.

The British follow-up was not as swift as the Jaeger officers had feared and no breakthrough occurred, but one wing of Eighth Army's offensive surrounded and cut off the 3rd Regiment which was holding Carlentini. In hand-to-hand fighting the Jaeger cut their way through the encirclement and after an exhausting night march gained touch with German forces at Paterno.

By this time, 20 July, the British thrust from the south and the US drive from the west had forced Hube to pull his troops back from their positions in Central Sicily. While that retrograde move was being made news came that Mussolini had been deposed. Immediately the Italian units in the island began to disintegrate, leaving only very few loyal units and with the majority of the Italian Service units now supporting the new regime of Marshal Badoglio.

By the beginning of August the German troops in Sicily were to all intents and purposes fighting the campaign without any Italian support. Their numbers were too few for them to defend the island without reinforcement, but there could be none. The mighty battles in Russia were the first priority in the matter of supplying new formations to the firing line. There remained no alternative, for OKW, but to order evacuation. The need still remained to hold the bridgehead against Eighth Army whose Divisions were now closing in upon it, and the Para units were put in to close gaps in the line, to restore a shattered front of to win back a lost position in a gallant charge.

An example of this was the action fought on 1 August, by the remnants of Nos. 1 and 3 Companies of the Engineer Battalion. These were hurried by road to Centuripe to support the 2nd Battalion of 3rd Regiment which was struggling against the attacks of British 78th Division. The Assault Engineers arrived during an artillery barrage and were distributed in small groups among the hills to the south of the town. Before they could organize a defence they were attacked by a small group of British infantry holding positions on the higher ground. Loaded down with weapons, hand-grenades and explosive charges, the Engineers climbed under fire towards the crest of the mountain, their own advance covered by the fire of a single machine-gun and that of a four-barrelled light anti-aircraft gun.

Arriving breathless on a plateau, the assault group leader quickly identified one of several stone-walled cottages as a British strong point. The Paras stormed it, charging through a hail of machine-gun fire and flung explosive charges into the open door. The British fire stopped abruptly. There was more firing from a short line of sangars set up on the crest and the Engineers swung their attack towards them. Suddenly, out of his sangar rose a British infantryman firing his Bren gun from his hip.

A burst of Schmeisser fire cut him down, but he tried to get to his feet and continue firing. The attack at Centuripe was the final action in which the Para Engineer companies were involved before they were ordered to pull back.

On 6 August Catania, whose approaches had been defended so tenaciously by 4th Regiment, was given up. The 1st Para Division formed a rearguard while the other units of the German Army in Sicily took ship for the Italian mainland. On the night of 16/17 August, the last elements of 1st Para Division crossed the Straits of Messina. The huge stocks of bombs which had been brought into Sicily for the bombing of Malta had to be destroyed to prevent them falling into Allied hands. The night sky lit with flames and detonations was a Wagnerian backdrop to weeks of hard and costly battle.

The campaign in Sicily was at an end.

The collapse of Mussolini's Italy produced a struggle for power between those who were still loyal to the Duce, those who supported the new conservative government of Marshal Badoglio and radical elements who wanted chaos and revolution. The new Prime Minister had indeed declared his intention to remain a fighting ally of Germany, but such a declaration lacked conviction. For Kesselring it was a time of delicate political manoeuvring. If Badoglio ordered the Italian Army in the homeland to rise against its former allies, the Germans would suffer heavy losses and while the military forces of the former allies fought each other the Anglo-Americans would exploit the situation so that the whole of Italy would pass into their control. Far better for the German Supreme Commander, South, who was still *persona grata* in the highest circles of the Italian Government, to pretend to believe Badoglio while moving strong German units into the country. If the need arose these would be in sufficient strength to disarm the Italian Army, and could then go to occupy the principal areas of Italy and thus ensure that German control was clamped upon an ally who had ceased to be reliable.

During this period of political change the units of 1st Para Division and the Corps troops evacuated from Sicily, were in Calabria recovering from the strain of the weeks of fighting, but anticipating orders that would send them off to some new campaign. Spread thin across southern Italy, 1st Para Regiment took up position in the Gulf of Taranto, ready to defend the area and its vital naval base against a British sea-borne invasion. The 3rd Battalion was detached to serve in the Salerno sector, and 2nd battalion of 4th Regiment, together with a sub-unit from the Para MG Battalion, were sent to the 1st Regiment as replacement units. It was during this time when 1st Para

Division was moving northwards through Calabria to a concentration area, that news came of the Badoglio Government's capitulation. This was a shock for it might soon be the case that German troops would be considered the enemy against which a new Italian Army would be employed in battle. The units of 1st Para Division were isolated in a land that might at any moment become a hostile one.

British troops landed in Calabria on 9 September; they were attacked and halted by 2nd Battalion of 4th Regiment. But that was not the only assault landing made that day; the one at Taranto was successful. The British were back on the European mainland but they were not alone for on the same day, and at Salerno, the US Fifth Army landed. Remnants, and they were only remnants – of 3rd Regiment went into the attack at Battipaglia and halted the advance in that area. The initial successes gained by 1st Para Division's regiments, however, could, not conceal the fact that the Germans were too few in number to hold the Allied invasions and drive them into the sea. On US Fifth Army's sector, reliance would have to be placed upon natural barriers and standard Army units to contain the assault, while the Jaeger of 1st Division would be moved to the Adriatic side of Italy, there to meet the swift thrusts of Eighth Army. The units of 1st Para Division were taken out of the line at Salerno, regrouped and put in against the formations of Montgomery's Army,

principally 1st British Para Division, which were striking northwards out of the heel of Italy.

Slowly, and delayed by furious Allied air attacks, the groups of 1st Para Division reached the combat zone and were put into the line piecemeal as they arrived. They were too few to do more than form a loose perimeter of strong points and certainly too weak to resist the overwhelming British pressure. Fighting hard in desperate rearguard battles the Jaeger were forced back. Other units arrived in support, but it was not until late in September that Para divisional headquarters was able to begin the concentration of its widely spread units into a cohesive battle front. A fresh assault landing at Bari on 22 September, brought new pressure and forced Division to pull back still farther, first to a point north of Barletta and then to retreat even farther in a movement which lasted until the first days of October.

It was at this time that Kesselring began to construct the German winter positions in southern Italy – the Gustav Line. It had been the intention of the German Supremo to hold the Allies south of Foggia. At that place there was an airfield with facilities for flying off the heaviest aircraft, ones with which the British and American Air Forces could bomb southern Germany and the Balkans, Kesselring was unable to hold the Allies south of Foggia; the advances by both US Fifth and British Eighth Army had pushed the battle line past the vital airfield. But if the

Above left: Following Italy's surrender in the autumn of 1943, paratroops were rushed to hold Rome. This picture shows a Fallschirmjaeger patrol guarding a crossroads. (Brian L. Davis)

Above: An episode during the brief battle for Rome. The picture shows Fallschirmjaeger reinforcements travelling on an ammunition carrier. (Brian L. Davis)

Supremo could not prevent the Allied air forces from using Foggia he could, certainly, ensure that their ground forces would be held south of Rome. He would construct defences along a number of rivers behind which rose high mountains and which, on the Tyrrhenian side of Italy, ran almost down to the sea. Along this line the Allied armies would be bled to death while his own forces could be rested for battles yet to come.

During October the 1st Para Regiment, together with divisional troops, were taken out of action on the Adriatic side of Italy and set to the task of building the Gustav Line defences, leaving the 3rd and 4th Regiments still in the line but subordinated to 29th Panzer Grenadier Division. The continuing pressure by Eighth Army forced the Jaeger to give even more ground and resisting doggedly they reached, by mid-November, the River Sangro, one of the natural defence positions of the Gustav Line. The Jaeger were then taken out of the battle and moved inland to construct defences around the Castel di Sangro and other

fortifications set up during medieval times to defend the river line. Eighth Army pressure continued and under the furious assault by a succession of British Divisions the Sangro was crossed, and it was feared that the British might break through the Panzer Grenadier positions.

To meet and weather that crisis the regiments of 1st Para Division were taken from their building tasks and rushed to the Ortona sector. Para Regiment 3, the first unit to reach the threatened sector, set up a blocking force, putting 2nd Battalion into positions on each side of the coast road to the south of the town. The 1st Battalion took post on Ortona's south-western approaches while 3rd Battalion was postioned to thicken 2nd Battalion's battle line and to act as mobile reserve.

The first fury of a new British offensive struck 26th Panzer Division, which was holding the ground around Orsogna. To strengthen it Jaeger units were rushed to the threatened sector and placed temporarily under the command of the Panzer Division. Once again, as had been the case on the Eastern Front in late 1941, individual Jaeger battalions were committed to battle. These were the 3rd Battalions of both 4th and 6th Regiments. The latter, which had been detached from 2nd Para Division, was taken, temporarily, on to the strength of 1st Para Division. Fighting furiously in appalling weather the Jaeger held Montgomery's northward drive and the British offensive died down. Not for long however.

On Christmas Eve, 1943, a new assault opened to drive in the outer defences of the Gustav Line. The offensive gained initial successes and the losses suffered by 1st Para Division in the bitter fighting caused it to be regrouped and relocated from the Castel di Sangro area to an even more sensitive sector near the coast road. The furious fighting on the Adriatic side of Italy was concentrated chiefly on the sectors which Montgomery was determined to gain. To achieve these he mounted his heaviest assaults using his finest formations. To meet the strong attacks by these élite Divisions; 8th Indian, the Canadian and 78th British, the fighting abilities of the finest regiments of the German forces in Italy were needed. The Jaeger who had been brought in held their ground. The battle was fought in such appalling weather that both sides were forced to call a halt. The fighting which had been both fierce and widespread, dwindled to just patrol activity and even that was carried out at a lower level than usual.

The Gustav Line, on the Adriatic side, had held. The 1st Para Division backed by a few battalions of Jaeger regiments had fought a good fight. Late in January 1944, the Allies moved the emphasis of their operations to the Tyrrhenian side of Italy where Eighth Army was about to undertake its own offensive to smash the Gustav Line. The German defences on Eighth Army's front were based on the Rivers Garigliano and Rapido, and the mountain ranges around the town of Cassino, mountains which ended only a handful of kilometres from the sea, leaving just a narrow valley through which ran the River Liri.

We must, at this point, leave the Gustav Line operations to go back to the autumn of 1943, and to consider the operations carried out in Italy and the Mediterranean area by Jaeger units other than those of 1st Para Division.

As we have seen, the political crises of the late summer of 1943, led eventually to a point where the Italian Army had to be disarmed and to carry out this delicate task a strong, well-led German formation was needed. The 1st Para Division was fully employed in fighting in Calabria. The only other unit available was the fledgling 2nd Para Division. It was during March 1943, that the formation of a second airborne Division had begun around a cadre of battle-tested soldiers, including men from the the Ramcke Brigade who had escaped from Africa, elements of 2nd Para Regiment and the 4th Battalion of the Assault Regiment. From its concentration area in Brittany, the 2nd Division, still not completely raised, moved in May to southern France where it became part of XI Flieger Corps, a formation in the strategic reserve of Tenth Army in Italy.

The crisis in Italy caused OKW to alert 2nd Para Division and to send it with all due speed to an area south-east of Rome; far enough distant from the capital not to be provocative, but close enough for the Jaeger units to take

over the city if the situation deteriorated. With the announcement of capitulation by the Badoglio Government clashes broke out between Italian and German troops. To prevent the trouble from spreading XI Flieger Corps ordered 2nd Para Division into the city to disarm the garrison of Rome. The Jaeger entered the Italian capital on 9 September. They acted swiftly and within a day the city was under their control and calm had been restored. Resistance to their operation had been light. But a more determined resistance was put up by the troops at Monterotondo, to the north-east of Rome, where the Headquarters of the Italian Army, was situated. Major Gericke's 2nd Battalion of 6th Para Regiment, jumped on the headquarters complex on 9 September and having overcome Italian opposition, arranged for all units of the Italian armed forces to cease hostilities against the Germans.

Below: Street fighting in the heat of summer: Fallschirmjaeger pause in the wreckage of a small Italian town, September 1943. (M. Klein)

10. 'Duce, I have been ordered to rescue you'
GRAN SASSO, SEPTEMBER 1943

Gericke's 2nd Battalion withdrew from Monterotondo but did not return to its parent unit; 6th Regiment. In November 1943 it became one of the cadre units of 11th Jaeger Regiment of a proposed 4th Para Division.

Two other operations which were undertaken at this time illustrate the skill in planning and the speed of execution shown by Para units as well as the *élan* which the Jaeger demonstrated in their military actions. The first operation was that of 12 September, to rescue the Italian dictator, Mussolini; the second was the Para drop which captured the island of Leros in November of that year.

Mussolini, under arrest by the Badoglio Government, was moved frequently, from one prison to another, for the Italian authorities were aware of Hitler's determination to rescue his former ally. In August the former Duce was taken to the area of the Gran Sasso Massif. German wireless-operators monitoring signals between Italian units, picked up a message which indicated unusual activity in the Gran Sasso. Discreet inquiries established the presence of a very important personage in the Albergo Rifugio on the peak of a mountain. It could only be Mussolini and plans were made to rescue him from his prison.

It must be pointed out here that there are two versions to the story of how the Duce was rescued. The version which has been accepted for years is the one in which SS Major Skorzeny claims to have carried out the mission using men from his SS Commando group. Skorzeny played down the role of the Fallschirmjaeger and the Nazi propaganda media ensured that only his account received publicity. The other version is that Jaeger units were the principals involved; from the planning to the execution stage of the operation. The Jaeger story is less well known; indeed, so widely accepted was Skorzeny's version that no word of thanks was ever written or spoken by Mussolini to the Fallschirmjaeger or to their commander, Student. It is clear that the Duce believed that the group which had rescued him were under the command of the SS Major.

Let us accept, although even this claim is rejected by the Paras, that Skorzeny was the man who personally liberated Mussolini. It is how he came to be that man which is interesting.

The rescue story begins during the night of 10 September 1943, when General Student, advised of the location of the dictator's prison laid plans to rescue him during the morning of the 12th. It was clear that only an airborne operation could succeed. The hotel which was being used as a prison was on the top of a mountain. The only means of access were by hours of climbing or by using the cable-car system. Mussolini's guards were under orders to kill him if any escape attempt were made. Neither a foot march nor an assault from the cable-car could succeed. The unusual wind conditions of the Gran Sasso made a parachute drop impossible even from the lowest altitude of 60 metres. The option remaining was a glider-borne assault. Major Mors, commander of the Paratroop Training Battalion, was ordered to prepare one of his Companies for a glider landing. While that unit was making its assault the rest of the battalion would reach and occupy the valley station of the cable-car system. The valley detachments would then make contact with the mountain top Company, reinforce it if necessary and prevent the Italians from interfering while the operation was in progress.

The next task was to assemble the men and machines. The nearest glider group, in Grosseto, was ordered to fly in to Practica di Mare airfield on the morning of the 12th. Only then would Student brief the glider pilots, the Jaeger of Major Mors's No. 1 Company who would be flying the mission, and the SS. Student allowed Skorzeny to accompany the Paras since it was the SS Major's task to protect the Duce once he was rescued. There was, in Student's eyes, a sharp distinction to be drawn between the military part of the operation and the political. His men would carry out the former; the SS officer would provide for the latter. Student was not pleased when Skorzeny brought a detachment of men with him but he accepted that they would participate in the mission.

Quite late in the evening of 11 September, Major Mors

Above: One of the DFS gliders that carried the Fallschirmjaegers into the attack. (M. Klein)

Below: The Storch aircraft piloted by Major Gerlach, Student's personal pilot, to fly Mussolini and Skorzeny to safety. The take-off was risky in the extreme: an ultra-short run downhill to a cliff edge. (M. Klein)

having reported that his battalion would be unable to reach the cable-car station by the time specified, a new zero hour, 14.00 hours was agreed. Shortly after dawn on the 12th, the trucks bearing Major Mors and his men drove out towards the valley below the Gran Sasso. At 09.00 hours Student arrived on the airfield at Practica di Mare to brief those who were to take part in the operation. Among the men assembled was the Italian Carabinieri General Soleti whom Skorzeny had persuaded to collaborate. Student gave his accustomed, detailed briefing on the purpose of the mission and how it was to be accomplished. General Soleti, who now learned for the first time what he was expected to do, was visibly upset and attempted suicide. Having been restrained he agreed to accompany the Germans because of their assurance that his presence would prevent bloodshed. Student closed his briefing by expressing the belief that the landing would be so great a surprise to the Italian guards that they would not fire a shot. There would be no need to alarm them by making crash-landings or employing the parachute brake system.

Each commander has his own particular worries. Those of Captain Langguth, commander of the tug aircraft group, included whether his machines and the gliders they were towing could gain enough height to bring them safely over the 4,300ft (1.300m)-high mountains to the east of Tivoli. The distance between the airfield and the mountains was not great, the angle at which the machines would fly was shallow and no other route could be flown without compromising the mission by betraying to the Italians the fact that something unusual was happening.

Lieutenant von Berlepsch detailed the arrangements for the glider force. He, as leader, would fly in the first machine of the first chain, together with his Company HQ group. Skorzeny and his men would fly in the second chain of aircraft. Take-off was at 13.00 hours and as Captain Langguth had feared the machines did not seem to be gaining height quickly enough. It seemed to him that those of the third chain were flying so low that they might not clear the mountain peaks. He decided to gain height by circling and immediately swung his chain of machines in a great curve expecting that the other pilots would follow his example. There was no wireless communication between the aircraft for him to give direct orders. To his surprise the other chains did not conform to his movement but maintained the original course for the Gran Sasso. Thus, the second chain, the one with which Skorzeny was flying, had now become the lead group.

At 10,000 feet (3,000 metres) and often flying blind in the culmulus clouds which had gathered over the Gran Sasso, the gliders began their descent. Lieutenant Meyer-Wehner's machine which was carrying Skorzeny, was the first to touchdown and was followed within seconds by the others whose Jaeger quickly set up defensive positions and gained contact with Major Mors and the remainder of the battalion in the cable-car station. One glider, whose pilot realized that he could not make a smooth landing on the spot he had chosen, was forced to crash-land, injuring all the occupants.

Major Mors then set out for the summit by cable-car and reported to Mussolini that the first part of the mission had been accomplished. The Paras, using the tactics of surprise and daring, had liberated him. Now it was the task of the SS commander to escort the Duce to Germany. In the interests of speed and security Student had decided that Mussolini would be flown in a Fieseler Storch from the summit of the mountain to the airfield at Practica di Mare. A second Storch, which was to land in the valley, would carry Skorzeny to the same field where an He III would fly to Vienna carrying the Duce, Skorzeny and a doctor from Flieger Corps staff. The first Storch, was flown by Captain Gerlach, Student's personal pilot, who landed it on the only available spot, a downhill slope. Gerlach was only able to accomplish that difficult feat by running the Storch up the slope and against the wind. The second machine, the one which should have carried Skorzeny, could not be used, the undercarriage had been damaged in landing. The SS Major insisted on flying with the pilot and Mussolini although this dangerously overloaded the light aircraft. The only way in which Gerlach could take-off from such a small areas was to fly downhill and into the wind. The Luftwaffe captain brought the machine to Practica di Mare and when Mussolini entered the He III the paratroop role in the operation was nearly concluded. There remained only the need for Student to telephone and advise Goering of the rescue.

The Commander-in-Chief of the Luftwaffe was surprised. The operation had been ordered and executed in such secrecy that even he had not been informed. Goering did not pass the news to Hitler immediately. When finally he did it was to learn, to his chagrin, that Skorzeny had already telephoned Himmler who had given Hitler the news of his ally's liberation. Student's subsequent attempts to gain for his men the recognition they deserved met only with Goering's resigned comment that the Fuehrer had accepted the SS story and had rewarded Skorzeny with the Knights Cross of the Iron Cross. There was no way either could be revoked. Thus, a Para operation, skilfully planned and carried out, went unacknowledged. Today the legend persists that it was Skorzeny and not the Jaeger of Major Mors's Training battalion who brought Mussolini out of captivity in September 1943.

11. The last Para drop in the Mediterranean theatre
LEROS, NOVEMBER 1943

Among the crises that faced the Germans in the Mediterranean theatre at the end of 1943, was the British seizure and occupation of several of the Dodecanese islands shortly after the Italian surrender. Not only did these islands lie across the sea routes between the German bases in Rhodes and those on the Greek mainland, but there was the fear that the Allies might use the Dodecanese as a spring-board to invade the Balkans. Faced with the need to act, OKW prepared an operation to recapture the lost islands.

The first move in the German operation went in on 5 October, when their forces attacked and captured Kos. The choice of that island as the first objective had been dictated by the fact that it had an airstrip from which aircraft could cover future operations. Just as its capture was a prize for the Luftwaffe so was it a particularly serious blow to the British, for now the RAF had no local base from which to operate. It could now give no air cover over those islands against which the Germans would be certain to act and of which Leros was strategically the most important as a naval and a seaplane base.

Leros, only nine miles (fourteen kilometres) long and three miles (five kilometres) wide, is shaped like an hourglass, with two huge indentations, the one on the western side named Gurna Bay and that called Alinda Bay, on the eastern side, which all but bisect the island. Both bays are surrounded by bleak mountains, rocky outcops and precipitous cliffs. Chief among the mountains which cover the island are Appetici and Germano from whose tops most of the island can be seen. Among the few flat parts of Leros is the area of ground, little more than a kilometre wide, which lies between the two bays.

Command of the operation to recapture Leros was invested in Lieutenant-General Mueller, commanding the 22nd Air Landing Division, whose formation had already stormed and captured a number of other Dodecanese islands, including Kos on 3–4 October. To lead the assault he had Captain Kuehne's 1st Battalion 2nd Para Regiment and the Para Company from the Brandenburg Regiment. The sea-borne part of the operation would be a two-part

landing; Captain Aschoff's Western Force which would land in Gurna Bay and Captain von Saldern's Eastern Force which would land in Alinda Bay. The naval task forces would carry men from the Kuestenjaeger (the special boat service) of the Brandenburg Regiment and 3rd Battalion of 1st Brandenburg Regiment could be used as reinforcement. To compensate the lack of artillery support the Germans could rely upon Stuka and other bombers and a vast number of fighter aircraft which would be used in ground support roles. German Intelligence established that the British garrison was 234th Infantry Brigade whose 2nd Royal Irish Fusiliers, and King's Regiment were in the south of the island while 2nd Buffs held the north. The British garrison was later reinforced by 2nd Queen's Own Royal West Kent Regiment. Backing the British Brigade was an Italian garrison of gunners manning the coastal guns which dominated the approaches to the island.

German High Command demanded that Mueller make his attack in October, but he refused to undertake the operation until action had been taken against the Royal Navy in the eastern Mediterranean, since he had no intention of risking his sea-borne forces. He did, however, order the Luftwaffe to begin its bombardment of the gun positions and permanent defences on the island. This was Part 1 of Mueller's four-part operational plan. Not until the start of November did he consider it safe for his battle groups to undertake the second part of Operation 'Leopard' – the sea-borne invasion. The third stage would be the exploitation from the beachheads and then his troops would go into the fourth and final stage, the defeat of the British and Italian forces.

Emboldened by the recapture of Kos, High Command detached Captain Kuehne's battalion of 470 men and had it flown from Ferrara to Ekali, north of Athens. There Kuehne's 1st Battalion, 2nd Regiment, trained hard for the operation, clambering over rocky slopes, practising close-quarter warfare and tactical exercises using sand-tables to show the terrain in which they would be operating. General Mueller briefed the battalion commander on the mission. The task of 1st Battalion would be to capture the narrow waist of Leros between the two bays and go on to capture Monte Meroviglia, a dominant height in the north-west of the island. In conjunction with the seaborne detachments the battalion would go on to capture the island's capital.

Although the Luftwaffe carried out more than a thousand raids upon Leros the guns had still not been knocked out, but Stuka and Heinkel bomber attacks had 'softened' the Leros garrison. General Mueller then ordered the second stage of Operation 'Leopard' to be launched and convoys of ships carrying the German assault troops set off. As these neared the coast of Leros the airborne units, waiting at three airfields near Athens, were ordered to emplane. It was dawn on 12 November; D-Day for the operation. Forty Ju 52s swept southwards, flying almost at wavetop height, towards the island, but after an hour's flight and almost within sight of their objective, they were recalled. The reason for aborting the drop was that Captain Aschoff's Western Force had come under fire from the coastal guns and had been driven back. There had been no landing on Gurna Bay, but the assault by the Eastern Force had been successful and two beachheads had been gained.

At about midday the Paras emplaned again and two hours later the aircraft, changing formation from 'arrowhead' to 'in line', were nearing Gurna Bay. Only a minute or two from the target the files of twelve machines in line astern climbed from wavetop height and began the run in to the drop zone. The Jus now at an altitude of less than 500 feet (150 metres) were flying lower than the anti-aircraft guns which had been sited on the neighbouring mountain peaks. These poured fire at the slow-flying targets. Over the small strip of ground between the two bays the Paras began to leave their aircraft. Captain Kuehne had chosen the drop zone (a triangle based on the villages of San Nicola, San Quirico and Alinda) since it seemed to him, from air reconnaissance photographs, to offer the most favourable terrain in which to concentrate after landing. The area was cut about with wadis in which the Jaeger could group. For this operation they carried personal weapons so that they would be in a position to go into action once the landing had been accomplished.

What the battalion commander did not know was that deployed across the jump zone were the Companies of 2nd Royal Irish Fusiliers. At a jump height of only 600 feet (180 metres), the paratroops were in the air for less than twenty seconds, too short a time for the Irish Fusiliers to

Right: A training flight; Fallschirmjaeger check their gear before emplaning. Braunschweig, May 1941. (R. Hoffman)

react and the Paras had soon gone to ground in the rocky, scrub-covered lower slopes of Monte Germano. Within minutes the scattered groups of Paras had concentrated and were ready for action. Kuehne ordered his No. 1 Company to face northwards and to cut the roads in their sector. His No. 3 Company was ordered to face eastwards and to cut the road between Alinda Bay and the small town of Leros. A secondary task for that Company was to carry out reconnaissance northwards. These two small screens of Paras would have to hold any British assaults while Nos. 2 and 4 Companies. together with the Brandenburg Para Company, attacked the dominant Rachi ridge and secured it as a base for future operations. British reaction was not slow in coming, but it was weak because part of the garrison was in action against the sea landings on the eastern side of the island.

There the Brandenburg Kuestenjaeger had made their sea-borne landings; one striking for the sheer cliffs to the north of Pandeli while a second force made course for Alinda Bay. Despite furious and accurate fire from the coastal artillery the Brandenburg troops gained footholds and opened their assault upon their objective, Monte Appetici. This was unsuccessful; the air strikes for which they had called dropped the bombs on the Brandenburgers and forced them back. The Kuestenjaeger, deciding that the mountain was too large a target to capture, selected a new objective, the 15cm gun battery on Castle Hill, to the south-east of Leros town, attacked and captured it.

On the Gurna Bay sector the Paras had consolidated their hold upon the drop zone and had begun to move out from the original perimeters. By 13 November, D-Day plus 1, the 1st Battalion's aggressive patrolling had cut the island in two, dividing the Buffs in the north from the Irish and the King's in the south. Reinforcements for 1st Battalion of 2nd Regiment were dropped during the day. These were a Company of Brandenburg Paras who arrived in the middle of a storm which caused many of them to be dropped over the Bay of Alinda. In this operation two transport planes were lost. Other reinforcements came in by seaplane. Throughout the following days British counter-attacks, supported by fire from the British destroyers *Echo* and *Belvoir*, sought to smash the Para cordon across the neck of Leros, but these assaults lacked strength whereas the Germans were being reinforced with new men and weapons. This reinforcement allowed an attack to be carried out at dawn on the third day of the operation (14 November). Two of Kuehne's Companies, Nos. 2 and 4, supported by Stuka attack, moved out from their positions on Monte Rachi to take Monte Meroviglia, but were unsuccessful.

One unit which did come in to reinforce the British garrison, 2nd Battalion of the Queen's Own, was caught as it made its approach march towards the Buffs' positions. Under German mortar and machine-gun fire backed by constant Stuka attack, the West Kents formed up, but their assault died before it had time to develop. The Kents reformed, advanced through the Para fire and retook Germano where they gained touch with the Buffs. That link-up offered the chance that the German Paras in Leros town area might be contained by capturing the little village of St Nicola. Despite hand-to-hand fighting with the Jaeger garrison the combined Kentish force was too weak to seize the village.

The ferocity of the fighting caused Operation 'Leopard' to lose momentum. The German senior commander on Leros decided to withdraw from Monte Rachi and to use the units freed by that action, together with infantry reinforcements, chiefly 3rd Battalion of Brandenburg's 1st Regiment, to carry out an assault upon Monte Marovigilia where British Brigade Headquarters was sited. By 17.00 hours on 16 November, they had captured their objective and the fighting was all but over.

Operation 'Leopard' had been successful and Leros, the most strategically important of the Dodecanese Islands, had been captured. The 2nd Para Regiment's 1st Battalion was flown back to Greece and went back into action, now however on the Eastern Front, where the other units of 2nd Division had been posted, but as the cadre around which 10th Para Regiment (4th Fallschirmjaeger Division) would be built.

Captain Kuehne's battalion lost 68 men killed in action and 100 wounded, of whom two died of their wounds, but the operation had been successful. An island defenced by 24 batteries of artillery, of which 43 were coastal defence pieces, 58 heavy anti-aircraft guns and a further 49 light AA guns backed by a British and Italian garrison, had been captured in less than a week. One interesting aspect of the operation is that on 14 November, that is the third day, a German thrust so alarmed a Royal Navy signals detachment on Monte Meroviglia that they burned the signal code-books. Thereafter, every message sent by that station was in clear and was picked up by the German wireless intercept service.

There was no time for Kuehne and his men to rest on their laurels. Within days an advance party had been flown back to Italy, with the remainder of the battalion returning by sea. But the parent regiment, the 2nd, was no longer serving in the Mediterranean: it had been rushed to Zhitomir on the Eastern Front. Kuehne's battalion was then posted to Lake Trasimeno, north of Rome, where it formed the nucleus of veteran soldiers around which the 10th Fallschirmjaeger Regiment was raised.

12. 'He who would rather die than lay down his arms cannot be defeated'

THE EASTERN FRONT, JANUARY-DECEMBER 1943

The Soviet winter offensive, which had begun when Sixth Army was surrounded at Stalingrad in November 1942, rolled on, threatening the formations of Army Group Centre which were holding the line round Smolensk and Vitebsk. One Soviet thrust driving out of the Rzhev salient struck 7th Flieger Division, but despite the mass employment of armour against the Jaeger positions the Russians achieved little more than local penetrations. There were heavy casualties on both sides in the battles for Starova and Duchov-shchina, but the Red Army was not able to force a break-through of the Fallschirmjaeger front. This was not the case in other sectors of the German battle line whose units were less able to hold the sweeping advances. In those places the Red Army tore gaps in the line and poured through in huge masses, advancing with the confidence that a decisive victory was almost within its grasp.

A massive Soviet thrust in the third week of February 1943 shattered the right flank units of 2nd Panzer Army, which were holding the Orel sector. To seal off the breach 1st Jaeger Regiment was taken from its sector of the front and rushed to Orel where it was placed under the command of 46th Panzer Corps. In savage fighting against fearful odds the Jaeger were able to prevent the gap at Dmitrovsk from being widened and then in a series of attacks and counter-attacks fought on until they had closed the Orel breach by the end of March. On the last day of that month 7th Flieger Division, soon to be re-numbered and renamed as 1st Fallschirmjaeger Division, was taken out of the line and posted to France for rest and recuperation.

Although the bulk of the Division had left the Eastern Front, the Corps troops; the Assault Regiment, the Anti-aircraft Machine-gun Battalion and detachments of the

Right: March 1943 on the Eastern Front. Tiredness shows itself in the eyes of these young Fallschirmjaeger. The weapon is an MG 34.

Right: The ideal of comrade-ship, as epitomized by the Fallschirmjaeger élite: help for a wounded paratrooper in the snows of the Eastern Front. (M. Klein)

Below: Fallschirmjaeger sentry in snowbound Russia. 'Egg grenades' are ready to hand as laid down in the regulations. (Brian L. Davis)

Anti-tank Battalion, remained in Russia grouped as Battle Group Meindl and placed under the command of 6th Division. The Para detachments fought in winter battles around Sobakino and in the defence of Yuknov airfield before they were moved north-west to Lake Ilmen. The Assault Regiment's 1st Battalion, which was heavily committed in the fighting around Shaikovka, could not be taken from the battle to accompany the other battalions but remained in action until April when the shattered Companies returned to the depot in Germany. By the time that 1st Battalion was relieved the other Para detachments had been posted to Germany, except for 4th Battalion of the Assault Regiment. That battalion was still fighting in the lonely forests and swamps of Volkhov where, more than a year earlier, 1st Jaeger Regiment had suffered appalling losses in the fighting connected with the siege of Leningrad. It was not until July 1942 that 4th Battalion could be taken out of the line and it then left the Eastern Front.

The manifold tasks which had been laid upon 2nd Para Division during 1943 had taken its component regiments from France to Italy, Sardinia and Leros. These, however, were not to be the last entries in the Division's battle calendar for that year.

Following the defensive victory at Kursk in July 1943, Stalin and the Supreme Stavka went over to the offensive and in two successive operations, 'Kutuzov' and 'Rumyantsev', had flung back the Central and Southern German Army Groups. By the middle of October Koniev's 2nd Ukrainian Front had set up three bridgeheads across the River Dnieper and it was only a matter of time before it burst out of these and went on to capture the important industrial complex of Krivoi Rog. Nothing, it seemed, could halt the advance and by 25 October Dnieper-petrovsk had fallen.

No effort by the German forces could, it seemed, do more than delay the onslaught. The First Panzer Army, of Army Group South, conducted a successful counter-attack against Koniev's flank and forced a temporary halt, but the Red Army's assault merely swung from the stalled sector to that held by another Soviet Front. With Koniev's thrusts thwarted, emphasis moved south and was carried on by Tolbhukin's 4th Ukrainian Front. Then, during the first week of November, when 4th Ukrainians' assault began to lose momentum, the Soviet point of maximum effort moved to Vatutin's 1st Ukrainian Front. His offensive, deploying thirty infantry divisions, 24 armoured brigades and ten motorized divisions advanced quickly to the north and south of Kiev. The city fell on 6 November and a week later the forward elements of Vatutin's host were in Zhitomir. The massive Red Army offensive struck along the seam connecting the inner wings of Army Groups Centre and South and, under its weight, the danger grew that they would be torn asunder.

To meet that crisis there were only a few élite divisions that German Supreme Command could put into immediate action. The 2nd Para Division was one of those few and during the first week of November it received movement orders. It was to proceed at best possible speed and to take up positions near Zhitomir there to seal off the Russian penetrations. Because the Division had had to carry out missions in a number of areas of Europe it was no easy task to retrieve the scattered battalions and regiments. Indeed, when the 2nd left for the Eastern Front it was short of three battalions, each of which was still needed in those other areas.

The journey from Central Italy to the Ukraine took a week; on 17 November, the divisional advance party arrived at Berdichev. Not until ten days later did the rearguard arrive. The move to the operational area was quickly accomplished and within two days the Division, as part of Fourth Panzer Army's, 42nd Corps, was concentrated to the west of Kiev.

Shortly before midnight on 28 November, General Wilke was able to report to the commander of 1st SS Panzer Division. 'Leibstandarte SS Adolf Hitler' that the 2nd Para was ready for action. The time was opportune for the SS Division was about to undertake a mission to clear a wooded area between Belka and Teterev near Radomysl. A group of Fallschirmjaeger were to collaborate in that operation in order to familiarize them with local conditions. The 2nd Para would relieve the SS from their positions as soon as Corps had reached the line Gardov–Teterev. The attack to clear the Belka woodlands opened on 29 November at 05.30 hours, but even before it got under way it encountered a Russian thrust coming from the Tolstoy Kolkhoz. The élan of the first German assault drove back the Red troops, but the terrible weather, the ground conditions and the tenacity of the Soviet defence combined to slow the advance, and also made it impossible for 2nd Para to concentrate its regiments and relieve 1st SS Division from its positions near Kotcherovo. Corps directed that the relief be carried out by 2 December.

At 06.00 hours on 30 November, the battle group from 2nd Para went in to clear the woods and at 11.00 hours had opened its successful attack. The veteran Jaeger had trained the replacements well. During the afternoon of that day 2nd Para Regiment arrived in Sobolev and with its arrival the relief operation began. By 20.00 hours on 1 December it had been completed ahead of schedule. Both 2nd and 7th Regiments were in the line and responsibility for the whole sector then passed from the SS to the Fallschirmjaeger.

Although the SS had fought their battles with accustomed flair and thoroughness, the strength of the Soviet forces on that sector had prevented a full victory. Nevertheless, the German gains had worried Stavka who then grouped Sixtieth Red Army to the north-east of Zhitomir and ordered it to hold the Germans, to fling them back and to break through to the River Dniester. The first Soviet assaults were met by counter-blows in which 2nd Para took an active part. As a result of its well-conducted operations it had not only smashed a number of Russian formations but had also closed those gaps in the German line which the Red Army had created. Stavka was still determined to smash a way forward to the Dniester and it was against the sector of front held by 2nd Para that the heaviest Russian assaults were made. By day and by night, punctually and unremittingly, the attacks were repeated. Heavy losses did not deter the Soviet soldiers as they strove to reach the river. Line after line advanced into the fire of the Fallschirmjaeger machine-guns. Unwavering they marched forward through the heaviest artillery and mortar fire until the shattered survivors, convinced at last of the hopelessness of their efforts, turned back in retreat. The respite would be brief. Punctual to the minute, for most of their attack were launched at regular intervals, the next assault would come in, the Russian infantry marching over, across and through the ranks of their dead comrades; victims of earlier and futile attempts to crush the Jaeger.

Tank assaults were as unsophisticated. Masses of vehicles driving in columns or in solid blocks, unheeding of how many of their number burned or swung hopelessly out of control. 'The Ivan tank crews did not seem to notice our tank-busting teams which ran alongside them and blew them up with satchel charges or hollow-charge grenades. It was clear that to them the need to reach the objective was more important than how many of them were lost. Casualties were less important. Some of the tank regiments would get through; that was what was important.'

When 2nd Para and the other Divisions and Corps fighting around Radomysl had at last closed the line they went over to counter-attacks intended to drive the Red units back across the Dniester. At that moment of victory a new crisis developed. Soviet troops had begun to break through at Kremechug, some 186 miles (300 kilometres) distant, and in order to seal off the gaps which their thrusts had made, 2nd Para was airlifted on 15 December, and taken to the Kirovgrad area. Almost as soon as the units landed they were rushed into the line. Supported by 11th Panzer Division and 286th SP Brigade the Jaeger carried out their first attack in this new area. This was at Klinzy, some five miles (eight kilometres) to the south-west of Kirovgrad. The SP Brigade support for this operation was exclusively with 7th Para Regiment and for the attack the Brigade committed 18 SP guns and 9 SP howitzers. The attack would go in on a 7-kilometre front

Left: A company headquarters on the Volkov front: neighbouring commanders confer. Officers too carved sticks to ease the boredom of life in the swampy wastes. (Brian L. Davis)

through the valley of the Kamenka with the intention of reaching the southern edge of Novgorodka. Nos. 1 and 3 Batteries supported 1st Battalion of the 7th Regiment and the 2nd Battery the 2nd battalion. The SP reserve group was positioned between both battalions so as to bring forward extra support wherever and whenever needed.

The impetus of the assault halted the attacking Soviet units and knocked out a number of their tanks and anti-tanks guns. Bad weather and the onset of night prevented the Jaeger from reaching the given objective. Most of 17 December was taken up with the Jaeger regrouping and preparing to renew the advance, but the SP Brigade was active and destroyed another six enemy tanks as well as other targets. The combined attack went in again at first light on the 18th. The immediate objectives were two hills and the first of these, Point 170.3, was taken at the charge. The few daylight hours were coming to an end when the assault went in to take Point 163.7, and darkness fell before the objective could be taken. On the 19th, it fell. During the attacks that day 7th Para Regiment reached but could not take the western edge of Novgorodka, and as the SP guns had to be taken out of the line for servicing, the assault was halted until the 21st. The named objectives for that day were the town and the hills behind it and with the exception of the northern suburbs and one hill, all the targets were taken. The Soviets, frustrated in their own attacks, were determined to halt any farther German advance on that sector and brought forward massive reinforcements. Against that concentration of power the advance by 2nd Para slowed. The fighting during those dark December days was bitter – often man to man – and on this sector, too, the Paras saw with horror the wastefulness of the Red Army's attacks. Wasteful or not, those attacks achieved their objective. The 2nd Para's attacks were finally halted and on 23 December the Division was forced on to the defensive.

Stavka was not content just to halt the German drive, and issued orders that Novgorodka was to be retaken without delay. In the days before and after Christmas the Red Army flung wave after wave of tanks against the thin defensive line. Depite the persistence of the Soviet armoured assaults and against the fury of every type of attack that the Red Army could mount, as the old year died, the Jaeger and SP line was still holding firm. The year 1943, had been an eventful one for the 2nd Para Division.

The year 1943 had been for Germany a succession of disasters. It had begun with the loss of Sixth Army at Stalingrad and that had been followed in May by the defeat of the Axis forces in Africa. In July a campaign to crush the giant salient around Kursk and to win back the initiative on the Eastern Front had had to be abruptly called off when the Western Allies invaded Sicily.

The success of that seaborne and airborne assault produced a ferment in Italy so strong as to overthrow

Right: Preparing for the assault on the central sector of the Eastern Front, 27 April 1943, in the Zhitomir area. (Brian L. Davis)

Left: In bright, but bitterly cold weather, Fallschirmjaeger bring forward supplies of ammunition, ducking below the sky-line. (Brian L. Davis)

Mussolini who had been in power for more than twenty years. In September the British and American Armies invaded the mainland of Italy and the Government of Marshal Badoglio, which had succeeded that of the fallen Duce, promptly surrendered. With the armed forces of her principal ally no longer sharing the burden of the war, Germany was forced, from her own resources and dependent upon the help of the armies of a few European nations, to garrison occupied Europe as well as to fight in Russia, in Yugoslavia and in Italy. Partisan activity had become more widespread, tying down more military units and it was to be expected that the Western Allies would soon invade north-west Europe.

So, at a time when manpower resources were running low, as a consequence of four years of bloodshed, the Reich's armed forces were now called upon to carry out even more tasks if the war were to be prosecuted successfully. There followed a comb-out of non-combatant units which produced some men, other men whose duties had become redundant were redesignated as infantry, and women were encouraged to volunteer for work as signallers and clerical duties so as to release yet more men for the front line.

At this time, in November 1943, the decision was taken to create an Airborne Army. The Luftwaffe High Command accepted that the greatest number of men who would serve in it would never be carried by air to battle, to jump or be landed by glider on enemy territory, Indeed, it was doubtful whether it would be possible to give them a complete and thorough Jaeger training in ground warfare. Accepting these limitations, the High Command hoped that the expansion would bring semi-trained recruits who, grouped round a core of experienced veterans, would absorb the combat skills, experience and spirit of those 'originals'.

The Fallschirmjaeger had gained a reputation for fighting ability, for *élan* in attack, staunchness in defence, of comradely self-sacrifice and unit loyalty to a degree found in only the finest of élite troops. The Luftwaffe High Command hoped that the new volunteers for the Para Army would absorb these ideals and traditions to maintain the awesome reputation which the first Jaeger had won. From 1940 to 1943 it had been possible to employ them only in Company, battalion and, occasionally regimental strength, but they had fought against overwhelming odds and had triumphed.

The Allies were fully aware of the potency of the Jaeger in small groups. How much more impressed and fearful would they be, argued Luftwaffe High Command, if they knew that the German Airborne forces had expanded from just a few Divisions to a complete Army. The psychological effect of the expansion would have an enormous effect upon Allied military planning.

The Luftwaffe High Command order was issued. A Fallschirm Army was to be created. It was one of the very few positive actions to come out of a year of disaster.

1944

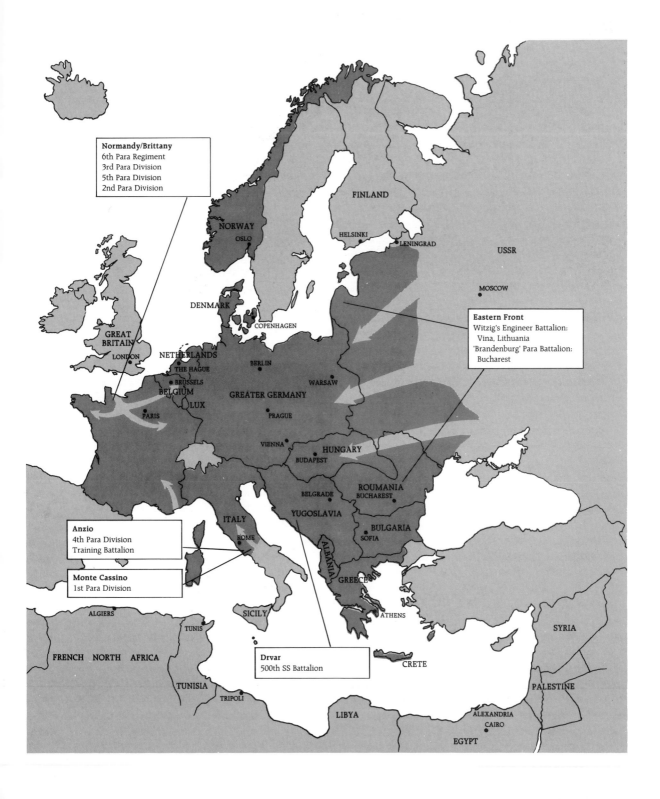

Normandy/Brittany
6th Para Regiment
3rd Para Division
5th Para Division
2nd Para Division

Eastern Front
Witzig's Engineer Battalion:
Vina, Lithuania
'Brandenburg' Para Battalion:
Bucharest

Anzio
4th Para Division
Training Battalion

Monte Cassino
1st Para Division

Drvar
500th SS Battalion

ICELAND

NORWAY
OSLO

FINLAND
HELSINKI
LENINGRAD

USSR
MOSCOW

DENMARK
COPENHAGEN

GREAT
BRITAIN
LONDON

NETHERLANDS
THE HAGUE
BRUSSELS
BELGIUM
LUX
PARIS

BERLIN
WARSAW
GREATER GERMANY
PRAGUE
VIENNA
HUNGARY
BUDAPEST

ITALY
ROME

BELGRADE
YUGOSLAVIA

ROUMANIA
BUCHAREST

BULGARIA
SOFIA

ALBANIA
GREECE
ATHENS

ALGIERS
TUNIS

SICILY

CRETE

SYRIA

FRENCH NORTH AFRICA

TUNISIA
TRIPOLI

LIBYA

ALEXANDRIA
CAIRO

PALESTINE

EGYPT

13. 'Not every bullet finds its mark'
THE EASTERN FRONT, JANUARY-JULY 1944

In the first days of January 1944, the Red Army resumed operations against the 2nd Para Division and the 286th SP Brigade. The Fallschirmjaeger were forced to depend upon the Army's SP Brigades because OKL had made no provision for Para units to be equipped with heavy weapons. It was not until the creation of 11th and 12th Para SP Brigades that the Jaeger had support groups under their own control. Stavka did not conceal its offensive intentions. It made a deliberate show of the forces which it would deploy in an effort to intimidate the German units upon whom the full fury of the assaults would fall. The SP guns were moved to those points at which the Red Army would make its maximum effort. This would be at Plavny, along the widely over-extended front held by 2nd Para Regiment and 1st Battalion of 5th Regiment on both sides of the highway to Kirovgrad. To support 2nd Battalion of 5th Regiment SP Brigade moved five guns and two howitzers into that sector and three guns and one howitzer into that held by 2nd Regiment.

At 07.00 hours on 5 January, the Russian offensive began with strong tank and infantry masses striking against the 5th Regiment's battalion. The first wave of 25 T34s that rolled forward was a bait to test the strength of the German opposition. The entire Red Tank regiment was destroyed within half an hour, but two SP guns were hit and knocked out. That first attack was soon succeeded by a second and then by others. By the end of the day the batteries supporting 2nd Battalion had destroyed no fewer than 36 Russian armoured fighting vehicles. On the sector held by 2nd Battalion of 2nd Para Regiment the fighting was as bitter and as costly to the Russians, but slowly the weight of their attacks forced back the Paras and broke their line at certain points. The SPs went forward to help the Jaeger close the gaps. The fighting was intense and, particularly in the area held by 2nd Battalion of 5th Regiment, at times hand-to-hand. Russian tanks broke out of a wadi to the east of Plavny and drove southwards to where the TAC HQ of the SP Brigade and the 2nd Para Regiment were located. The last remaining vehicles of the SP Brigade were ordered forward into the attack and

crushed the Red assault before it could destroy the Headquarters. Captain Bausch of the 2nd Battery of the 286th SP Brigade destroyed two T34s in that operation and a troop of SPs, hurriedly recalled from the battle in the north of the sector, drove forward and knocked out another four enemy vehicles. The Para HQ then moved, covered by the guns of one part of the SP group while others drove out to hunt for more Russian armour.

As the Russian attack rolled on it flooded past the isolated detachments of 2nd Regiment and these then stood 'like green rocks in a flood of Red Army khaki'. The 2nd Battalion of 5th Regiment, which held the ground to the north of the highway, was submerged in the Russian torrent and lost contact with regimental headquarters. Its Nos. 5 and 7 Companies were almost completely destroyed. Three SPs which had been hunting Soviet tanks were ordered forward and smashed through the Russians to reach the survivors of 2nd Battalion. The Paras boarded the vehicles and a fighting retreat was successfully accomplished.

Late in the afternoon reports came in that Russian armoured forces had cut the Novgorodka-Kirovgrad highway near Ruptschina. At 22.30 hours the SP Brigade was ordered to remove that obstruction. Three SP guns and one howitzer were put into the assault with the Paras mounted in the vehicles. It was a bright moonlight night, but the SP group got to within 220 yards (200 metres) of a Red tank detachment before the alarm was raised. The T34s were being refuelled and replenished with ammunition. Under the shells of the SP guns eight of the tanks and all the trucks were destroyed. The successes gained by the SP Brigade during that one day of battle included sixty T34s, six anti-tank guns and four mortars.

Soviet pressure during 6 and 7 January, forced the Paras to pull back out of Novgorodka and despite the most strenuous efforts of the Red Army to reach Kirovgrad the Jaeger line held. On 10 January, thirty men, the survivors of 2nd Battalion of 5th Regiment, finally reached the Division's lines having been cut off for days. So great had been that battalion's losses that it was no longer an

operational unit. It was, therefore, withdrawn from the line and sent home to Germany where if formed the cadre around which 16th Regiment was to be formed.

Total exhaustion on both sides reduced the scale of the fighting for Novgorodka and as a result of the lull the SP Brigade was taken away from 2nd Para and moved to a more active sector of the front. The battle line was held until the next Soviet offensive which opened at the beginning of March. Stavka intention was to strike southwards from Kiev and to roll up the flank of Army Group South. The 2nd Para, in positions at Svenigorodka, held off the Soviet thrusts until a massed armoured assault thrust past Division's flank forcing a withdrawal. By the end of March the Division had pulled back behind the River Bug and had taken up defensive positions near Ananyev, but within days these too had had to be given up. On 10 May, the numerically weak regiments of the Division, which had been out of the line for a short spell, were rushed back to strike at a Russian bridgehead in the bend of the River Dniester at Butor. This was to be the last action of 2nd Para Division on the Eastern Front. It returned to Germany at the end of May, but its period of rest and recuperation was to be a brief one. On 6 June

1944, the Allies invaded Normandy. The Second Front had begun and within a week of that landing the 2nd Para Division was under orders to move to this new theatre of operations.

Major Witzig, whom we first met in Belgium at the outset of the campaign in France and Flanders in 1940, and subsequently in Tunisia in 1942–43, led a Para Engineer detachment in one of the most dramatic battles of the Eastern Front during the summer of 1944. I am undebted for the details of this single-day action to a former soldier, Hans Christian Grasser, not himself a Fallschirmjaeger, who was serving in Army Group North at the time of the Para engagement. He wrote to me saying that the story of a single battalion of Fallschirmjaeger holding off a complete Red Army tank Division had swept through the Army Group.

'During the summer of 1944, there had been a shocking defeat for the German Army on the Eastern Front. Army Group Centre had been destroyed in Belorussia in June,

Right: Lithuania, July 1944. The two sole survivors of one of the companies of the SS Para Battalion at Kaven, near Memel. (M. Klein)

Left: Between pauses in the fighting in the southern sector of the line, a veteran of the capture of Crete looks bored as he waits in his slit trench for a new Russian attack. (Brian L. Davis)

Left: Para Engineers in Lithuania during 1944. They are carrying Teller mines and entrenching tools with which to plant them. The strain of the fighting can be seen in their faces. (Brian L. Davis)

and towards the end of July Russian spearheads were approaching the Baltic Sea. Among the units which were hastily gathered together and put into battle to halt them was the 1st Battalion of 21st Para Engineer Regiment, commanded by Major Witzig.

It was on 25 July that his battalion took up positions on the road from Dunaburg to Kovno, immediately south of the village of Dziewaltowe, with No. 1 Company north of the road and No. 2 Company to its south. Responsibility for defence of the road lay within the area of No. 1 Company. The under strength No. 4 Company was attached to No. 2 Company. No. 3 Company was not serving with the battalion. To support the Para Battalion there should have been SPs and anti-tank guns, but for some unexplained reason although these were in position they took little part in the battle and had soon been sent to other sectors.

The ground on which the battle was fought was open. To the north of the road lay the little hamlet of Dziewaltowe from which a track ran south-westwards to join the road. About a kilometre to the west of the village was a small birch wood and behind that again a very large forest which overlapped the battalion area on both flanks. The road from Dunaburg entered a deep cutting in which No. 1 Company had its HQ and this cutting extended back as far as the track leading north-east to Dziewaltowe. To the south of the road, in No. 2 Company's positions, there was a low hill. The Company's outpost line ran along its forward slope and overlooked another low hill which was held by the Red Army. Behind No. 2 Company's hill there was a track, an extension of the cutting, running south-westwards.

The battalion was poorly off for weapons. There had been neither the time nor the mines to lay out a minefield.

A few Panzerfaust rocket-launchers, and one Panzerschreck per group of four men, formed the principal weapons of defence.

The noise of tanks moving forward was heard all through the night of 25/26 July, and Russian infantry patrols were also active attacking the Para outposts. At first light the Red Army tanks could be seen extending across a broad front so that they formed a wall of steel about a kilometre from the battalion's front line. Immediately behind them the artillery was ranked, clearly visible in the morning air, with field guns and the Katyusha rocket-launchers massed almost wheel to wheel. The silence which had endured since sun-up was broken within an hour by the opening of the Soviet barrage. This lasted for more than an hour. The bombardment lessened in intensity and through the smoke and dust of the explosions the tanks could be seen rolling forward, each with Red Army infantry clinging to the outside of the vehicles or with other infantry groups trotting alongside them.

The Jaeger held their fire until the first line of enemy tanks was only 20 metres distant. Then small groups of them raced among the steel giants fixing high-explosive charges on the outside plates or attacking them with Panzerfausts. As the Russian infantry sprang to the ground they were shot at close range by fast-firing MG 42s. Within minutes the men of No. 1 Company had wiped out fifteen T34s, most of which stood on the open fields burning in the bright morning air. Then it was the turn of the Red Army infantry. They charged forward shouting their battle-cry but in the face of massed machine-gun fire their attack crumpled and died. The first Soviet attack had been halted, but at what a cost. Of No. 1 Company there were just over 30 men left to hold the line.

To the south of the road there had also been heavy fighting but on that sector the Russians had had a success. A group of tanks had managed to fight its way through the Para positions, cross the small track running through the cutting and cut the Dunaburg–Kovno road. The SP guns which might have defeated the T34s had already left the battlefield together with the anti-tank guns and without that support the Para position was now indefensible. There were Russians to the front, on the right flank and behind the battalion's positions. Now it was a matter of withdrawing the forward Platoons and bringing them back to a regroup line set up in the woods to the west of the village.

By this time the Russians who had broken through had been reinforced with infantry who fired at any movement. The small groups of Jaeger making their way from No. 2 Company positions had more than two kilometers of open ground to cover before they reached the safety of the thick woods. Few made it. At the regroup line the survivors of No. 1 Company, twelve unwounded men in all, came in. From No. 2 Company only ten men reached the line. Major Witzig led the shattered remnants of his battalion through the forest, along little tracks, bypassing Red Army positions and avoiding confrontation at every step until the German line was reached. Over the course of the following days other Jaeger came in, men determined not to be taken prisoner. Soon the Para Engineer Battalion numbered 65 men and they were soon put back into action again and served until October when the unit was taken out of action and broken up. Major Witzig and some of the battalion officers went off to the the Western Front; the rank and file were dispersed among other Para battalions. Witzig's Para Engineer Battalion had fought its last fight.'

Right: Fallschirmjaeger prepare to interrogate a Russian prisoner taken in the fighting around Zhitomir. (Brian L. Davis)

14. 'We are the Green Devils'
MONTE CASSINO, JANUARY-MAY 1944

Although the first battle to capture the town of Cassino and the adjacent Liri valley opened on 17 January 1944, it was not until a month later that Fallschirmjaeger were involved in the fighting in that sector; fighting which was hard, bloody and remin-iscent of the trench warfare of the First World War. Like the offensives of that great conflict the several battles for Cassino featured heavy artillery barrages, long approach marches on foot and by night, and repeated attacks with fearful loss for very small gains.

To set the picture it must be understood that despite Montgomery's assertion that, 'The basic problem was we [the Allies] had become involved in a major campaign lacking a predetermined master plan,' the capture of Rome was seen by the West as one of the prime objectives of the war in Italy. Certainly the capture of an enemy capital city would be a prestigious prize to the Allies. The shortest distance to that objective was up the western side of the Italian peninsula, using Route 6, the Via Casilini, the main road from the south. That ran across the fast flowing River Rapido, through the town of Cassino and passed through the narrow valley of the River Liri. No advance upon Rome could begin until those three obstacles had been overcome, but once through the final one, the Liri valley, the Allied tank forces would be in the good 'going' which leads to Rome. The task of Fifth Army was to open an offensive, overcome the three obstacles and then go on to capture the Eternal City.

To draw the attention of the German defenders away from the defence of the Rapido and Cassino town British X Corps, forming part of Fifth Army and serving on that Army's extreme left flank, opened the offensive on 17 January. The second blow was made deep inland, among the Appenines, where French forces, on Fifth Army's right flank, began their assault. Finally, American Army units opened the attack upon the centre of the German line, aiming to seize Cassino town and the adjacent mountain on which stood the Benedictine monastery. The two flank attacks achieved limited gains, but the central thrust by the US troops was a total disaster.

That initial assault was bloodily repulsed and the Allied commanders carried out sea-borne assaults at Anzio, hoping to compel the German commanders to withdraw troops from the Cassino sector to meet the Anzio landings. These had not fulfilled the hopes which had been set upon them. The Allied troops failed to move inland from the beaches and the German commanders, exploiting that hesitation, moved down all available units to seal off the penetrations. Among the groups which Kesselring sent racing down to Anzio, and certainly the first to reach the Allied landing areas, was Battle Group Gericke, comprising a battalion each from the 11th and 12th Para Regiments. Major Gericke's battle group reached the combat area and went immediately into the attack. The *élan* with which it fought brought it swiftly to those positions from which a German coastal defence battalion had been driven when the Allied landings came in. Other German units which came speeding down from Rome included the Para Corps Assault Gun Battalion. By the afternoon of 22 January a ring of German troops had been set up around the beachhead areas, a ring which though flimsy held firm against the breakout attempts by US VI Corps (British 1st and US 3rd Divisions). In the last week of January Gericke's battle group, which for administrative purposes had been incorporated into the 3rd Panzer Grenadier Division, received reinforcements. The first unit to arrive was the Para Corps Training Battalion which was quickly followed by the Corps Machine-gun Battalion, the Engineer Battalion of 4th Para Division together with the 1st and 3rd Battalions of 12th Regiment. As a result of these additions to its strength Gericke's battle group became strong enough to fight independently of 3rd Panzer Grenadier Division.

The 11th and 12th Regiments, named above, were part of 4th Para Division. This was a new formation whose raising had been delayed by administrative difficulties. But it was essential that the Allied invasion forces be confronted by German units at full strength and com-pletely equipped. Splinter groups and *ad hoc* detachments were now insufficient to master a situation which grew

Above: Cassino. A Fallschirmjaeger NCO keeps a
sharp lookout in the ruins.
(Brian L. Davis)

Right: In the wreckage of
Cassino, a Fallschirmjaeger
team fires a short-barrelled para
version of the 81mm mortar.
(Brian L. Davis)

Left: A para NCO giving instructions to a mortar group in the ruins of Cassino. (M. Klein)

Right: At Monte Cassino, the Fallschirmjaeger made use of flamethrowers in the close-quarters fighting among the ruins; this photograph of a Para Engineer Unit is from a pre-war training exercise. (Brian L. Davis)

more complex with every day. It was this need for full-strength, properly administered formations which speeded up the raising of the new Division. That task was completed during February 1944; the 4th became operational and was taken on the strength of I Para Corps. At about the same time, 1st Para Division, which was fighting against the British Eighth Army, was ordered to switch from the Adriatic side of Italy to the Tyrrhennian where it would face Fifth Army.

The first units of 1st Para Division to arrive in the Cassino sector were Nos. 1 and 3 Battalions of 1st Regiment, together with No. 3 Battalion of 3rd Regiment. The Para Corps Machine-gun Battalion was pulled out of the Anzio beachhead and posted to the Cassino area. Those four battalions were grouped temporarily under the commander of 1st Para Regiment, Colonel Schulz, and placed on the left wing of the German forces defending the Cassino sector. The task of Battle Group Schulz was to halt attempts to outflank the German line which the Allies might make through the Appenine mountains. On 7 February the battle group took over the stretch of ground from the Benedictine monastery on the summit of Monte Cassino to Point 593, known otherwise as Monte Calvario. Because of its dominating position, Calvario was one of the most important of the heights surrounding Cassino town.

Michael Klein, a former Jaeger in Battle Group Schulz, remembered his unit's arrival in Cassino. 'The town was being shelled when we marched into it and we climbed to our positions passing through a hail of shells. The Amis – I know now that it was the 34th Division which opposed us – were making the most determined efforts to force a way

through and for a short period part of the 3rd Battalion of US 135th Regiment actually captured Monte Calvario. My unit of 3rd Regiment, was portering for a Company which had been ordered to recapture the hill. We were resting in a gully on the western side of Calvario when an NCO ordered us to join an assault platoon. We rushed the first enemy positions, killed or captured the disorganized Ami group and carried on uphill. The Americans had had little time to consolidate their hold on the crest and we swept them off it. We immediately prepared for defence against their counter-attacks and when these came in drove them back. Their attacks were bravely made but unco-ordinated. The worst feature of those days was not the frequency or severity of the infantry assaults but the constant artillery fire. The rain of shells falling on our positions seemed to last all day, to which were later added the aerial bombing raids. These created a lot of noise and dust but caused few casualties. The worst memory – the most nerve-tearing thing – was the unending noise of explosions. That really wore down our nerves.'

From 11 to 18 February, the battle reached a crescendo as 36th (Texas) Division carried out massive frontal assaults to capture the town and Monte Calvario. While these frontal attacks were going in, 34th US Division struck out through the mountains to take Monastery Hill from the north. In appalling weather the infantry regiments moved off, but snowstorms blinded the US artillery observers and the guns could give no real support to the attack.

The Jaeger of 3rd Regiment crouched, frozen, in their sangars on the hill and watched the thin lines of 142nd Regiment climb up the mountain slopes. Then the Para

machine-guns and mortars opened up a fast, destructive fire. The 142nd Regiment was destroyed on the frozen hillsides of Monte Calvario. Roll calls when the scattered US units reassembled in those positions from which they had advanced so confidently, showed that in most cases the strength of battalions had shrunk to less than one hundred men. The veteran US II Corps, shattered by its terrible experiences at the hands of the Fallschirmjaeger, had to be withdrawn from the Line. The first battle of Cassino had ended and the Paras who had defended the area not only increased their already high reputation as warriors, but had had bestowed upon them by their US opponents the nickname 'green devils'.

Allied historians describe the continuation of the battle by the New Zealand Corps as the second battle of Cassino. To the Germans this assault, which followed almost immediately and which was fought by three Divisions: 4th Indian, 2nd New Zealand and 78th British, formed part of the first battle. The British formations had been brought across from Eighth Army and grouped into Freyberg's, New Zealand Corps.

The most important aspect of the second battle of Cassino was the bombing of the Abbey, ordered because it was believed that German troops were using the building as an artillery observation post. At 09.45 hours on Tuesday, 15 February the first group of the 142 Flying Fortresses which were employed, dropped their bombs and were then followed by 87 other aircraft. When the bombers flew away the German point of view was that the Allied bombing had violated the sanctity of the abbey and their troops could now use it. The Paras found inside the damaged building shell-proof subterranean passages and shattered walls which they quickly converted to little fortresses.

The Jaeger of Battle Group Schulz, who had endured the fury of artillery fire and a succession of infantry attacks, had now had added to their battle experiences that of being bombed from the air on a massive scale. They were aware that so great an effort on the part of the Allies could only mean that new infantry attacks were imminent. Throughout the whole of 15 February, from the monastery to the summit of 593, the Jaeger waited for these to begin. None came. There had been a communications failure in New Zealand Corps. Freyberg, who had intended to open the offensive on the 16th, had brought it forward by one day. He had, however, forgotten to advise the 4th Indian Division which was under orders to attack immediately behind the aerial bombing. Because of this administrative blunder the 4th Indian was still preparing for an attack on the 16th, when the abbey was bombed on the 15th. The advantage of a quick follow-up was lost.

Not until the evening of 16 February did 4th Division move and then it was a single battalion which struck up the slopes of Monte Cassino. It was cut to pieces by the Para Machine-gun Battalion. On the following day six battalions of the Division attacked all along the line held by Battle Group Schulz. That assault, too, was flung back in confusion as machine-gun fire, mortar fire and the terrifying Nebelwerfer shells raked the leading Companies. Bowed but unbroken by the Para fire, the battalions reformed and moved forward in a fresh advance. By a tragic error shells from the New Zealand Corps barrage crashed down upon them and the cohesion of the advance was lost in the confusion of that bombardment. The Jaeger exploited the situation and opened up at close quarters with machine-guns and mortars which smashed the attack. But on one side of Calvario a single battalion had gained a slight foothold.

Determined to capitalize upon success, however minor, Freyberg, decided to switch the main effort of his attack from Monastery Hill and to seize 593. This was more difficult than the Corps Commander had thought it would be. It is no easy task to halt a battle while it is in progress and some units which did not receive Freyberg's order continued to fight for Monastery Hill. One such unit was a battalion of Gurkhas which was trapped in a minefield and lost 243 men in a couple of hours to Para machine-gunners who traversed their weapons backwards and forwards across the files of men. Despite these terrible losses the Gurkhas fought to press their attack home, but when daylight came the Companies were seen to be isolated and they were pulled back. The attack on 593 which Freyberg had ordered had also been disastrous. On the 19th, the offensive was called off.

Bitter weather and the exhaustion of the Allied infantry brought a pause in military operations. German Tenth Army regrouped and its commander placed the whole of the Cassino sector, a stretch of some eight miles (thirteen kilometres), under the command of 1st Para Division. Starting on 20 February, Jaeger units began to replace those of 90th Panzer Grenadier and 44th Hoch and Deutschmeister Divisions. The 3rd Regiment was given responsibility for Cassino town. The 1st Battalion took over Monastery Hill. The 4th Regiment held Monte Calvario and the 1st Regiment held the ground on Division's left flank as far as Monte Cairo where 5th Mountain Division was positioned. The burden which 1st Para now had to bear was a heavy one to place upon a formation, some of whose units had been continuously in action since the first landings in Italy during September.

Now holding the most vital stretch of front in Italy, the Division underwent some bitter experiences, of which the first was the Allies' attempt, on 15 March, to obliterate Cassino town by 'carpet bombing'. The Allied commanders were determined to destroy the German garrison and it has been calculated that in their determination they dropped a weight of bombs equivalent to five tons of explosive for each German soldier in the Cassino sector. The Allied commanders were convinced that any troops who survived that terror would have been driven mad by the experience. The 775 bombers came and

for four hours the aerial attack continued upon the 350 Paras and Engineers in the town.

As soon as the first aircraft appeared Captain Foltin, commanding 2nd Battalion of 3rd Regiment, ordered his No. 6 Company to change position. The men left the cellars of the Hotel Excelsior and took shelter in a cave at the foot of Monastery Hill. They were among the few complete units to survive the bombing. When the aircraft departed the greatest part of Colonel Heilmann's 3rd Regiment together with all its equipment had been smashed and buried metres deep in rubble. Four of the SP Battalion's five guns had been destroyed together with all the light arms, rifles, machine-guns and mortars.

The bombers flew off, the Allied artillery opened up and in a barrage which lasted from 12.30 to 20.00 hours, the guns fired 196,000 shells into 1st Para Division's positions. Behind the barrage Freyberg's infantry marched forward with orders to take a tactically important feature leading up to the Abbey, the Rocca Janula (Point 193). This was a sector that had been defended by No. 2 Company of 3rd Regiment. When the assault battalion of the Indian Division, the Rajputana Rifles, overran the German positions, only one man, a corporal, was found alive, but at Point 236, a determined group of survivors from No. 3 Company, halted the advance. Then another Allied artillery barrage fell short crashing down around the unfortunate troops. Through the Rajput dead and

Left: In the darkened devastation of Cassino, the 'Green Devils' make ready to repulse yet another Allied assault. (Brian L. Davis)

Right: The sky warriors went underground at Cassino, hiding in the ruins of the monastery and emerging from cellars and tunnels to beat off successive attacks in fierce hand-to-hand fighting. (Brian L. Davis)

wounded, a second Indian battalion, 1/9th Gurkha Rifles, carried the advance and moved towards Hangman's Hill, less than 600 yards (500 metres) from their objective – the Abbey.

At dawn the Gurkhas were seen on the bare rock of Hangman's Hill and in that position they were pinned down by the machine-guns and mortars of No. 3 Company. The battalion held out on the open slope for nearly eight days and was all but destroyed.

On the New Zealand sector inside the town, the silence after the great barrage was broken by the sound of tank engines. A mass of armoured fighting vehicles had been committed to the attack, but their employment in the shattered ruins of Cassino town was a tactical mistake. The Jaeger who had survived the bombing and the bombardment opened fire on the 26th New Zealand Infantry Battalion which was attacking the Hotel Continental. A troop of tanks rolled forward to support the 26th Battalion. Out of the ruins of the hotel entrance rolled the only Para SP gun to have survived and in a furious burst of fire it knocked out the Allied machines.

One SP gun and less than a hundred Jaeger, sixty of them from Foltin's No. 6 Company, held the New Zealand Corps' attack. The Para line was holding but only just, and during the night of 16 March, the last reserves of 1st Division were put in to defend the town; 2nd Battalion of 1st Regiment, parts of the Para Corps Engineer Battalion

and the divisional motor-cycle Company. By concentrating the fire of all the artillery and Nebelwerfer rocket batteries under his command, General Heidrich was able to support his own units and to dominate those of the Allies.

He did more than that. Even the best soldiers lose heart if they are always on the defensive. They need to attack and to know that they are superior to their opponents. Heidrich decided to let his men counter-attack. The first of these went in at dawn on 17 March. An assault group drawn from No. 1 Battalion of 3rd Regiment struck at the Gurkhas holding out on Hangman's Hill, but was flung back. Then the motor-cycle Company, which had entered the town only the previous night, waded through the icy, fast-flowing waters of the River Rapido to recapture the railway station. The battle inside Cassino was being measured in gains or losses of just metres.

The motor-cycle Company struck heavy New Zealand infantry opposition backed by tanks, and the Para assaults although made with great *élan*, could not gain the objective. A day later, with the unit strength now reduced to just nineteen unwounded men, the survivors were pulled back across the river.

Once again a composite account must describe the highlights of the second battle. 'It was a time whose events were so overwhelming that it is difficult to describe them in words. It was something which had to be experienced. The principal impression was of unending noise. The Allied artillery did not stop for any length of time and that whole fury of Allied fire-power was concentrated upon our divisional sector, an area just over 1,500 yards (1,400 metres) long by 450 yards (400 metres) wide. On to that small strip of ground bombs and shells fell in an unending rain. The barrages were worse than anything we had experienced on the Russian front.

On 15th March, waves of aircraft, holding rigid formation flew over us but we did not believe that we could be the target. We knew that the Tommies' front line was less than a hundred metres from us. What we did not know was that they had pulled back during the night from those positions. That first cluster of bombs was, therefore, a total surprise and many of our casualties were suffered because our men were caught in the open.

The noise was deafening, the explosions rocked us from side to side. I know that I did not expect to live through that inferno and prayed that when death came it would be instant and total. To be badly wounded would be to die slowly, for the stretcher-bearers could not be expected to leave their cellars in such conditions.

When the bombing ended there was a short period of total silence. Then the barrage fell. Again the ground shook and shuddered. Some of us linked arms, others crouched in a circle their arms around each other's

shoulders to steady themselves and also to gain comfort from physical contact. The barrage seemed to last an eternity and when it stopped there was again that frightening silence. We had lived through it. But who else had? Then from our left came the sound of a short burst of fire from a German machine-gun. We were not alone. Then other groups fired. We of 1st Division were still there holding Cassino. The Allies had done their worst but we had survived.

The attacks by Indian troops were alarming. We had been told about them and knew that they were all mountaineers from the Himalayas. They were quite small but very agile, used ground well and persisted in their attack in the face of frontal and enfilade machine-gun fire.

Shortly before the Allies halted their assault [18 March], they made major attacks along the whole of the Divisional front. These came in, on our sector, under cover of smoke. The infantry which attacked us that day were coloured New Zealanders [Maoris] who were good but we held them. For all their skill and determination they could not break into our positions.'

On 19 March, continuing Heidrich's series of counter-attacks, groups from 1st Battalion of 4th Para Regiment struck at Rocca Janula at first light. One of the principal objectives was to seize or neutralize a large stone sangar on the knoll, which had been enlarged by its Indian garrison to become a small fort. That stone position was also an advanced base and was therefore a danger. The stone sangar was only one of the objectives of the day's operations and fighting became confused because German and British operations were being carried out across the same sector. While the Jaeger were fighting to seize the Rocca Janula from the Indians, two British battalions from the Indian Division were above them on the higher slopes of Hangman's Hill going in to reinforce the Gurkhas. The confusion continued and each day saw attack and counter-attack succeed one another in a bewildering kaleidoscope. That first assault by 1st Para Battalion was repulsed. A second and then a third attack were launched; these in turn were driven off. Eventually, so many dead and wounded covered the ground that both sides agreed to a two-hour truce to recover them.

A tank attack unsupported by infantry went in. The New Zealand and Indian armoured regiments reached a point to the north of Cassino and then the lead vehicle was halted, having entered a minefield. The other vehicles of the column halted and were immediately attacked at close quarters by the Jaeger holding the area. Only eight of the sixteen Sherman and Stuarts which had begun the attack were able to reach the safety of their own line.

The second offensive of Cassino was broken off on 22 March. At its conclusion Field Marshal Alexander wrote a report to Churchill and in describing the bombing and barrage of 15 March, included the sentence, 'No other troops in the world but German paratroops could have stood up to such an ordeal and then gone on fighting with such ferocity.'

In the interim before the next offensive opened, 1st Para Division reorganized its units, moving 4th Regiment and the Machine-gun Battalion into the town and on to Monastery Hill. Para Regiment 3 formed the link with the Mountain troops on Monte Cairo. The 1st Regiment went into divisional reserve. The words of a divisional Order of the Day issued on 26 March, illustrate the pattern of the fighting. It described how the HQ of 2nd Battalion of 3rd Regiment was attacked and how hand-to-hand fighting took place before the enemy seeking to overrun the headquarters could be driven off. In the afternoon of the same day, 19 March, a second attack was beaten off. On the 20th a Jaeger tank destruction team tried unsuccessfully to knock out two enemy machines using Panzerfaust rocket-launchers. The missiles faild to explode and the enemy infantry now aware of the presence of the tank-busting team moved in to destroy it but was driven off with loss. Also on the 20th, an attack was carried out upon an enemy strong point in the town's fish market, the house being seized and blown up. A later Order of the Day mentioned specifically No. 1 Company of the Para Engineer Battalion and its young commander, Lieutenant Cords. The work of the battalion had not only included mine-laying, building defences and leading assaults with flame-throwers, but had also included the more unhappy aspects of warfare, burying the dead of both sides. At one point the only way of overcoming the smell of the corrupting corpses was to soak rags in eau-de-Cologne and to bind the cloths around the noses of the mules on which the dead were loaded. In such circumstances there could be no question of individual burials, and mass graves were dug and quickly filled with the fallen on both sides.

The offensive which opened the third battle for Cassino, on 11 May, bypassed the town by driving across the River Gari and thus into the Liri valley. French troops attacked from the south and Polish troops from the north. A Polish patrol seized the Abbey ruins, but the Jaeger had evacuated them leaving only their wounded behind in the care of a Medical Officer. Fighting continued on other parts of the Cassino sector and there, as in former battles, the Jaeger fought hard and well. Where an attack drove back the German defenders, counter-attack groups, drawn principally from the Pioneer Battalion, went in with flame-throwers and, often in hand-to-hand combat, flung back the attacks.

It was the threat of encirclement by an enemy now more than ten miles (16 kilometres) behind the defenders

of Cassino, which forced Kesselring to order 1st Para Division to evacuate the town on 18 May. The Jaeger began a fighting retreat northwards. Strong pressure by units of Fifth Army struck into a gap in the German line and only an immediate counter-attack by 12th Regiment, stopped the danger from developing into a crisis. The two divisions of I Para Corps pulled back through Rome. The last German unit to leave the city was 1st Battalion of 10th Regiment, which crossed the Tiber bridges only hours before the Allies arrived.

While 1st Para Division had been embattled in Cassino, on the Anzio sector the 4th Para Division, now fully raised and forming part of the newly created Fourteenth Army, had been in almost continual action. The two Divisions now formed part of I Para Corps although they were serving on different sectors of the Tyrrhennian Front. The fighting at Anzio had been in essence a struggle by the Allies to expand their beachhead and by Fourteenth Army to confine and destroy it. When, at last, Fifth Army broke through at Cassino, Tenth Army on that sector and Fourteenth Army at Anzio, were forced to withdraw northwards. The Allied armies pursuing Fourteenth Army more closely were halted by elements from 4th Para Division grouped along a line between Lanuvio and Campaleone. A surprise landing by British commandos at Practica di Mare overran 10th Para Regiment positions and only by hand-to-hand fighting was the mass of the regiment able to

break through and to escape northwards. A forced march which lasted all night brought the Jaeger out of Allied encirclement.

Rome had fallen, but the excitement of its capture was lost in the wider excitement of D-Day, the invasion of Normandy. Italy had suddenly become a side-show and the bravery of the defenders of Cassino was not fully acknowledged by the German public whose attention was now focused on France.

The withdrawal by I Para Corps contined and there were a number of major missions fought by 4th Division during their retreat. The Division was in action around Florence and then carried the major burden in the defence of the Futa Pass during the Gothic Line offensive of autumn 1944. The bitter fighting in front of, through and then behind the Futa Pass cost 4th Division more than 600 killed and missing and double that number in wounded. The 12th Regiment, which suffered more than 50 per cent losses, had to be withdrawn from the Line. Only a massive reinforcement of Luftwaffe volunteers brought the regiments up to something like combat strength.

The principal task of the 1st and 4th Para Divisions had been to delay the northward advance of the Allied Fifth and Eighth Armies. At the year's end both divisions were positioned below Bologna, holding the approaches to the Po plain and the foothills of the Alps in anticipation of the offensive which the Allies would certainly open once campaigning weather returned.

Right: Anzio: rations are brought forward by Fallschirmjaeger wearing US helmet nets. In the background is a Panther tank. (Brian L. Davis)

15. 'Though others may be unfaithful...'

THE DRVAR CAMPAIGN, MAY 1944

While, during the spring of 1944, in Italy 1st and 4th Para Divisions were striving to hold Cassino and Anzio and the 2nd Para Division was fighting in Russia, there was one airborne formation, not part of the Luftwaffe establishment, which was in action in Yugoslavia.

Even in an arm of service of such ability and renown as the German airborne, there were units which attracted special notice. With some we are already familiar, as for example, the Assault Battalion. Not so well known was an SS unit created around a cadre of military criminals. That unit was Para Rifle Battalion 500/600.

The background to the creation of the battalion is of interest. There was a great rivalry for power among the leaders of the Third Reich which manifested itself in the efforts each of those men made to control a private army. Reichsmarschall Hermann Goering was Commander-in-Chief of the Luftwaffe and, therefore, of the airborne forces which were on the Air Force establishment. His boast that 'everything that flies in Germany is under my control', was total and unchallenged until Reichsfuehrer Heinrich Himmler, Commander of the SS, which was another private army, decided, in the autumn of 1943, to challenge Goering's monopoly. From the earliest days of the Nazi Party the SS had sought to gain power within the Reich by infiltrating and controlling every aspect of German life. Himmler had successfully infiltrated political Germany, taken over the Reich Intelligence services, and raised an army of more than thirty Divisions which were outside the authority of the Regular Army, in the autumn of 1943. He was poised to penetrate the Luftwaffe. It was a favourable time for Himmler to undertake such an operation for Goering was out of favour. He had failed to fulfil his boasts to supply the troops at Stalingrad. As a consequence, in February 1943, Sixth Army, encircled, outnumbered and starving had been forced to surrender. With the Reichsmarschall in disgrace, Himmler's opportunity to infiltrate the Luftwaffe had come.

Who spoke to whom recommending an expansion of SS authority into the German Air Force cannot now be determined, but soon an official order came from Fuehrer HQ to SS Central Office that an SS battalion of paratroops was to be raised. This unit would be used for special operations. More than half the strength of the formation would be made up of volunteers. The remainder would be drawn from men who had served sentences in military penal establishments and who would be given the chance to redeem their lost military honour through service in the SS battalion. The 500th first went into action at the beginning of 1944. That initial mission was not a parachute drop, although all ranks had been trained or given refresher training at the Kralyevo Para School, but a ground operation against partisan forces in Yugoslavia, Greece and Albania. The baptism of fire as airborne troops was not long in coming. Within six months of No. 500 battalion undertaking military operations, it was selected for a very special mission. The battalion was to be airlanded by parachute and glider on to the hillside plateau at Drvar where Tito, the Yugoslav partisan leader, was known to have his Battle Headquarters. Paratroops would seize and hold the ground. That initial task accomplished, the gliderborne element would land, and capture the partisan commander. The battalion would then hold the area until relieved by a battle group from 373rd Division. That battle group was under orders to carry out the relief, without fail, during the first day of the operation.

Let us see, in more detail, what exactly what was involved. The SS Para battalion, numbering just over 600 men, was to be landed in the centre of an area held by at least 12,000 partisans. Because of a shortage of transport aircraft the paratroops could not be dropped in a single 'lift'. The initial one would be made at 07.00 hours and the second, a reinforcement wave, would come in at about midday. Nor were there sufficient DFS 230 gliders for more than one glider assault. The one positive factor was that the Luftwaffe ruled the skies over Yugoslavia and could, thus, bomb and strafe known or suspected partisan positions without fear of retaliation. To counterbalance that was the negative factor that German airborne troops went into battle with strictly limited amounts of ammunition and no heavy weapons. Thus, an airborne unit had to fight under the double inferiority of being outnumbered and by an enemy who was better and more lavishly armed. The surrounded paras could only receive supplies from an air drop and the aircraft which would bring those supplies would have to fly through a corridor of fire.

The reason why the operation known as Unternehmen Roesselsprung ('Knight's Move') needed to be mounted was that the Yugoslav partisan forces, the JANL, (Jugoslav National Army of Liberation), had so grown in strength and numbers since the German attack upon and occupation of Yugoslavia during 1941, that it had recaptured whole regions of the country from the Germans and was threatening the other, as yet still occupied areas. Conventional offensives by German ground troops had had little military success although they had caused the JANL much inconvenience. When the partisan forces were low in strength they had simply avoided direct confrontation and when faced with a superior enemy force had dispersed into the mountains. In the early months these tactics, which they had been forced to adopt, had worked well. Once the JANL set up a formal organization of Corps and Divisions and, once a national headquarters had been established, however, such evasion was no longer so easy.

The effort to disperse Main Headquarters and then to set it up again not only consumed time but also disrupted partisan operations. As a result of German offensive operations in 1942 and 1943, JANL Headquarters had several times to be moved.

This inconvenience was repeated when a fifth German offensive opened in the autumn of 1943, during which Tito had once again been forced to move his HQ from Jajce and into the small Bosnian town of Drvar. There, in a cave set in a narrow cleft in the hills which surround the town, the new HQ was set up. This choice of location was dictated by the fact that the Luftwaffe was very active and the Stukas came down with frightening fury upon any partisan target. Tito's cave was not only hidden in a narrow cleft and, therefore, an almost impossible target to detect and to hit, but also it had an exit through which the partisan leader could escape if German ground forces threatened to capture him. The words 'ground forces' in

Below: The company HQ of 500 SS Para Battalion during the fighting for Drvar in May 1944. (M. Klein)

this sentence qualified the operation. The partisans were prepared to meet an assault on the ground. They had not reckoned with one from the air.

Space does not permit me to describe the German operational plans or the whole course of the resulting battle. German XV Mountain Corps, was to encircle Drvar. Into the constricting ring 500 SS Para Battalion would be airlanded. The calibre of the troops which would form the circle was high and included the SS Mountain Division 'Prinz Eugen', many of whose men were natives of Bosnia. Also included in the order of battle for this offensive were detachments of a Brandenburg battalion who were specialists in Intelligence and Counter-Intelligence operations, together with Croatian units that were religious and political enemies of JANL which was dominated by Serbians and Communists.

D-Day for the operation was 25 May, a choice which may have been deliberate for that was also the date of Tito's birthday. Just after 07.00 hours on the morning of that day, 314 paratroops of Rybka's battalion had flung themselves from their transport machines, had landed and within minutes had captured the deserted town and the area around it. The young commander dropped with 'Red' Group, one of the three detachments into which the first wave was divided. With the landing area secured the gliders circling above the town swooped to land the assault detachments of 320 men. This was divided into six groups each of which had been given a special objective. Rybka and his group were to attach themselves to 'Panther', the largest glider group, of 110 men, whose task it was to attack the 'Citadel', Tito's cave headquarters.

Rybka and 'Red' Detachment marched from the town towards the area on the hillside where the six gliders of 'Panther' Group had come to a halt. The glider pilots had each landed within yards of the objective – the mouth of the cave. Seeing how close the machines had touched-down Rybka anticipated that he would be able to lead these men into the final assault that would capture the partisan commander. He found instead that the site was a slaughterhouse. So speedy had been the reaction of the men of Tito's escort battalion and of the other Yugoslav troops around the cave entrance that the flimsy wooden

machines had been riddled with fire even as they skidded along the rocky ground. Rybka fired a red flare which brought most of the SS troopers in the town rallying at the double. A concentrated effort was made to take the 'Citadel'. It was an unequal battle. The partisans, superior in number and possessing heavy weapons, had the advantage of holding ground that had been extensively prepared with field defences. The SS Paras had nothing but their training, their ethos as SS soldiers and their personal courage to pit against those terrible odds.

The first attack collapsed under the superior fire-power of the defenders. The SS group reformed and went in again, and then again and again, attacking throughout the morning. Some attacks gained ground; in others ground was lost. Never in the fury of that morning did the SS manage to enter Tito's cave and by midday it was clear that 'Roesselsprung' had no hope of gaining its objective. The partisan forces, now heavily reinforced, had begun to take the initiative and to counter-attack. The arrival of the second wave of Paras at midday brought little change in the situation. Obermeier's group, more than 220 strong,

dropped on to a landing zone swept by machine-gun and mortar fire and suffered heavy losses. The survivors linked up with the main body of the battalion and yet another assault was made. That, too, failed. On the Yugoslav side, fresh units were arriving and were put into the fight to relieve those who had borne the burden of the first German drive. There were no fresh troops or replacements arriving to relieve the SS paratroopers.

Late in the afternoon Rybka took the decision to withdraw from the cave area. It was not until long after dark that the remnants of the battalion were concentrated inside the walls of the town cemetery. They had had a long and exhausting day. The battle group from 373rd Division, which had been under orders to relieve them, had failed to do so. The SS battalion was surrounded by an enemy who was now supremely confident of being able to take on and destroy this German formation. The losses which had been suffered in killed and wounded had weakened the battalion, but its morale was still high.

Each partisan attack during that long, cold, dark night was fought off. Then with the dawn came a familiar,

Left: The second wave arrives, midday 25 May 1944. Companies which have been in action since early morning watch as their comrades in the follow-up wave drop from Ju 52s (M. Klein)

Right: During the afternoon, Stukas pounded Tito's headquarters after the failure of the attack on the ground. SS Paras observe the bombing from their hastily excavated positions. (M. Klein)

Right: Wounded were concentrated in the town cemetery, where the survivors of the SS Para Battalion held out all night. (M. Klein)

rattling sound, far away but drawing ever closer, the noise of MG42s in action. The roar of engines was heard near the cemetery. A group of *Schwimmwagen*, carrying a battle patrol from 13th Regiment of 'Prinz Eugen' Division had broken the partisan ring. The battle was over. It had been short but disastrous. The objective, to capture the partisan leader, had not been achieved, and at the battalion roll-call after the battle only 200 men answered their names. The rest were dead or wounded. It had been a costly experience.

Those who came forward to make good the losses were all volunteers. The battalion was fast losing its reputation as a penal unit. The flood of men fleshed out the Companies and in the autumn of 1944, the battalion went into battle in Lithuania striking into the flank of the Red armies which were thrusting for the Baltic. In November the battalion ceased to have military criminals posted to it and became instead an all-volunteer unit. In recognition of the new status the number 500 was dropped and a new number, 600, was given.

In common with most élite German units at that time of the war, Para Battalion 600 was used as a 'fire brigade', rushing from sector to sector, from front to front, wherever a disastrous breakthrough threatened, or else was used to form a special spearhead unit whenever an offensive was launched. In that role elements of 600 Battalion served in the Ardennes operation, forming part of Skorzeny's '150 Panzer Brigade', a commando unit

Above: The SS Para Engineers remain vigilant during a lull in the fighting for Tito's HQ at Drvar, May 1944. (M. Klein)

disguised in American Army uniforms. With the failure of that last German offensive in the west, most of the crack, major units, including 600, were sent east again to counter the Russian winter offensive on the Oder. The battalion was one of the groups defending the bridgehead at Schwedt on that river's eastern bank. Not until 1 April 1945, did the handful of survivors of 600 Battalion pull back across the Oder to the western shore.

In various other 'fire brigade' operations the battalion, now desperately low in numbers, fought in a counter-attack at Bernau, to the north-east of Berlin, and then formed the rearguard to the German forces pulling back from the River Oder line. It was the end of April 1945. The war in Germany was coming to an end. Berlin was about to fall and the territory of the Third Reich had shrunk to a narrow strip of land running from Prague to Yugoslavia and to a small number of isolated patches of territory in central and northern Germany.

In one of these small areas of northern Germany, what was left of 600, regrouped and conducted a fighting retreat until the war in Europe ended and with its end the survivors of the SS Para Battalion passed into American captivity.

Right: September 1943, new intakes of recruits train for battle. Here pioneers storm into the attack under cover of artillery fire. (Brian L. Davis)

16. Penny packets of Paras in a ground role
NORMANDY, SUMMER 1944

I n June 1944, four years after they had been driven from France, the British forces returned again, but this time reinforced and strengthened by the armies of their American, Canadian, Free French and other Allies. 'Overlord', the Allied operation to liberate Europe, opened in Normandy and although the Allies had brought artificial harbours with them, these would clearly be of limited and short-term use. To ensure a smooth and unbroken supply of *matériel* to the liberating armies in their advance through France, Belgium and Holland, it was imperative that natural harbours with sophisticated cargo-moving equipment be captured as quickly as possible. The nearest suitable ports to the invasion areas were Cherbourg, at the top of the Cotentin peninsula, and Brest, the great naval base at the tip of the Brittany peninsula. Both these objectives lay in the American operational area in which were also located the Fallschirmjaeger Divisions of General Meindl's II Para Corps.

The 1st Para Army, with its seat in Nancy, was not yet fully raised and thus had no direct operational control over the fighting in which II Para Corps was involved against the American units in the bridgehead or subsequently, in Brittany. In any case, the events of the summer of 1944 moved so quickly that the OKW intention to hold the units of First Para Army as a reserve could not be met. Instead its Divisions were put quickly into battle in an endeavour to contain the invading Allied armies.

The 3rd Para Division had been in Brittany since the beginning of February 1944, and it had been intended that it would be relieved when 2nd Para Division arrived from the Eastern Front. This was another intention that would not be realized. On 7 June, the second day of the invasion, the advance units of 3rd Para moved forward into the beachhead area and were followed soon after by the main body which took position to the east of St-Lô, at the base of the Cotentin peninsula. The 5th Para Division had already begun concentrating around and to the west of St-Lô before the invasion took place. The 2nd Para Division, which had been fighting on the Eastern Front since November 1943, had expected to be rested, re-equipped and reinforced in Germany. This was another vain hope; every formation that could be spared was sent.

Following the invasion of Normandy on 6 June 1944, the understrength 2nd Para Division was rushed to Brittany where the 6th Para Regiment was already located. The 6th, which had been raised as one of the constituent

regiments of 2nd Division, was held directly under the control of 74th Corps.

On D-Day, this Corps was forced to commit 6th Regiment to battle in an independent role, as the other formations of 2nd Para had not reached the invasion area. The Regiment was stationed at that time some five miles from the coast. A quick reconnaissance showed von der Heydte that certain tactically important villages had not yet been entered by the US troops, and he determined to seize and hold them. On his left flank he placed 2nd Battalion with orders to advance and capture St-Marie Eglise; the 1st Battalion in the centre was to take St-Marie du Mont, while 3rd Battalion on the right flank was to seize Carentan.

In the fierce fighting which marked the first week of the allied invasion, 1st Battalion was almost totally destroyed. Throughout the following six weeks the other two battalions fought a rearguard action to hold Carentan. No supplies could reach the units by road, but ammunition dropped by one single Ju 52, enabled them to continue fighting. The remnants of the Regiment fought their way out of an encirclement at Carentan, were then surrounded at St-Lô, escaped again and were trapped in the Falaise pocket. When the roll was called in August, fewer than 40 unwounded Jaeger answered.

The 2nd Para Division, with only 2nd and 7th Regiments, plus divisional units under command, was ordered to concentrate around the naval base of Brest. The task given to General Ramcke, the divisional commander, was, together with other units, to hold Brittany against Allied airborne or seaborne assaults.

The journey which 2nd Para Division made from its concentration area at Cologne to the operational area in Brittany had been both long and dangerous. In addition to the Allied air raids which caused damage and delay, French partisan operations against the railway lines and bridges as well as direct attack upon the forces travelling by train, delayed the arrival of German units. Not until 19 June, six days after they had left Cologne, did the advance guard of 2nd Para Division reach the new operational area and some battalions of the main body did not arrive until late in July. The Allied intention to starve the German battle line had succeeded brilliantly.

By the time that 2nd Para Division had finally completed its concentration at the top of the Cotentin peninsula the situation of German Seventh Army had begun to deteriorate. The Allied beachheads which had been established on D-Day, expanded as more and more troops arrived from the United Kingdom. A breakout from the confining perimeter could not be long delayed and the US formations which would bring about that rupture of the German battle front were the First and Third Armies. It

Above: SS Para Jaeger bring forward Panzerfaust, the one-shot anti-tank rocket projectors, during the fighting for Drvar in May 1944. (M. Klein)

was obvious that General Eisenhower would use these formations to seek a decision not only against the weakest-held sector of the German line, but also in an area which promised the greatest opportunity for exploitation once the breakout occured. The area which offered that potential was to the south of the Cotentin peninsula where 3rd and 5th Para Divisions were positioned.

Meanwhile, in Brittany, 2nd Division was still poised to repel airborne assaults for which it had been sent to the Brest area. The 2nd Para Regiment, with only two battalions on strength, was holding the high ground at Ménez-Hom and to the south of Châteaulin. The sector held by 7th Regiment, which was also short of its 2nd Battalion, was on the heights of Monts d'Arée. The divisional Engineer battalion held the sector around the Height of Douanenez and the anti-tank battalion the area to the west of the port.

The relative calm in Brittany gave the divisional commander time to train his inexperienced men. It will be recalled that the decimated Division had arrived from the Eastern Front and had expected to rest and refit in the Rhineland. The recruits to fill the depleted ranks of the Jaeger regiments may not have had experience of combat, but they could be taught much by the surviving veterans of the Russian campaign and the recruits were eager to learn.

The peaceful sojourn in Brittany held until late in July when Patton's US Third Army advanced into the peninsula. Its task was to capture Rennes and Brest and Patton succeeded in fulfilling the first part of his orders quite

Above: Fallschirmjaeger in Normandy move forward towards the Allied bridgehead. The leading man carries a Panzerschreck, the two-man rocket launcher. (M. Klein)

swiftly. This was hardly surprising since neither 6th Armoured Division nor 79th Infantry Division met serious opposition. The mass of the German units which had once been stationed in Brittany had been taken to fight in Normandy.

At this time the German military situation in that sector deteriorated dramatically. Their front around St-Lô, at the centre of the Cotentin peninsula suddenly collapsed. More US units were urgently needed to exploit that breakthrough. The highly mobile units of Patton's Third Army were ordered to change direction away from Brittany and eastwards, deep into France. Brest and the Breton harbours were no longer as vital as they had once been – now the sights were set on others higher up the coast – Calais, Dunkirk and Antwerp.

For the Allies there was the glittering prospect of encircling the whole of German Seventh Army. Obedient to his orders, Patton headed towards Le Mans, leaving only his VIII Corps to continue the advance towards Brest.

The reasons why Hitler wished to hold Brest and why the Americans needed to capture it were both grounded in prestige. For Hitler, maintaining his hold on the port would demonstrate to the world that he intended to reconquer France. Also he needed, but this was a secondary consideration, to hold the port as a base for his U-boats. For their part the Americans wanted to capture this major naval base as a sign that they were unbeatable. As Bradley had explained in a private talk with Patton, 'We must take Brest in order to maintain the illusion that the USA cannot be beaten.'

For that prestige objective Ramcke's 2nd Para Division, together with other German formations, was sacrificed and no fewer than 4,000 men of US VIII Corps were killed. When the end came Ramcke's formation had been weakened by casualties and by the withdrawal of units to serve in Normandy. As early as the end of July the Division had been ordered to send a battle group to restore the badly mauled 5th Para Division. The group set out on 2 August but during the following day was struck by tanks of an armoured division and driven back to Dinǎn. The US armoured Division thrust past the town and surrounded the battle group which fought its way out of the encirclement to reach St-Malo. Here its battalions went into defensive positions and held the seaside town until 5 August.

Not many days after the battle group set out for Normandy the mass of 2nd Para Division was also ordered to move towards the battle sector. The 2nd was without transport and was forced to comandeer French civilian trucks in order to carry the most essential units. Ramcke divided his force and the move began. Advised by Ultra intercept that this fresh and veteran Division was *en route* to the battle area, Allied High Command issued orders for it to be stopped or at least delayed. The divisional reconnaissance battalion was intercepted by an American armoured Division and totally destroyed. Then the US tanks turned to attack the two columns. The first of these made up mainly of 2nd Regiment, successfully fought off the armoured assault. The 7th Regiment column was not so fortunate. It withdrew into the woods around Huelgoat, where it had also to fight against French partisan groups and lost heavily in the battle against both enemies. During the battle 2nd Battalion of the 7th Regiment was surrounded for a short time but fought its way out of the encirclement. As an example of the ferocity of the fighting, no fewer than thirty US tanks were destroyed, some by the SP Company but most by the Jaeger who fought them at close quarters.

A withdrawal to the Monts d'Arée area followed and within days the Americans had surrounded Brest and had cut it off. The 2nd then fought its way from the Monts d'Arée on which it had been completely isolated and into the citadel area of the port. The US advances had not only surrounded the naval base but had also trapped a number of German units before they could reach the safety of the Citadel. Most were quickly overrun but one of them, 266th Infantry Division, still held out and to rescue it 7th Para Regiment mounted a counter-attack on 9 August. The attack was a complete surprise to the Americans who had thought the German forces to be defeated and in despair. The veteran Jaeger had taught the recruits well and the battalions cut their way through the US lines and brought out the German Division. This was not an isolated offensive operation carried out by the Paras in Brest but just the most important of many. But however heroic the attacks or staunch the defence the end could not be gainsaid and on 20 September, General Ramcke, now commanding all the German forces in Brest was forced to surrender them. With that the original 2nd Para Division ended its existence, but by the beginning of December a new one had been raised in the Hilversum area of Holland where it remained until relocated, later that month, to the west and south-west of Arnhem.

The headquarters staff of XII Flieger Corps became redundant early in 1944, when its Divisions were transferred from the Luftwaffe establishment to that of the Army. By a change of number and title XII Flieger Corps became II Para Corps, with 3rd and 5th Divisions under command, and was posted to Brittany as a component of Seventh Army.

The two Para Divisions were located in the Cotentin peninsula and shortly after D-Day were ordered to move up to the invasion area there to participate in a general counter-attack to drive the Allied forces into the sea. That was an order easier to give than to execute. The attitude of the General Staff had always been that the Fallschirmjaeger were airborne troops and that they did not, therefore, need the vehicle establishments of standard infantry formations. Although it had long been accepted that the Jaeger WERE élite infantry the General

Staff had still made no provision to increase the vehicle scale. As a result neither Para Division had transport sufficient for its needs.

When the order came to move to the invasion areas 3rd Para's solution to the lack of transport was to send the motorized detachments to the battle area loaded with Jaeger. These would be dropped near the area of operation and the trucks would then return to pick up the other units which were foot-marching to the sound of the guns. The Division's motorized units set out carrying one Jaeger battalion from each of the regiments as well as divisional troops. At Torigny the advance guard halted waiting for the bulk of the Division to join it in the assigned concentration area. Divisional HQ, for its part, received orders that it was to advance from Torigny north-eastwards through St-Lô and to drive the Americans out of the thick woods around Cerisy-la-Forêt. En route to the woods was the dominant height, known as Point 192, an important objective. Its capture would give observation over the enemy-held area when the second part of the attack struck forward to reach the Baie de la Seine. Since the bulk of Division had not yet arrived in the concentration area south of Caumont, only the advance guard detachment took part in this successful operation.

Four days later, on 14 June, US forces struck down the Bayeux–St-Lô road and towards the divisional concentration area which was held only by the rear echelons of the advance guard. The mass of the Division, still foot-marching from the Cotentin peninsula, had not yet arrived. The American attack was driven back with heavy

Left: Von der Heydte, commander of 6th Regiment, with SS Brigadefuehrer Ostendorf, GCO 'Goetz von Berlichingen', outside Carentan about 11 June 1944. (M. Klein)

Right: Major Alpers interrogates a US prisoner shortly after the Allied landing in Normandy. (Brian L. Davis)

loss in men and armour, the greatest number of tanks destroyed being attributed to the 12th Para SP Gun Brigade which had been raised in Melun at the end of March 1944. Since 5th Para, the other component of II Corps, was still not fully operational, the SP Brigade was able to give full support to the units of 3rd Division. Switching his detachments from one sector to the other, Captain Gersteuer, the Brigade Commander, beat back the US tank thrusts down the vital main road. By June 17 the main body of 3rd Para Division had arrived in the concentration area and the divisional commander found that his orders had once more been changed. His Division was to go over to the defence of the ground which the advance guard groups had won in their first battle; a line running from the Cerisy woods across Point 192, and St-André to Caumont. On the right of his 15 mile-wide (24km) stretch of front the Divisional commander placed 8th Para Regiment, with 5th Regiment in the centre and the 9th on the left. For three weeks the Division held the line, its staunch defence preventing the US First Army from capturing the important communication centre of St-Lô. That town was vital for any advance into the Cotentin peninsula and all American efforts were directed towards its capture. Their units made little progress. The US infantry had not been trained for this type of campaign. They had anticipated a campaign of sweeping movement and found that they were trapped in a lush jungle. This account of the fighting in Normandy was supplied to me a number of years ago by a paratrooper who had written it for one of my earlier books, *The Killing-Ground*.

'The ground over which we fought although not dense bocage country, was still one which favoured the defender over the attacker. The area was made up of little fields each enclosed within old and tall hedges set on the top of earth banks usually over a metre in height. Some of those hedges and trees along the road were so tall and their summer foliage so thick that they formed, like aisles in a church, cool, green tunnels in which we could move without fear of being seen and attacked from the air.

Although we were mostly young soldiers our training had been so thorough at the hands of the veterans that we adapted better to the close country conditions than did our enemies. Because of the close nature of the terrain the Americans could not use units as large as a battalion and they felt unease in small unit actions. We, on the other hand, had been trained for such operations and were completely at home in the thick hedges. The US armour could not deploy in mass against us and our Panzerfaust projectors were more than a match for those tanks which they brought in against us. The other great advantage which the Americans had was their air cover, but again, hidden beneath the bocage we were invisible and, in any case, we and the Americans were so close together that an air strike would have caused them as many casualties as to us. It was only when we were south of St-Lô that the material advantages which the Americans enjoyed could be used to great effect against us. Their artillery, tanks and aircraft supported their infantry magnificently.'

The great offensive by US First Army to capture St-Lô went in on 11 July behind the heaviest barrage that any of

the veteran Jaeger had ever experienced. The American assault struck for and captured the important Point 192, and then went on to drive the Jaeger units southwards towards the principal objective. Losses mounted and there were so many casualties in 9th Regiment that it had to be withdrawn and replaced by the 8th. The divisional Signals Company was then converted to infantry and ordered to take over the positions vacated by 8th Regiment. The US First Army's drive to capture St-Lô had so weakened German Seventh Army that its Commanding General demanded fresh units to replace those which had been bearing the brunt of the fighting since D-Day. One of the units sent forward was 5th Para Division which had only completed its raising by the beginning of July. It would be blooded near St-Lô.

The 5th then suffered the fate of so many other Para units before it. It was not able to fight as a complete unit. Rather its regiments were taken from it and inserted into other formations to bolster them. Thus, the divisional commander was not able to exercise any tactical control over his own units. The 14th Jaeger Regiment was placed under the command of Panzer Lehr Division north of St-Lô. The 15th Jaeger Regiment went to 353rd Division fighting to the west of Carentan and 13th Regiment to the east of Marigny.

The second and major part of the US offensive, Operation 'Cobra', was intended to open the German front wide enough to allow Patton's newly arrived Third Army to break out into Brittany. From intercepted German signals it was clear that the German forces had been so weakened as a result of the British 'Goodwood' offensive that they would not be able to withstand Operation 'Cobra'. Among the signals decoded by Ultra were those which passed between Meindl, commanding II Para Corps, and Student, commanding First Para Army. Meindl complained that the fighting power of his Jaeger was dwindling daily. His last two requests for reinforcements had been ignored and the critical situation forced him to commit the few replacements which had come up as soon as they reached the combat area. As a result 90 per cent soon became casualties because they had had so little training. Meindl declared that most of the replacements had never thrown a hand-grenade, fired more than a few rounds or knew anything about digging-in or camouflage.

Student, in his reply, promised 2,000 reinforcements, but Meindl asked that half of these should have further training in Germany. He later signalled that if the Americans did carry out their offensive they must breakthrough because there was nothing to stop them. Meindl knew that it would be upon his depleted Corps that the full force of the US attack would fall. Already the signs

were there; aerial bombardments and artillery barrages, heavy, sustained and damaging.

In 'Cobra', Bradley, commanding US First Army, planned that VII Corps would penetrate west of St-Lô and that its armoured and motorized units would strike deep into the German rear towards Coustances. The offensive opened on 25 July and to create a gap through which his armour could advance Bradley used nearly 2,000 heavy and medium bombers. The fury of that bombardment was an experience that shattered the German units. Under its weight 14th Para Regiment was destroyed and then behind the aerial assault and a subsequent crushing barrage the 30th US Division attacked with armour support.

In vain the 3rd Para Division supported by the 12th SP Brigade fought to hold the storming American advance. Its rapid succession of blows began to shatter the German southern wing. Patton's Third Army swung away from Brittany and, returning to Normandy, thrust deep in its advance turning the left wing of Seventh Army and forcing its flank units back towards Putanges. The Americans had not only broken the German line but had by that time reached an area of France in which there were no more German combat units and those fighting Divisions which were to the north were pulling back rapidly. But not rapidly enough to outpace the tanks of Patton's 5th Armoured Division which was spear-heading Third Army's advance to Argentan. Between the Franco-American armour advancing towards Argentan and the Anglo-Canadian-Polish tank forces striking down from Falaise a pocket had been created which was beginning to encircle the German Seventh Army and Fifth Panzer Army.

Against the forces trapped in that pocket the Allies unleashed the full fury of their great superiority in the air and on the ground. This was a *material Schlacht* in the fullest sense of the term. The Germans could set up no firm defence. Defence lines were smothered in furious barrages which became even more concentrated as the Falaise pocket shrank in size. If the two trapped armies were to escape they would have to reach the eastern side of the Falaise pocket before it was completely closed; and the danger of its being closed became more acute with each passing day. There was still military order and good discipline within the pocket and frequent attempts to stabilize the front. The 84th Corps was placed in charge of all troops on the north side of the pocket and its Order of Battle included 3rd Para Division and a battle group of the 'Hitler Youth' Division.

The commanders within the pocket prepared for a breakout. Army HQ was in a quarry to the east of Villedieu-lès-Bailleul and those of the SS Corps and the

Right: Major-General Schimpf, commander of 3rd Fallschirmjaeger Division issuing orders at his tactical HQ. (Brian L. Davis)

Right: Donkeys too could serve with the Fallschirmjaeger; a commandeered beast of burden during the campaign in Normandy, 1944.

Right: A front-line slit trench in the jungle-like conditions of the Normandy *bocage*. The Fallschirmjaeger uses a field telephone to tell his comrades of the enemy's movements. (Brian L. Davis)

Hitler Youth Division in a stone hut near the eastern end of the pocket. The plans to breakout were made by candle-light during a night in which the Allied gunfire rose to a peak of intensity. Amid the unceasing detonation of shells discussions went on, runners fetched and took messages and time-tables were co-ordinated. SS General Hausser gave orders that 3rd Para Division would breakout in conjunction with the SS Corps to which 'Hitler Youth' Division belonged. The Fallschirmjaeger would move at 22.30 hours from a concentration area north of Montabard and breakout through the area of St-Lambert where the encircling ring was not yet completely closed. The Para assault was to be a silent one. There would be neither a barrage nor machine-gun fire to carve a way through the Allied units. The Paras would hold open a gap through which the other units would escape. The Fallschirmjaeger units would spearhead the assault. Then would come Army HQ and following that the Grenadier regiments of the Hitler Youth.

En route to the stone hut which was SS Corps HQ, Meindl and Schimpf discussed the breakout plans. They decided that the Jaeger would form two columns and march by compass bearing south of Coulonces and Magny to reach the high ground to the east of Coudehard. There the units would form and hold open the gap for the other units before they too moved back away from the butchery, destruction and desolation that was the Falaise pocket. The Para artillery unit was to fire off all its ammunition, blow up its guns and the gunners would then join the rearguard detachments. The Jaeger would be accompanied by a battery of 88mm guns and anti-tank guns, as well as by the last two Tiger tanks of the Hitler Youth Division. These would beat off any attempts by Allied armour to interfere with the escape.

In the SS HQ hut there were further discussions with the commanders of the 'Hitler Youth' Division. It was decided that 1st Battalion of 26th SS Grenadier Regiment would follow the Paras through St-Lambert and across the River Dives. A battle group led by Sturmbannfuehrer Olboeter would cover the rear of the escape group. There were to be liaison groups between the SS and the Paras so that the evacuation would go without a hitch and so that contact would not be lost between the units.

At 22.30 hours the 3rd Para detachments left the woods north of Montabard in which they had been sheltering. Silently, the columns moved through the night each man maintaining touch with the man in front of him and the one behind him. To the east of the Argentan-Trun road the head of the column had to divert to avoid Canadian tanks on the road ahead of it. A sudden barrage of artillery fire fell on the escaping column wounding General Schimpf. The Corps Commander, Meindl took over

command of the Division. Just after midnight the advance guard reached the river and crossed near a mill a kilo-metre to the south of Magny. A vigilant Canadian patrol discovered the escape attempt and tanks and artillery opened fire upon the gap in their line through which the German were filtering. To avoid the artillery barrage and the growing enemy infantry opposition Meindl moved his units eastward, but was then forced to change direction again to pass an armoured group blocking the road. By first light the Jaeger had reached the area of Coudehard beyond which was a high ridge which Meindl saw to his chagrin was occupied by a group of Canadian armoured fighting vehicles.

In the growing daylight, it was by that time 05.30 hours, Meindl made an appreciation of the situation. He decided to make the breakout point along a path which threaded its way through two high stretches of ground and sent out patrols to ensure that the path was free of the enemy. Moving slowly and cautiously the Jaeger passed out of the encirclement and held open a corridor through which some SS units passed. The main body of the Hitler Youth Division had lost contact at some point during the night and had made its breakout elsewhere. While the Jaeger units of 3rd Para marched eastwards, Meindl and his officers waited at the breakout point to meet the Fall-schirmjaeger rearguard which did not arrive until about 07.00 hours on 21 August.

The Para Division had lost heavily both in men and equipment. The 12th Para SP Brigade lost 40 per cent of its battle strength and more than 90 per cent of its ration and ammunition Trains. The Jaeger were exhausted after months of combat, but they were not to rest yet. Instead the regiments were regrouped and their remnants ordered to form the rearguard for Fifth Panzer Army and Seventh Army as those withdrew towards the Seine. Not until the first week of September were the survivors of 3rd Para Division able to leave the line and they were taken to Cologne where the regiments were to be brought up to strength with new recruits and issued with new weapons and equipment.

The other unit of II Para Corps, the 5th Division, after the shattering experience on 25 July near St-Lô, was still not serving as a single formation. Its regiments continued to serve with the formations to which they had been allotted or else were used to create new Fallschirmjaeger regiments. By the end of September the broken remnants of 5th Division had been taken out of the line and posted to Cologne where it was reformed and fleshed out with new men.

The campaign in Normandy was ended and the German Army in the west had been defeated. In obedience to

Hitler's statement that 'one yard of Normandy is worth a kilometre of ground on any other battle front', Army Group B had stood and its stand had proved to be disastrous and wasteful. A quarter of a million German soldiers had been killed, wounded or taken prisoner in pursuit of that insane policy. The Falaise pocket had witnessed the destruction of a major part of Army Group B. Nearly one-third of its infantry Divisions were either destroyed or immobilized – bottled-up in the coastal fortress towns. The remaining 40 were worn out, under strength and shattered as were its Panzer Divisions and the three Fallschirmjaeger Divisions which had been used in Normandy. All that sacrifice had proved unavailing. The Allies were on the mainland of Europe and were preparing to advance towards Germany.

By the time that the last flickers of resistance were dying away in the Falaise area, Allied armies were driving towards the Seine and Paris. Hitler had ordered German Seventh Army to stand fast and, in pursuance of that order, together with Fifth Panzer Army, it had been almost totally destroyed in Normandy. It is true that men and vehicles had escaped from the Falaise pocket and had crossed the Seine, but these did not form an army in being, rather a collection of fragments which could be capable of only limited opposition to the Allied advance.

German military leaders in France, from Field Marshal Model, Commander-in-Chief, West and of Army Group B, down to those officers commanding the remnants of Divisions, all emphasized that their men needed rest, refitting and re-equipping – but principally, rest. A battle line of sorts still existed but the Divisions manning it were just names and numbers; sub-units lacking the most basic military necessities. The only major formation which remained still reasonably intact was Fifteenth Army which Hitler had held in the Pas-de-Calais in anticipation of the REAL invasion. Fifteenth Army had not been involved in the heavy fighting for Normandy, but it had been reduced in strength as its units were taken away to bolster up the battle line in the invasion area. By the middle weeks of August it held no more than six of the original nineteen Divisions which had once been on strength.

So great had been the destruction in Normandy and so weak the Fifteenth Army, now threatened with encirclement at Antwerp, that it would be no exaggeration to say that from the estuary of the Scheldt and extending as far as Liège in the far east of Belgium, there was a vast and almost undefended gap in the German battle line. Why that gap was not exploited and why the German Army in the west was given time to reform its front in northern

Right: Fallschirmjaeger of the 6th Regiment wait behind a camouflaged 7.5cm Pak anti-tank gun in the Carentan area. (Brian L. Davis)

France and Belgium, forms no part of this narrative. But reformed that front was, and quickly too. On 4 September, von Rundstedt was recalled as Supreme Commander, West, leaving Model in charge of Army Group B.

Into the gap across the whole of Belgium von Rundstedt inserted Student's First Para Army, a formation still not completely raised. Of that time Student said, '. . . we had no disposable reserves worth mentioning, either on the Western Front or within Germany. I took over command of the right wing of the Western Front on the Albert Canal on 4 September. At that time I had only recruit and convalescent units and a single coast defence unit from Holland. These were reinforced by a Panzer detachment – 25 tanks and SP guns. . . .'

Student's black picture was lightened by the fact that he had von der Heydte's 6th Jaeger Regiment, a veteran formation which had been withdrawn from Normandy and refitted. In addition there was a battalion of 2nd Jaeger Regiment, five new Para regiments, an anti-tank battalion and Para Army's service units. Behind that thin screen of veterans and recruits Student created a front and to strengthen it formed battle groups from non-Para splinter groups and military fragments which entered his area of Command. By mid September the worst of the crisis was past and Student now commanded five Divisions which were strung out across Belgium and linked up with the reconstituted Seventh Army, holding the Siegfried Line sector. His battle line was made up of, 719th Infantry Division holding the right wing, Battle Groups Chill, principally 85th Infantry Division, and Walther, a Fallschirmjaeger group. Erdmann's Para Training Division, the 176th Division, 59th and 245th Infantry Divisions were the other units under Student's authority. There was later to come on strength a Panzer Brigade and II SS Panzer Corps, which was refitting near Arnhem.

Throughout September and for much of October, the First Army fought to hold its positions against the Anglo-Canadian assaults, but under that pressure was forced back, contesting every yard in a dogged defence. By 27 October, the 10th Canadian Infantry Brigade had driven 6th Jaeger Regiment out of Bergen op Zoom and the whole German line slowly gave ground. At the end of October 1st Battalion of 2nd Jaeger Regiment was taken out of the line. The losses it had suffered had reduced it to the strength of a very weak Company.

On other sectors of the Western Front the 3rd and 5th Para Divisions had also been in action. Both had raised battle groups to fight the 82nd US Airborne Division

Left: Fallschirmjaeger man a heavily camouflaged Flakvierling during the Normandy campaign. (Brian L. Davis)

which was engaged in Operation 'Market Garden'. From the end of that operation the Fallschirmjaeger Divisions held their defensive line all the way through the autumn of 1944, battling against 1st US Army's penetrations and probes. The 3rd Para Division which had had to be reformed, re-entered the line at Dueren during November and held its positions against American armoured and infantry assault and aerial bombardment. Even at this time of crisis and desperate pressure the Para Divisions were called upon to hand over units to strengthen other formations. Thus the 2nd Battalion of 8th Regiment was detached from its parent unit and sent in to help 344th Infantry Division. Despite the constant drain, the under strength Jaeger regiments and battalions continued to hold out and in so doing obstructed the advance of US First Army between Altdorf and the Huertgen forest. The subsequent battle for that densely wooded area was almost as bitter as had been the fighting in the dark forests of Volkhov, and Jaeger losses were crippling. Late on 16 December, the Para Divisions were taken out of the Huertgen sector and marched, without rest, into those areas of the Ardennes from which the attack to reach the port of Antwerp would go in. Both 3rd and 5th Divisions had been assigned to take part in 'Wacht am Rhein'.

An account of that period from September to December 1944, has been written by Adolf Strauch who volunteered to return to active service although not yet healed of wounds. On arrival at Elsenborn towards the end of August 1944, he was ordered to take over a platoon of No. 8 Company of 2nd Battalion, 2nd Jaeger Regiment. He was given the verbal instruction that in the event of the Company commander being killed and if there were no other officers, he was to take over. His immediate superior was a company sergeant-major who had no combat experience and who was made responsible for 'A' and 'B' echelons. Strauch's first introduction to the men of the Company was depressing.

'There they stood. Next to young volunteers there were the old NCOs of the Luftwaffe, men who had been taken from headquarters units and from Orderly Rooms. The heart of the Company consisted of just eight Fallschirmjaeger. We knew that we would soon be in action and that there would be too little time to train the men in the use of their weapons. On 5th September, No. 8 Company consisted of two heavy machine-gun platoons, one mortar platoon, one half platoon of light machine-guns, two Panzerschreck and Coy HQ.

On 7th September, our Company, forming part of Lipp Battalion, reached Helchteren and we were involved, as soon as we arrived, with British infantry and tanks of the Guards Armoured Division. The leading Troops of armoured fighting vehicles were attacked with Panzerfaust

rocket-projectors and driven back. We dug-in in front of the village and our Signals group linked us up with battalion HQ and with the RAP. On 8th September, the British attacked again and were driven back with heavy loss. We, too suffered casualties. We had had an 88mm gun supporting us but a few hours later this was pulled out and from that point on we lacked the support of heavy weapons.

The enemy repeated his attacks during the 9th, using flame-throwing tanks. We had only a few Panzerfaust and our Panzerschreck were out of action. By this time the Company Commander had been wounded and I took over. We were attacked constantly and under those assaults our units were practically wiped out. We could no longer defend the position and over the field telephone were ordered to withdraw. The British tanks were all around us but five comrades and I crawled through ditches to reach Battalion HQ. Some Panzerfaust were found and with these the British tank advance is halted. At the HQ I learnt that not only my Company, No. 8, but also No. 5 has been destroyed. Our wounded were not so much loaded on to the open, horse-drawn carts as bundled aboard. The carts set off but came under tank fire which killed the teams. It was a terrible picture.

My new orders are to collect the little groups of men in the area and to group them. To my great pleasure I see that some of the groups are from the platoons of No. 8 Company. The wounded have still not left the battle zone and in an attempt to hold back the British armour Captain Lipp and the officer commanding No. 5 Company, take some Panzerfauste and go out and attack the enemy vehicles at close quarters. Both are killed in action.

We pull back across swamp and heath land and march throughout the night. During that march we meet General Erdmann on a bridge across the Maas-Schelde Canal. He orders us to go to Kinrooi where a new battalion will be re-raised. The battalion was reformed on 17th September, and declared ready for action. The new commander is a Major from the Flak, as is the new commander of No. 8 Company. We are taken by truck to Liessel and Deurne, which we reach by midday and go straight into battle. On the Deurne road there is a battery of 88s manned by old men. Parallel to the road, and about 500 metres distant, enemy tanks appear, passing in front of the guns like ducks in a shooting-gallery. We all anticipate that the 88s will smash the tanks. A few shots are fired, but they fall short. The tanks halt and then the gun crews abandon their weapons and run away. The sights are faulty. Under the British tank pressure we have to abandon Liessel and move back to Deurne. We are not very happy.

During the following morning the battalion reaches Deurne and takes up defensive positions. Battalion orders

Above: An aircraft spotter was essential in the fighting in north-west Europe. Here a Fallschirmjaeger is a look out for enemy aircraft during the Normandy campaign. (Brian L. Davis)

Below: A lightly wounded Fallschirmjaeger in Normandy. It was a matter of honour that if a Para could still stand and fire his weapon then he stayed with his unit.

us to go forward with part of our Company through completely open country and to take up position along a railway embankment. I object that we shall lose the men who will be in position there as the area had no cover. The British tanks come in to attack Battalion HQ which is in a detached house in the village and their shells smash its walls. Thank God, we have not yet moved into it. The men who had been ordered forward to the railway embankment run out of ammunition and are forced to surrender. I must say it; it was useless to put officers of another arm of service in command of Fallschirmjaeger detachments. Determination, courage and bravery are no substitutes for combat experience.

Fighting is now being carried on only by small groups of Jaeger. We are out of touch with the rest of the Company. Battalion orders me to collect the stragglers and to lead them to Venray where we shall regroup. Arriving in Venray I am told that fighting is still continuing in Deurne and I am to return there by truck with the men I have just brought out. *En route* the Feldgendarmerie halt us and take our truck. We continue on foot and meet other groups from our battalion who are now retreating from Deurne. As our OC has been wounded I am ordered to lead the Company.

By the end of September, our decimated battalion is in Helenaven, a quiet sector. One morning I was called to Battalion HQ and accused of cowardice in the face of the enemy because I had led the stragglers to Venray. I am able to prove that I was carrying out orders and am cleared but the accusation depresses me and not even my promotion to Sergeant cheers me.

The battle comes nearer and then is all round us. There are frequent and heavy enemy bombardments. We take up positions in a marshy area between Horst and Sevenum and leave them in the night. During that night march I was swept away by flood water and nearly drowned. At a little village called America we take up positions in the marsh. It was uncomfortable but safe and there we stayed until the end of November. Then the line was taken back across the Maas and the Battalion marched via Venlo to Roermond. My No. 8 Company was then put in a bend of the Maas between Herten and Linne. In December we have a new commanding officer, Major Zander, a highly decorated man with combat experience in a Luftwaffe Field Division.'

What comes over very strongly in this, and other similiar accounts, is the flexibility of the German military system. Stragglers are formed into battle groups and fight as well with these strangers as with their old, former companies. Strauch's account continues with an account of a mission to test his leadership qualities and this follows in the section dealing with the Western Front in 1945.

17. Last flight of the Storming Eagles
THE ARDENNES OFFENSIVE, DECEMBER 1944

By the end of 1944, the tide of was war running against Germany. On the Eastern Front the Red Army was across the frontier; in the south, in Italy, the Anglo-American Armies were poised ready to resume their advance when campaigning weather returned, while in the west Allied forces were closing up to the Rhine and had already taken Aachen.

In reviewing the situation Adolf Hitler saw a strategic possibility. The great mass of the Allied armies in north-west Europe were in Belgium and Holland and were being supplied through the newly opened port of Antwerp. If the German forces were to attack out of the Ardennes, as they had done in 1940, the Panzer divisions could 'bounce' the Maas and reach Antwerp, the final objective, in a very short time. The Anglo-American Armies would be split and would be forced to retreat. A second Dunkirk, but one more disastrous than that of 1940, was anticipated.

The offensive would be fought by Army Group B, which had under command three Panzer armies: Sixth SS, the Fifth and the Seventh. The task of Sixth SS Panzer Army, on the right flank and the one with which we are concerned, was to break through the front of US First Army and then to advance so as to gain the crossing-points over the Maas between Liège and Huy. First SS Corps, of Sixth SS Panzer Army, had five formations on establishment: 1st SS Panzer Division (Leibstandarte SS Adolf Hitler), 12th SS Panzer Division (Hitler Youth), 3rd Fallschirm-jaeger, 12th Volksgrenadier and 277th Volksgrenadier Divisions. To support the operations of I SS Corps a Para drop was planned.

The military capabilities of the formations making up I SS Corps were varied. The SS Panzer Division (Leibstandarte) was an élite unit with a combat record of proven aggression. The 12th SS (Hitler Youth) Division, did not have the long fighting record of the 1st SS, but in its short history had won a name for itself for bravery bordering on fanaticism. The 277th Volksgrenadier Division had been so badly mauled in the fighting around Falaise in the late summer that its commanding General described it as only 'capable of defending itself ... with a few Companies

capable of offensive operations'. The 12th Volksgrenadier Division was a veteran formation, well armed and equipped. The 3rd Fallschirmjaeger Division, which had been in Normandy when the Allies invaded, had suffered severe losses since D-Day, particularly in its most recent battle, that of the Dueren Forest where it had also lost a great deal of transport. To give artillery backing to the 277th and the 3rd Para Divisions, each was advised that an SP battalion would be seconded to it for the forthcoming offensive. In the event neither Division received such support.

For Operation 'Wacht am Rhein', as well as for a follow-on operation 'Nord Wind', a number of Para formations and detachments were to be employed. In addition to 3rd Para Division, a Jaeger battle group was to undertake an airborne drop and there was a miscellany of other Para groups under the command of Otto Skorzeny. His unusual group, camouflaged under the bland title of '150 Panzer Brigade', included not only American-speaking commandos and the SS Para Battalion 500/600, but also the Jaeger of a Battle Group, 'No. 200'.

During the early hours of 16 December 1944, Field Marshal von Rundstedt, issued an Order of the Day. It was brief but impressive.

'Soldiers of the Western Front:
Your hour has come. Today, strong assault armies will attack the Anglo-Americans. I do not need to say more. You all know that everything depends upon this operation.

Carry with you the sacred obligation to give all and to achieve the superhuman, for our Fatherland and for our Fuehrer.'

The words of this Order inspired the men of Army Group B. The war diarist of a Panzer Company in the Hitler Youth Division spoke for most when he wrote, 'We knew that the hour had struck. It was an Order of the Day like those of the old times. There was the feeling that at last we had the opportunity – the final opportunity – to turn the War in the West in our favour.' This feeling of absolute

optimism was one repeated many times by Jaeger, both those who fought in the Ardennes offensive as well as by those who were in action in other sectors of the western battle front. That confidence grew when from Intelligence sources it was learned that the US troops facing Sixth SS Panzer Army, were the burnt-out remnants of Divisions which had fought in Normandy, or else were newly arrived in western Europe with little or no combat experience. The Amis were as good as beaten already.

The offensive would open with a short but intense artillery barrage supported by rocket fire. Searchlights would be shone on to the low clouds and in conditions of 'artificial moonlight', the infantry would go in. The time-table from its start to crossing the Maas, the most vital part of the operation, was put at four days. At 04.00 hours on Saturday, 16 December, a dark and bitter morning, the German assault Divisions moved towards their start-lines and at 05.35 hours the barrage opened.

We begin this account of the Para operations in the Battle of the Bulge, with the story of the drop made by Lieutenant-Colonel von der Heydte's battle group, in the mission called Operation 'Stoesser'.

General Student had selected von der Heydte to command the Battle Group, but when the two officers met on 8 December, the only details that the General could give his subordinate were that the unit he was to raise would be, for reasons of secrecy, not an established formation but would be made up of about 100 men from each Jaeger regiment of II Para Corps serving on the Western Front. These small groups were to report to the Para Army Weapons School, at Aalten in Holland. Battle Group von der Hedyte, numbering about 1,200 men, was to be ready for action by 9 December, but what the mission entailed Student could not say; only that it was vital. The battle group leader was allowed to select his own Company commanders and platoon officers. Since the battle group was in battalion strength it would be organized along conventional lines with four Jaeger Companies, a heavy weapons Company with twelve machine-guns and four mortars, a signals group and a pioneer platoon.

Nor could the General Officer Commanding Army Group B, give the Colonel any more than basic information. The final details would be given to him by Dietrich, Sixth Panzer Army Commander, under whose command he would be operating. That SS officer told him, on 14 December, that the task was to protect the open flank of I SS Panzer Corps by mounting an airborne drop on the Hoher Venn to block the roads Eupen–Malmédy and Verviers–Malmédy near Belle Croix, 8 miles (twelve kilometres) to the north of Malmédy. The intention of the mission was to draw off American units from attacking the SS Panzer spearhead group led by Jochen Peiper

Heydte's battle group was to hold its position until the spearheads of the SS Panzer Corps arrived on the following day. His operation was to be made in conjunction with the advance by Sixth SS Panzer Army towards Liège or the Maas bridges on the first day of the offensive. Thus, von der Heydte's battle group was to jump during the night of D-Day, immediately preceding the barrage. German Intelligence had no idea of the strength of the enemy in the area but this was thought to be not great.

Sepp Dietrich's orders continued. 'If for any technical reasons the Para drop is impracticable on the first day of the operation, the battle group will drop, early in the morning of the 17th, at the River Ambleve area or at Amay. It will secure the bridges there and hold them for the advancing Sixth Army.'

Von der Heydte was astonished at the SS General's orders; they were dangerously naïve. It was clear that Dietrich knew nothing of the limitations of a parachute operation. He pointed out to the SS General that only a few of his Jaeger had made a parachute jump and even fewer had made a night drop. There were high winds in the drop area whose force would disperse the Jaeger and the Colonel described the likelihood of limbs being broken from landing in trees. Dietrich remained unmoved by these objections. The burden of his reply was that it was hardly his fault if the Jaeger were poorly trained. Von der Heydte, aware of the baleful influence of mountainous regions upon wireless transmission or reception, then asked for carrier pigeons, which were, in his opinion, more certain means of passing messages. Dietrich replied that he was not running a menagerie and that if he could lead a whole Panzer Army without birds, von der Heydte ought to be able to lead a battle group without them. Nor could he supply aerial reconnaissance photographs, nor would he authorize recce patrols to be sent out. But then relenting he offered the services of Obersturmfuehrer Etterich from the SS Artillery and two signallers. They would be issued with a standard wireless. He also promised that dummy paratroops would be dropped behind the Allied lines so as to cause the maximum confusion.

There were now only days in which to prepare. Von der Hedyte's battle group had been moved from Aalten to Sennelager during the night of 10/11 December, and had liaised there with the air transport squadrons which had been detailed to fly the mission. To the dismay of the Jaeger officers many of the aircrews were untrained. They had neither experience in night flying nor in dropping paratroops. Worse was to come. The Jaeger detachments should have reached the departure airfields at Paderborn and Lippspringe at last light on the 15th, ready to drop on

the morning of the 16th. But fuel shortages meant that only a third of the battle group could be transported at any one time and the battalion had not arrived at the departure airfields by the scheduled take-off time. The operation was postponed and OKW ordered it to be flown during the night of 16/17 December.

It must be said that even if Battle Group von der Hedyte had reached the battlefield its presence would have had little effect upon the general course of ground operations for Sixth SS Panzer Army had failed to gain its first-day objectives. There was still a need for the Para drop to be made, but the Jaeger would not now be dropped over Ambleve or Amay, the secondary targets, but on to the Hoher Venn, the original objective. Reports coming to Army Group HQ told of American convoys bringing reinforcements southwards across the ridge and to the battle area at Elsenborn. It would be the task of von der Heydte's battle group to halt or at least reduce, that flow of reinforcement.

Just before midnight on the 16th the Jaeger climbed into their machines but although all the 80 aircraft took-off safely they did not all reach the drop zone. As they approached the Hohe Venn they encountered strong head winds which affected the pilots' judgement. Many of the inexperienced aircrews had not taken into account the fact that head winds reduce aircraft speed and, therefore, the distance it has travelled. Many pilots were working on a simple basis of hours flown to determine when they had reached the target area. The adverse winds gave them a false result. Few brought their Jaeger to the correct drop zone. Two hundred Paras came down near Bonn in Germany; others in Holland. A few aircraft crashed into mountain peaks which were hidden from view by the blinding snowstorms sweeping the area and others were shot down by accurate American anti-aircraft fire.

Only ten transports out of 80 found the drop zone and the klaxons to the Jus brought the Jaeger to the open doorways ready to jump. It was a frightening prospect. The night was dark, it was snowing, and wind was gusting at more than 30mph. Under normal conditions wind speeds of that velocity would have caused the mission to be aborted, but these were not normal conditions. Von der Heydte was physically exhausted and in great pain. His left forearm had been shattered some weeks earlier in a training accident and he had also damaged his right arm. Since being ordered to undertake the mission he had had little time to sleep. Now the moment had arrived and he would have to lead his untrained men in a jump into the darkness of the night and over a wooded area. The high winds dispersed the men who had jumped over the target area. By 03.50 hours von der Heydte had only six men of his battalion with him. An hour later and there were 26

and these he led to the crossroads which had been named as the Battle Group's rallying-point. Eventually 350 Jaeger had rallied among whom, he was pleased to note, was SS Obersturmfuehrer Etterich. He and his two signallers had made this their first jump without any Para training but had landed well. The men of the battle group, watching from the snowy woods, observed long columns of American vehicles heading southwards, and patrols which von der Heydte sent out returned with the locations of American artillery positions.

All this was vital Intelligence, but the SS Signals group could not raise Control and not knowing whether their messages were being received or not, continued to transmit the details. The 12th SS Division soon learned that Battle Group von der Hedyte was in position – but not from the messages which the SS group were sending out but from intercepted American signals. These reported that there were bodies of German paratroops hanging in the trees; men who had been killed during the drop.

During the afternoon the Battle Group commander pulled his small group back deeper into the woods, moving north-east and en route met up with a further 150 men of his Command. Only a few of the containers had been found and the group was to all intents and purposes armed only with personal firearms. Realizing the serious situation in which his group was placed, von der Heydte made the only decision possible under the circumstances. He released the American prisoners that had been taken during the morning patrols, together with some badly wounded Jaeger. This small group he left by the side of the north-south road, to be picked up by a US convoy. The presence of wounded Jaeger with the released Americans confirmed that there were paratroops in the area, but not how many, or exactly where they were. In moments of excitement soldiers have been known to exaggerate enemy strengths and aware of this the local US commander sent out patrols to comb the woods. Two and a half Companies searched, but met only slight resistance from a few Jaeger. The others had merely moved deeper into the woods away from the Americans. The patrol reports were inconclusive, but then word was received of Germans being seen in other sectors. A false impression was being built up of Jaeger strength.

The post-battle report of 1st Infantry Regiment stated. 'In conjunction with strong ground assaults the Germans also dropped Paratroops at a number of points around Malmédy, Eupen, Monschau and in the heavily wooded areas of this sector. At 15.30 hours on 17th, a convoy carrying the 18th Combat Team en route to organize a defence line and to block the Monschau-Malmédy road, observed paratroops numbering in excess of 500 in the woods and extending over a distance of several miles. We

received orders just before midnight to send out a task force to destroy the enemy who had cut the road between Eupen and Malmédy.' On the basis of that and similar messages it was widely believed that at least a whole Fallschirmjaeger Division had been committed. To meet this imagined concentration of enemy troops the Americans deployed troops who should have been employed in other parts of the Bulge and this overreaction kept combat units out of the line at a time when every man was needed. Paradoxically it was the fact that Battle Group von der Heydte had been scattered widely and not as a concentrated force that created confusion among the US units.

The Luftwaffe made attempts to air drop supplies but these were generally unsuccessful. Very few aircraft found the target area and those containers which were dropped fell wide of the mark and were lost. The one which was retrieved held drinking-water and damp cigarettes. For three days the battle group held out, but no SS panzer spearheads had arrived and even if they did there was little that the Jaeger could do to help them. The men were worn out, wet through, cold and hungry. Patrols had also established that the whole area was covered with American units. Discovery and a battle could not be far off. During the evening of 19 December, von der Heydte assessed the situation and concluded that if necessary he would conduct a fighting retreat towards the German lines. The wounded would only slow his group down and they were sent off in advance and in the same easterly direction. He grouped those Jaeger who were still capable of fighting and led them in an attempt to break through the encircling US ring. Marching through the trackless woods and in the bitter cold of the mountains, the group, starving and soaked, struck the US positions and sought to smash a way through.

The American defence was stronger than Heydte had anticipated and the Jaeger assault was smashed by the fire of US armour, artillery and infantry. The battle group melted back into the woods. Once again the commander assessed the situation and concluded that although a single large group would not be able not fight its way through, it might be possible for small groups to get through.

On 20 December, he broke up his command into small groups of three or four men and sent them out. Fewer than 100 reached the line held by 67th Army Corps at Kalterherberg. He, together with his adjutant and his runner, set out to reach Monschau, one of the first-day objectives and a town which he thought to be in German hands. It was not. Two days later, outside the town, von der Heydte ordered his companions to leave him. He was in agony from his broken arm and weak from lack of food

and loss of sleep. He reached Monschau went into a house and found it filled with Americans to whom he surrendered. For Lieutenant-Colonel Baron von der Heydte the war was over and the last parachute operation to be carried out by the German forces during the Second World War, had also ended.

During the night of 17 December, as Battle Group von der Heydte was dropping over the snowy, wind-swept forests of the Hoher Venn, the main body of Sixth SS Panzer Army, to which it was attached, had already been fighting for more than a day to break out of the steep hills and confining valleys of the Belgian-Luxemburg border.

Another Fallschirmjaeger unit on the strength of Sixth SS Army was 3rd Para Division although its allegience to that Army was of the briefest; a matter of two days only. The Division, which had been fighting for more than two weeks against the First US Army in the Dueren forest was taken from the line, late in the afternoon of 13 December, and posted to I SS Corps. The battalions of 3rd Para trudged out of the dark woods and with no time for rest were marched to the concentration area in the Eifel and into the positions from which they were to play their part in operation 'Wacht am Rhein' only two days later.

The 3rd Para Division had the task of seizing enemy positions in the Berterath–Mandersfeld sector and then of advancing to Hepscheid and Heppenbach. At those places their attacks would have cleared the way for the Panzer spearhead of Sixth SS Army – the 1st and 12th SS Divisions – which would advance westwards to the Maas and to the final objective of Antwerp. For the forthcoming operation all three Jaeger regiments were to be committed. The right wing regiment, 5th Jaeger, was to advance towards Losheimergraben – Bullingen and Schoppen to Faymonville. The centre of the Division's line was held by 9th Regiment whose task it was to pass via Losheim – Lanzerath and Buchholz to Moederscheid. The left wing regiment, No. 8, was to advance via Ormont and Holzheim to Ambleve.

The regiments moved forward behind the barrage and in the glow of artificial moonlight. Almost immediately their assault ran into difficulties. There were more extensive minefields than had been expected and the terrain made it difficult to maintain contact between the advancing regiments. Then, too, the defence of US V Corps, was not just firm but at times heroic. That defence was conducted with incredible skill and every pause in the Jaeger advance brought an American attack. The excellent marksmanship of the US infantry was a feature repeated over and over again, as was the speed with which American artillery units came into action and the accuracy with which they shelled.

Obstructed by minefields to the west of Ormont, the

attack by 8th Para regiment was stalled until two Companies of SS Engineers from 1st SS Division were able to force their way through the traffic-congested roads to reach the area and help the Para Engineers to gap the fields and lift the mines from the roads.

By midday I SS Corps had not gained the objectives they had been set. The US line had not been breached and only one of three roads had been cleared for the Panzer advance. The single positive result of the heavy fighting of that first day was that 3rd Para Division had captured Lanzerath and with that success a major section of the road from Losheim to Buchholz railway station had been cleared. The road could now be used by the Panzer units of I SS Corps to whom the problem of blown bridges was unimportant – the Panzer would simply divert round them. Late in the evening the difficulties of the morning and early afternoon were overcome in the sector held by 5th Jaeger Regiment whose attack also brought forward its right wing neighbour, 12th Volksgrenadier Division. Late in the evening of the 16th, there was evidence that the anticipated breakthrough might occur very soon. So seriously did the officers of V Corps consider a rupture of their line possible that when the 99th US Infantry Division, which was holding the line there, asked for a single infantry battalion as reinforcement it received not just that for which it had asked by also a squadron each of tanks and SP guns.

During that first evening of 'Wacht am Rhein', the SS Panzer Battle Group which should have been, according to Hitler's detailed planning, thundering along the roads towards the Maas, was still held up at Losheim. This battle group, commanded by Sturmbannfuehrer Jochen Peiper, was the spearhead of Sixth SS Panzer Army, just as that Army was the spearhead of the whole operation. Peiper,

never a patient man, felt himself frustrated by being unable to carry out his orders to drive westwards. Exhibiting that brand of ruthless determination for which the SS Panzer Divisions were renowned, he ordered his tank driver to run over the German horse-drawn artillery columns which were blocking the Losheim–Losheimergraben road ahead of him. Those who did not get out of his way were crushed under the tracks of the Panzers. Despite these measures it was not until early evening that Battle Group Peiper reached the start-line of his attack.

In books written by SS authors, the 9th Para Regiment is shown in a very poor light during that first night of battle. Peiper, according to these books, had arrived in Losheim shortly after 19.30 hours. There he received an order from Corps directing him to turn west to Lanzerath where the advance by 9th Para Regiment had stalled. As he marshalled his column ready to advance he was told that the road along which he was to take the battle group was still mined. The specialist Engineer Companies had not reached Losheim. The SS officer's method of clearing mined roads was draconian. He ordered his leading Company to drive on and lost five vehicles before the mined area of the road was clear. It was not quite as wasteful as it reads. Peiper knew that the speed and efficiency of the SS Panzer repair shops meant that his damaged machines would soon be 'runners' again. They would be ready for action when he needed them.

Driving along the Lanzerath road Peiper could see no signs of any Jaeger advance. It was clear that the attack had stopped and he could not understand why. Halting his King Tiger outside an inn he went in and found it filled with officers of 9th Regiment who told him that their units were unable to advance in face of strong enemy opposition in the woods along the road and railway line.

Right: General der Flieger Student inspects a parade of Fallschirmjaeger during May 1944. Firmly committed now to a ground role, they wait and prepare for the coming invasion. (Brian L. Davis)

Peiper went on foot to check the accuracy of that report and found no one in the Para regiment who could tell him just how strong the US opposition was. Infuriated by this display of inaction, Peiper soon became involved in a furious argument with the 9th Regiment commander whose 1st Battalion he promptly commandeered. He ordered the Jaeger to mount the outside of his King Tiger tanks and the column resumed the advance with the heavy reconnaissance vehicles of Haupsturmfuehrer Preuss's No. 10 Company leading the way.

The orders from I SS Corps for 17 December were that the attack was to be continued with the aim of breaking the front of US V Corps. Peiper mounted a strong attack which after initial obstruction broke the line and his Panzers rolled over 3rd Battalion of 394th US Infantry Regiment. The 3rd Para Division passed through the gap in the line which the SS commander had created and the direction of its advance changed from west to north-west taking it into the area of 12th Volksgrenadier Division.

On its sector, 5th Regiment, moving via Losheim-graben to Neuhaus, had reached the southern edge of Bullingen. In the centre, 9th Regiment, following the advance by the SS Panzer battle group on foot, took Moedersheid and by first light on the 19th had reached Schoppen. The left wing regiment, the 8th, striking from Ormont passed through Heppenbach and had reached Ambleve by the 20th. From these points which the regiments of 3rd Para reached during 19/20 December, there was to be little further progress, although by the end of the month the important north/south road between St-Vith and Malmédy had been cut at Ligneuville. A combination of heavy losses, determined American resistance and the exhaustion of the Jaeger after so many weeks of unbroken battle, first slowed and then halted the division's advance.

In addition, there were other difficulties, the chief of which was that the SS Panzer spearhead had moved farther northwards and westwards out of the sector held by 3rd Para. In the area of Stourmont and La Gleize, Peiper was still trying to find a way out of the hills and into the more open country leading up to the Maas. In that ambition he was frustrated by a strong American defence.

The end of the year found the regiments of 3rd Para still holding the line, but now deeply aware that the enterprise upon which they had entered with such anticipation of victory had failed.

The task of 5th Para Division during Operation 'Wacht am Rhein' was, as part of 85th Corps, to form the right wing of Seventh Panzer Army, to reach a line running from St-Hubert to Attert and then by a mobile defence to protect the southern flank of Fifth Panzer Army as that force advanced westwards towards the Maas.

When the offensive opened, 5th Para had only two regiments on its strength and these advanced towards the River Our with 14th Jaeger on the right and 15th on the left. The 13th Regiment had been detached to 'stiffen' the 352nd Volksgrenadier Division on 5th Division's left flank. Even during the first day of the offensive there were signs that the confidence felt at OKW on the outcome of 'Wacht am Rhein', would not be justified. In any operation the attacking force enjoys an initial advantage, that of surprise, and since the shock of battle would come in against only a few American divisions holding a great length of front, Hitler and the Supreme Command were convinced that an immediate success was inevitable; that the advance would be so fast that the US troops would be unable to form a solid front. The laws of *Blitzkrieg* would apply and in the panic that would ensue on the Allied side the River Maas would be reached on time and the storming advance continued until Antwerp itself had been taken.

This did not happen. Although on that first day 5th Division advanced on a broad front, the 11th SP Para Brigade had to be brought into action quickly to beat down US resistance in Nachthanderscheid and Walsdorf. Bridges across the rivers of the Ardennes were vital to the success of the operation and the 5th Para Engineer Battalion worked at full speed to put one over the Our across which the artillery regiment could pass and give support to the Jaeger regiments. The SP Brigade, whose vehicles' weight would have smashed the wooden structure, forded the Our and climbed the steep bank to move on and give more flexible fire cover to the battalions wading through deep snow towards their objectives.

The resistance which the US troops put up against the German assault was not everywhere so determined as that first encountered. At some places first-class formations retreated immediately while on other sectors rear-echelon soldiers, men from whom little could be expected, fought furiously to hold back the Para regiments. The situation was not good. The 352nd Volksgrenadier Division on the left could make only slow progress against determined American opposition; the advance of the two Para regiments in the centre of the line was delayed by the need to keep in touch with the 352nd as well as by repeated American counter-attacks. Only on the right flank was the Panzer Lehr Division pushing so strongly forward that its reconnaissance units had advanced past Hosingen. The battle line was, thus, echeloned north-west to south-east – a potentially dangerous situation offering the Americans the chance to make flank attacks once they had regained their strength.

The second day of battle saw both regiments of the 5th still fighting hard, forcing the advance but depending more and more upon the SP Brigade which switched from one regimental sector to another, on calls for its guns to beat down US opposition. The slowness of the Volksgrenadier Division in coming forward retarded the advance of the rest of 85th Corps and that delay gave the US defence time to coalesce. By 18 December the front had hardened as the initial uncertainties and panic which had beset some US units whose men were recruits and whose 'blooding' this was, was replaced by a determination to give as good as they got. Despite the stiffening resistance 14th and 15th Regiments were able to gain ground.

'Those days in the Ardennes were dark, short, cold and wet, and the nights were bitter. The snow was in places more than calf deep and there were no winter camouflage uniforms so that we stood out against the white background. It was hard work trudging through the snow along the narrow country roads, each of us wrapped in our own thoughts until machine-gun fire brought us back to reality. Artillery fire we tended to ignore unless it was clear that we were the direct targets, but when the machine-guns or mortars opened up we deployed and in short rushes moved towards the centres of resistance. The American troops had little idea of defensive tactics – we did not known at that time that they were in the line for the first time and were therefore completely inexperienced in fighting. Often just one single machine-gun would be firing and it would not be supported by a second weapon. It was also easy to work round the flanks of US units. When they realized that we were behind them they would often leave their guns and run, usually straight into our fire. They seemed genuinely astonished when we captured them that we had not gone to ground when their heavy-calibre machine-guns opened up, but had instead continued with our attack. It seemed that their standard tactic was to lie down under machine-gun fire until their artillery started a barrage upon our machine-gun positions.

There were some units which fought with great bravery. There was one supplies dump where the men held us off for a couple of hours and might have continued to resist, but their ammunition ran out. They all expected to be summarily shot after surrendering. Our advance was further delayed by the fact that we stayed a while to sample the food supplies which were in the store.'

The period from 18 to 20 December was one of fluctuating fortunes with first the Paras and then the Americans holding the advantage. Attack was succeeded by counter-attack and every gain at one point by a loss at some other place. On the 18th, the 14th Regiment, which had had no time to regroup since 'Wacht am Rhein'

opened, was halted on the western edge of Weiler in order to do so. During the following day the opposition which had been delaying 15th Regiment crumbled and the Jaeger battalions moved smoothly forward via Bourscheid towards Nothum. The 14th was less lucky and as it renewed its advance towards Hocher it was struck by strong American armoured forces and driven southwards until it reached Goesdorf where it collected and regrouped. During that day the Para Engineer Battalion was brought forward and, covered by the fire of Nebelwerfer projectors, its attacks broke the resistance of the garrison at Wiltz. By midday on 20 December, the town had fallen with nearly 1,000 prisoners and many trucks which the Engineers put into immediate use together with the 25 fully intact and undamaged Sherman tanks.

At about this time 5th Para, which had been recreated out of the remnants of the original Division lost in Normandy, became the spearhead of the advancing Seventh Army. Their neighbours on each flank were in difficulty and to bring them forward the 5th's two regiments extended their own fronts and their attacks got the advance moving again. But the continuing failure of the left wing formations to come forward into line with 5th Para faced it with the threat of a flank attack and the Division halted, changed its front to face southwards and went over to defence. To strengthen the Jaeger line the 13th Regiment was detached from the Volksgrenadier Division and returned to the 5th.

On 22 December, the situation in the Ardennes changed dramatically. Hitler's expectations of a victory had been based in part upon the bad weather which would prevent the Allied air forces from flying and thus allow his ground operations to develop without interference from fighter-bombers and rocket-firing aircraft. On the 22nd the low clouds were suddenly blown away and the blue skies were filled with Allied aircraft bombing and strafing the German formations. Under the massive blows of British and American squadrons the German forces staggered and slowed. Another factor was active in reducing the German effort; supply difficulties meant that little fuel was coming forward through the congestion on the narrow country roads, and without petrol the advance could not continue. Operation 'Wacht am Rhein', lost momentum and by Christmas there were no more hopes that it might succeed. By this time, too, Eisenhower's counter-moves to contain and then destroy the bulge were having effect.

On 23 December, the front held by 5th Para, the Jaeger regiments and the SP Battalion came under heavy and repeated attacks by the tanks of 4th US Armoured Division as Patton's Third Army, having completed its change of front from west to north, began to smash at the walls of the German salient. Under that pressure the Para regiments were forced more and more towards Bastogne and then formed part of the ring of German units encircling the town.

Determined American probing attacks to relieve Bastogne found the boundary between the right wing of 5th Para and the neighbouring Fifth Panzer Army. These American probes developed into heavy attacks and in the fighting to defend Chaumont, 14th Jaeger Regiment suffered severe losses. The whole Division was now fighting desperately, not only to hold the positions it had gained, but also to prevent a link-up between the American 101st Airborne Division besieged in Bastogne and Patton's armour. In a desperate endeavour to smash the defenders in Bastogne, von Manteuffel, the Fifth Panzer Army Commander, opened an attack covered by an air raid on the town by Luftwaffe bombers. He committed as many troops as he could spare. The 15th Panzer Grenadier, the 26th Volksgrenadier Division, the Panzer Lehr Division and, from the south-east, the Jaeger regiments of 5th Para. The attack was timed to go in at 03.00 hours on Christmas Eve and the assaulting units had barely crossed their start-lines when they were struck by well-controlled and co-ordinated US artillery fire. Anti-tank shells and conventional artillery crashed down upon von Manteuffel's attack. Twenty-seven of his tanks were destroyed or left burning outside Bastogne and the German infantry and Jaeger, now without armoured support, tried frantically to dig into the frozen ground to escape the fury of the American artillery fire and to prepare themselves for the counter-attack that would inevitably come in against them. In despair von Manteuffel ordered his forces to go over to the defensive. They could do little else.

On 26 December, the men of 37th Tank Battalion, the point-unit of 4th US Armoured Division, reached the high ground south of Bastogne and saw the little town lying in the valley below them. Colonel Creighton Abrams ordered the advance. 'We are going into Bastogne. Everybody ready? Right, then straight down the middle, lets go!' The Lead Troop was made up of the new super-heavy Shermans, 40-ton giants armed with 75mm guns. At more than a mile range they opened fire and headed by those King Cobra tanks the assault wave of Abrams's 37th Tank Battalion charged downhill. Their thrust-line took them across the shallow slit trenches manned by the Jaeger of 5th Para whose men sought to engage the American vehicles at close range. Those who made the attempt fell in the fire of the US Infantry riding into battle in halftracks. The German ring around Bastogne was broken. The town was relieved and with little pause the 4th US Armoured, in conjunction with other armoured and airborne units, then began to push the German forces eastwards and back to the lines from which their offensive had started. It was upon 13th Regiment that the first furious attacks fell and under the pressure of 80th US Infantry Division the regiment began to give ground until the flank of 5th Para at Nothum was threatened. The very last reserves of the Para Division were brought into the battle line. These were the Nebelwerfer Battalion and the Anti-tank Battalion. The latter had lost all its vehicles and guns in the advance; victims of Allied air attack. The gunners were put in as infantry but even that reinforcement did not increase Jaeger strength to a point where the line could be held. By the end of 1944, the defiant remnants of 5th Para Division, exhausted by weeks of continuous battle, fought in appalling conditions, were withdrawing along the southern wall of the Ardennes bulge back to the start-lines from which they had entered upon Operation 'Wacht am Rhein'.

The evidence that the Third Reich was doomed to go down in defeat piled up during 1944. There could be no hope now that she could win the war. The best that could be hoped for was a stalemate and that was unlikely for her prodigious efforts to divide the Allies politically had failed.

Militarily, her situation was nearly hopeless. In the south the mountain barrier of the Alps might delay the Allied armies in Italy in their advance towards Austria and southern Germany, but in the east the Red Army had crushed Army Group Centre and had driven through its shattered front to reach the eastern provinces of the Reich. Then, in the June of 1944, the invasion of north-west Europe had been accomplished.

The employment of rocket missiles against the United Kingdom would not bring about a stalemate. For every indiscriminate rocket that fell on England, one hundred tons of aimed bombs fell on Germany's industries. The attempts to destroy the armies of the Western Allies by the offensive in the Ardennes in December had been unsuccessful and, as early as October, American troops stood on German soil at Aachen. The Third Reich was dying.

Throughout 1944, the Fallschirmjaeger had demonstrated their tenacity in defence and skill in attack, particularly at Cassino and at Anzio. They had shown the qualities of self-sacrifice in such forlorn hopes as the raid on Tito's Headquarters, in the Falaise pocket and during the Battle of the Bulge. Not until late in the year did the Para Army go into action as a single force and then only fighting in a ground role. The bitterness felt by many Para commanders who saw the demonstration of Allied strength when the Anglo-American Airborne Army dropped on the east bank of the Rhine during the spring of 1945, must have found an echo in the hearts of the rank and file. . . . 'If only we had such strength. . . .'

18. 'On the far bank of the Rhine'
THE RHINELAND CAMPAIGN, DECEMBER 1944

As a corollary to Operation 'Wacht am Rhein' as well as in an effort to revive the failing momentum of that offensive, Hitler planned and launched Operation 'Nordwind', an attack by Nineteenth Army intended to recapture north Alsace and to destroy the US Seventh Army. Fuehrer Headquarters confidently predicted that the Allies would have to draw off strength from the Ardennes in order to contest 'Nordwind' and that as a consequence of dividing the enemy's strength one of the two German assaults must succeed in its intentions.

For 'Nordwind', a force of eight Divisions was assembled, including 6th SS Mountain, 17th SS, 15th and 21st Panzer and 7th Para. General Erdmann, commanding the Fallschirmjaeger, received orders in the week before Christmas to move his Division and on 25th December, the advance party marched to positions north of the Hagenau forest. The Fallschirmjaeger Division now passed out of the control of II Para Corps and under that of Supreme Commander West who intended, initially, to use this élite formation in an attack against the flank of the advancing Canadian Army. That operation was cancelled and the Jaeger Regiments were pulled out of their positions along the Maas where their place was taken by units of 190th Division.

Details of 'Nordwind' were known to Allied Intelligence Officers who were concerned that several German Divisions were 'missing' from the Intelligence picture; that is to say their exact location could not be determined. Intelligence was convinced that these missing Divisions would undertake the new offensive. As we have seen from the account of the Ardennes offensive, Patton's Third Army had swung 180 degrees from its eastward thrust to form the southern wall of the Allied salient. The only major formation available to fill that gap in the line where Patton's Army had once stood, was Seventh Army and orders were issued for it to extend its front. Thus, that single formation now held a battle line which had once been covered by two US armies. The German High Command department, 'Foreign Armies West' was well aware of the Allied weakness on that sector and proposed that it should be against Seventh Army's thinly held lines

Right: Urban warfare in the West as the Allies close up to the Westwall. (Brian L. Davis)

that the main blow of 'Nordwind' should fall.

There was an additional reason for the new German offensive to be undertaken. On the west bank of the Rhine a large force of 100,000 German soldiers was holding a bridgehead around Colmar. Were a strike by that force in the Colmar pocket able to link up with the assault out of the Hagenau forest, not only would Patch's US Seventh Army be destroyed, but Strasbourg could be recaptured, gaining a prestige victory, and pressure would be taken off the Ardennes front.

The greatest number of General Patch's soldiers were raw recruits, without adequate training and mostly lacking in combat experience. They would, within days, be attacked by élite German units with years of campaigning behind them. The result was, initially, a series of humiliating reverses for the US Divisions. The first German attacks on 1 January 1945, were overwhelming and swept away most of the inexperienced 44th and 100th Divisions. Although the German units in 'Nordwind' were not up to establishment in weapons, those they had were used to good effect. As an example of this, some officers of the SS Mountain Division, fired 'whistling' cartridges from their Very pistols. The strange and piercing sound which was produced, caused panic flight among the green troops who believed themselves to be under bombardment by missiles with 'sledge-hammer force'.

For days the troops in the Hagenau area and in the Colmar pocket fought their way forward and it seemed as if Strasburg would soon be lost. Then, on 10 January, the American front hardened and the US units began to mount counter-attacks. One of these went in against a bridgehead at Gambsheim and such was its fury that the units being attacked asked for immediate help. The 7th Para was sent forward. The Division had only been raised during September 1944, and it was a strong formation up to establishment in men and weapons. The task which it was given was, in conjunction with the 15th and 21st Panzer Divisions, to crush the US forces in its sector, and from that position of strength smash a way through to Hagenau there to link up with the Gambsheim bridgehead. The first Jaeger attack was a classic one in which they advanced with great élan, forcing back the US 79th Division. The attacks began well, but then in the deep, snowy woods to the north of Hagenau, American resistance stiffened and the Jaeger regiments were involved in heavy fighting. Losses mounted and slowly the initiative on that sector was lost. On 8 January, the 12th and 14th US Armored Divisions, supported by 79th Infantry Division, struck the German line in a series of strong counterattacks. One curious fact emerged from these operations. An American post-battle account illustrated the amazing prodigality of the American tank men. One task force fired

in the few hours of that winter day, no fewer than 170 HE shells and 6,500 rounds of .30 calibre machine-gun ammunition, without hitting a single German.

At Colmar, on 20 January, the Franco-US counter-attack went in to beat back the German offensive which had advanced to within eleven miles (seventeen kilometres) of Strasburg. Under that pressure the German Nineteenth Army collapsed and by 9 February, its last units had been flung back across the Rhine. In the Hagenau sector 7th Para had managed to hold the line against the US armoured assaults, but in the confused battle fought out in the heavily wooded area, there were heavy losses on both sides.

'We were put in', recalled one man of 18th Jaeger Regiment. 'at those places were other German units had had their fronts penetrated by the Americans, had been outflanked or simply given way. What surprised us was the sheer power of the US artillery in support of quite small operations. But it was fire which was quite indiscriminate, not being directed at specific targets, merely a blanket coverage. Under that fire their tanks would come on, hesitatingly and without much confidence. They did not advance in any sort of fire and movement tactic, but would halt for long periods while their commanders studied the ground through binoculars. A salvo of shells or the appearance of a pair of Tigers was sufficient to cause them to turn back, leaving the infantry without protection. We soon worked out a tactic which was to drive off the tanks and then to cut up the infantry with our machine-guns and mortars.

Although the American infantry were quite inexperienced they were very brave. One of their attacks came in with their lines properly spaced out and as well lined-up as if on manoeuvres. It was a very brave attempt which persisted despite the heavy losses which we caused them. Our losses were also heavy, chiefly from the shelling, but also from air attack, as well as in the missions which we Jaeger undertook south of Hagenau. The terrible weather added to the general misery although we occupied houses and barns when we were not actively in the line.

It was not long after we reached the battle area that our attacks went in and as a result we had soon restored the situation. The front stayed almost immobile from that time on and did not become alive again until the American offensive opened. We had most casualties during the first days when we were fighting to hold the American tanks and to close the gap in our front. On 26th January, the advance party of our Division left the Hagenau positions and by the first days of February, the remainder of the Division was back in reserve in the Kevelaer positions. We had barely settled down when the Allied offensive opened in the Reichswald and we were sent to that sector.'

1945

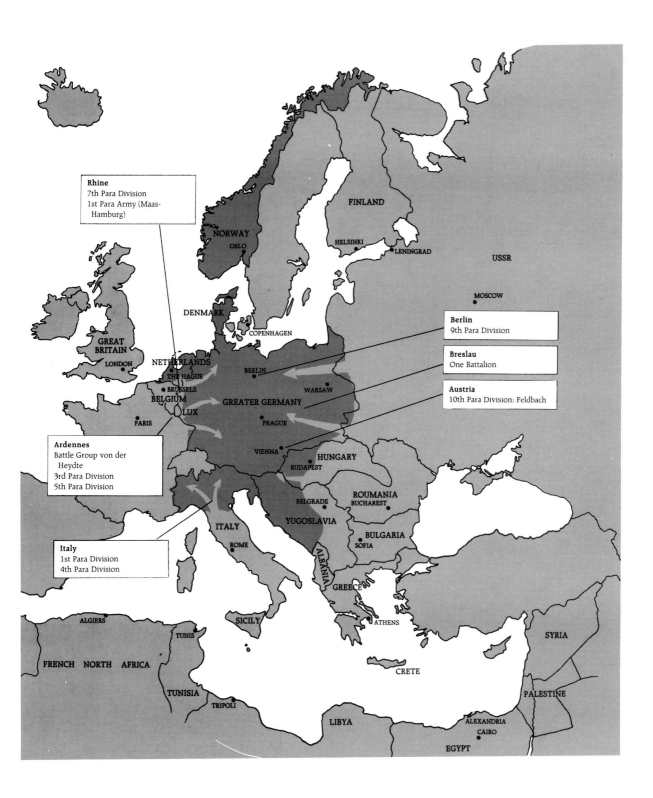

Rhine
7th Para Division
1st Para Army (Maas-Hamburg)

Berlin
9th Para Division

Breslau
One Battalion

Austria
10th Para Division: Feldbach

Ardennes
Battle Group von der Heydte
3rd Para Division
5th Para Division

Italy
1st Para Division
4th Para Division

ICELAND

NORWAY
OSLO

FINLAND

HELSINKI

LENINGRAD

USSR

MOSCOW

DENMARK

COPENHAGEN

GREAT BRITAIN
LONDON

NETHERLANDS
THE HAGUE
BRUSSELS
BELGIUM
LUX
PARIS

BERLIN

WARSAW

GREATER GERMANY

PRAGUE

VIENNA

HUNGARY
BUDAPEST

ROUMANIA
BUCHAREST

BELGRADE

YUGOSLAVIA

BULGARIA
SOFIA

ITALY
ROME

ALBANIA

GREECE

ALGIERS

TUNIS

SICILY

ATHENS

SYRIA

FRENCH NORTH AFRICA

TUNISIA

TRIPOLI

CRETE

PALESTINE

LIBYA

ALEXANDRIA
CAIRO

EGYPT

19. 'We have done our duty to the last...'

THE END IN THE WEST, JANUARY-MAY 1945

Despite the best efforts of the German forces in the west to carry out Hitler's demands, Operation 'Wacht am Rhein', had failed and in the first weeks of January 1945, the Ardennes bulge began to deflate under the pressure of Montgomery from the north and north-west, and of Patton from the south and south-west. Nor had operation 'Nordwind' gained the objectives which the Fuehrer had set. As a consequence of these failures by mid-January the German armies in the west were everywhere giving ground in the face of Allied pressure.

To summarize briefly, the events which were to occur on the Western Front between January and May 1945. Montgomery's Army Group opened its drive towards the Rhine in Ferbruary and this was followed by the assaults of American Army Groups. In March Allied pressure forced the Fallschirmjaeger Divisions back across the Rhine. Once established on that river's eastern bank, the British and American forces opened up major, new offensives against the German Army Groups opposing them. Aggressive American thrusts to the north and south of the Ruhr split the German battle line in the west. First Para Army, together with the other formations which were positioned to the north of that divide, were pushed north and then north-eastwards by the pressure of the British and the Canadians. The other German forces on the Western Front were driven eastwards towards the Elbe, where the US and Soviet troops would meet at the end of April. First Para Army, maintaining a dogged defence, moved slowly back towards the harbours and ports of the north German coast but under the hammer blows of Montgomery's Twelfth Army Group the cohesion of the German forces on that part of the Western Front began to fail.

It was not that the component units did not fight well. They did. Indeed, the Fallschirmjaeger Divisions did more than their duty demanded. Without counting the cost, these young soldiers – for there were few veterans left now in the ranks – swung into the assault with the same élan as the early regiments had shown in Crete and in Africa. Where the Jaeger were forced on to the defensive

they held their positions with the same fortitude as the Jaeger had shown at Volkhov and Cassino. But raw courage availed the units little. Under the crushing burden of Allied superiority in men and weapons, the Para Divisions were forced apart until, by the beginning of May, there was so little cohesion between them that those final bitter battles were fought usually in isolation and as regimental groups. Despite the crises which occured during those fateful weeks it was still not unusual for small units of Jaeger to be removed from their parent formations and committed to 'fire brigade' actions. As a consequence of these secondments a clear, comprehensive and chronological account of Fallschirmjaeger operations east of the Rhine is not possible. It is, therefore, my intention to describe the actions of each of the Para Divisions individually and not as part of First Para Army.

But we have not yet reached that point. It is still only the first week of the New Year and the German Army in the West is still embattled along the Maas holding a number of bridgeheads on the western bank of that river.

The front held by First Para Army ran from the Reichswald in the north to Roermond in the south. On the right flank was 47th Panzer Corps (6th Fallschirmjaeger Division, 15th Panzer Grenadier and 116th Panzer Division). In the centre was II Para Corps whose order of battle was, 84th Division, 7th and 8th Para Divisions. Army's left flank was held by 86 Corps with 180th and 190th Infantry Divisions. The 20th Jaeger Regiment had been inserted between 84th and 180th Divisions to close a small gap in the line.

It was to be against Schlemm's Para Army that the full force of an Allied offensive would come in. For that operation Eisenhower laid the main emphasis on the northern flank which was held by Montgomery's Twenty-First Army Group and Simpson's US Ninth Army. This Anglo-American force was ordered to open Operation 'Veritable' on 8 February 1945. German Intelligence anticipated the offensive, but believed that it would not start until the Allies knew that OKW had weakened the Western Front by withdrawing troops and sending them eastwards. Von Rundstedt's appreciation concluded, '. . . the attack is expected to be launched from the Roermond – Venlo bend of the Maas against the Rhineland area. . . . The fate of the Reich depends upon a successful defensive battle against this major, new, Anglo-American offensive. . . .' There was, however, little unison among the German commanders concerning Allied intentions. Blaskowitz, commanding Army Group H, was convinced that the main blow would be against Venlo. General Schlemm disagreed. It was his opinion that Montgomery would strike in the Reichswald sector in order to gain the Rhine at Kleve. The success of such an operation to outflank the Siegfried Line would also bring the added danger that the northern wing of the German armies in the west would be rolled up. Rundstedt accepted Blaskowitz's prognosis and moved his reserves to the left wing in anticipation of the thrust in that sector. The 7th Para Division was consequently withdrawn from the 'Nordwind' operation and moved from its positions at Hagenau into others east of Venlo. The 21st Regiment of 7th Para occupied the Siebengewald area and that Division's 19th Regiment moved into the sector around Weeze. Para Nebelwerfer Battalion No. 21, a formation under Para Army command, took post in the Lobberich area.

Late in the evening of 7 February, the area between Kleve and Weeze was subjected to a concentrated artillery and aerial bombardment. The history of Second British Army recorded that, '. . . over a thousand guns were employed in the preliminary bombardment, which was one of the most concentrated and terrifying of the whole campaign. It was not surprising that when the attack started at 10.30 hours on 8 February, it gained immediate success against little enemy opposition at first. . . .' The Headquarters of First Para Army was near Bocholt, in the village of Dixperlo, and the officers there could tell from the weight and direction of the British fire that the offensive had begun and that its main weight was upon 84th Division in the Reichswald position. Reports coming in confirmed that Schlemm's appreciation had been correct but Blaskowitz remained unconvinced. The Army Group Commander was still certain that the main blow would be at Venlo and when Schlemm reported, during the afternoon of 8 February, that he had moved 7th Para Division to support 84th Division, Blaskowitz was furious and ordered that it be brought back to Venlo. Schlemm was in a difficult situation; he had to obey an order that was in his opinion militarily unsound. He compromised and halted 7th Para as it moved northwards, holding it until the situation was resolved. Clarity came on the 9th, when it was finally agreed that Operation 'Veritable', was part of an offensive aimed at seizing the Reichswald. A second operation which was launched in conjunction with

'Veritable', was Operation 'Grenade' by US Ninth Army on the right wing of Montgomery's Army Group. Between these two Allied pincers the German forces on the west bank of the Rhine would be encircled and destroyed. As a preliminary move to meet the thrust in the north, Schlemm put 7th Division into movement again and it was taken by truck to the combat zone. U. W. Best, of 7th Para Division, who had been in the Hagenau operation, recalled that the British barrage could be heard from a great distance and as his unit neared the front the noise of the explosions made a frightening impact. 'One long continuous growling . . . indicated that a barrage of shocking intensity was falling on the positions in the Reichswald. Our units had all been at instant readiness so that we lost no time in moving out. After leaving the trucks we marched to where the barrage was falling. We found a situation that was very alarming for it was clear that the Army units in the Reichswald had been overrun. We were told that it was to be our job to drive the Tommies back and regain our former front line.'

Blaskowitz's delay in releasing the 7th Para Division meant that its units did not arrive in the battle area as a whole and, therefore it could not be committed as a complete formation. The situation in the Reichswald had deteriorated too far to permit any delay. The Allied attack already threatened a breakthrough at several key points and it was into these positions that the individual Jaeger battalions and regiments were flung in.

Now it was a case of each and every unit that could be released being sent to the Reichswald. Among them was 16th Para Regiment, already serving away from its parent 6th Para Division. The 16th was taken from the positions it was holding along the River Lek near Brakel and put into the Reichswald where its determined resistance helped to halt the British advance. The next Fallschirmjaeger regiment to arrive was the 20th which opened its attack from Zelderheide and had soon gained contact with detachments of the splintered 84th Division. U. W. Best describes the situation in those February days. 'We knew that we were fighting for the soil of our country. This was our Fatherland and we were determined to defend it at all cost. But it was a hard struggle; truly very hard. Despite its bitterness there was mutual respect between ourselves and the British. We and they respected the Red Cross flag – we all knew that in the winter weather the wounded had to be brought in quickly. For them to remain on the battlefield unattended would be to condemn them to death. We respected the Red Cross flag – after all, it might be we tomorrow who would be wounded and have to be brought in under its protection.

The British brought small tanks [Bren gun carriers] into the Reichswald. These were fitted with flame-throwers and were fearsome until we realized that they could not move off the forest paths. Also they were often not supported by infantry. Our engineers mined the roads which smashed some of the little tanks. Others were knocked out by satchel charges or hollow-charge grenades. We found it very easy to break the rhythm of the attack of the British infantry. Snipers and some well-sited MG 42s would drive the leading files to ground, where they would lie inactive until their barrage came down, whereupon they would stand up and resume their advance.'

The second week of February saw continuous attacks by British Divisions along the front of First Para Army. The southern edge of the Reichswald, between Bedburg and Gennep, was held until 12 February, when 2nd Battalion of 19th Para Regiment, exhausted, without heavy weapons and completely isolated, was overrolled in the open country to the west of Bedburg. The other units of 7th Para pulled back towards Goch with 20th Regiment holding the left flank and 21st Regiment the right one, and it was against 20th Regiment's left flank on the River Maas that 51st (Highland) Division made a violent thrust on the 12th. Only after days of battle could the Scots capture the tactically important town of Gennep. It was now vital for First Para Army to hold the sector running from Gennep to Goch and to the defence of that area a miscellany of units was committed. Groups from 2nd Para Regiment, from 180th Division and 20th Para Regiment were moved forward.

On 13 February, Schlemm moved Army TAC HQ from Dixperlo to a farm near Xanten. In the new area he would be nearer to the front and thus better able to control the Reichswald battle which was now reaching its climax. An order from Hitler then directed Schlemm to move the headquarters to Rheinberg, in the south of Para Army's sector. The Fuehrer *Befehl* declared, despite all evidence to the contrary, that the vital wing was in the south. In order to hold the area which Hitler had declared to be the most important, Schlemm was forced to pull out most of the units on the Reichswald front, leaving only the decimated regiments of 7th Para Division to hold the advancing British.

In support of the Jaeger regiments in the Reichswald the heavy weapons battalions of 7th were moved up together with the 12th Para SP Gun Brigade which was taken out of the Para Army reserve for this battle. On 13 February, the SP Brigade, supported by 2nd Battalion of the Para Training Regiment, attacked towards Heijen but was forced back to its start-line by an infantry and tank defence backed by rocket-firing Typhoons of the RAF. British attacks came in all along the line between the Maas and the Rhine, with the main weight upon the small market towns of Hassum and Hommersum, where 20th Regiment was positioned. The attempts by British XXX Corps to tear the Para's left flank away from the Maas were made with an unprecedented ferocity in which long and continuous barrages, flame-throwing tanks and low-level attacks by fighter-bombers were prominent. The battle along the railway line between Hossum and Hommersum, finally concentrated itself around the Hussum railway station which the Jaeger had converted to a fortress. In that small area the Paras of 20th Regiment were subjected to incessant attacks, barrages, bombardments, flame-thrower assaults and aircraft bombing. The regiment's losses were fearful, not only in numbers but in the way in which they were killed. Only with difficulty could the survivors of that terrible fight disengage from the British and pull back southwards across the railway line, away from a town which held for them all memories of the most frightful suffering.

The assault across the Maas, by 52nd (Lowland) Division behind another heavy barrage, failed to win ground against 2nd Para Regiment. The battle for Afferden, which began on 16 February, lasted for days and during the fighting two battalions of the Royal Scots were so badly mauled that all their officers and NCOs were lost and a private soldier was commanding the remnants. The regiments of 34th Armoured Brigade, which were supporting the Royal Scots, were crushed by 12th Para SP Brigade and had to be taken out of action. It was not only the SPs which won victories against the British armour during those days. The Para Training Battalion and 2nd Regiment went into action with Panzerfaust launchers, smashing the tanks and flinging back the Scottish infantry. The fighting ability and resolution with which the Jaeger defended their positions was acknowledged in a tribute in the divisional history of 52nd (Lowland) Division. German post-battle reports spoke of 300 British armoured fighting vehicles destroyed after that four-day battle.

Despite these local successes, the advances of Second British Army and First Canadian Army in the north, and Simpson's US Ninth Army in the south, could not be halted. Slowly the Germans were forced back towards the Rhine. By 1 March the SPs of 7th Para Division, which were forming the rearguard, reached Kevelaer. There were still victories to be won against the masses of British tanks pressing forward to the Rhine, but individual heroism could not stem that flood. At Xanten the Jaeger of the 7th were forced to give up the bridgehead they held at Wesel. At Bruedrich the last Fallschirmjaeger on the west bank of the Rhine embarked on ferries and crossed to the eastern side, there to prepare themselves for the assault which the Allies would soon undertake to vault that river barrier.

At this point let us take up again Adolf Strauch's account of the last months of the war. His name had been put forward as an officer cadet, and to test his leadership qualities Strauch was ordered to undertake a reconnaissance mission across the Maas. During the night of 5/6 January he and two comrades crossed the river and entered enemy territory, Marching by compass the group struck out for Heel but soon found themselves among enemy units. Without being detected they managed to bypass the positions and, getting through a swamp, crossed the Heel road and entered a wood where there were a number of enemy tank units. At daybreak the group moved to the Venlo–Maastricht road where they carried out a road watch. For hours they observed columns of vehicles and guns moving south. After leaving their observation point they were seen by a civilian who warned the British. The patrol was pursued and fired upon, forcing it to hole up for the rest of the day. At last light Strauch and his comrades moved back to the Maas destroying telephone lines as they pulled back. They crossed the river and made their report that a major offensive was being prepared.

At the end of January the Allies opened their attack south of Roermond. The 2nd Battalion was moved from the Maas positions to Montfort. A Fuehrer *Befehl* (a directive from Hitler) ordered that the town had to be held to the last. Artillery fire smothered the positions and neither rations nor ammunition reached the battalion area. Montfort was abandoned and the Company Commander was accused of refusing to obey the Fuehrer's order. The battalion then took up defensive positions at St Odilienberg where there was patrol activity – not always successfully carried out. At the end of February there was a move into the bridgehead at Wesel after which the battalion held the line from Sonsbeck to Xanten. When the Wesel bridgehead was given up, Strauch's unit moved across the Rhine in assault boats and was taken by truck to Rees. This was a bitter disappointment to the Jaeger, who had been in action without rest since September, and had hoped to spend a period out of the line. Instead they had to set up defensive positions, and established Company HQ in the cellar of a mill. Replacements arrived, including a number of Volkssturm, untrained Home Guards whose presence brought to all the Jaeger the realization that there was now no chance of final victory but only the certainly of a final battle. Without hope Strauch's burnt-out detachments prepared themselves to do their duty to the last.

Twenty-five Allied Divisions opened their assault against the weak and exhausted German units holding the Para Army line along the Rhine. The British barrage opened with fire from more than 3,000 guns. The Jaeger were ready. The signs of the offensive had been clear for days. The whole area was shrouded in smoke from shells fired to hide from the Germans the preparations which the Allied forces were making. The man-made features of the landscape disappeared under the fury of that bombardment, orchards were torn up, houses set alight. The commander of No. 5 Company entered the cellar in which Strauch and his men were sheltering from the barrage. The Company Commander ordered the detachment to take post but as he emerged into the open he was shot dead. British troops had surrounded the building. One Jaeger used a Panzerfaust to shoot his way out, but for the remainder of Strauch's group the war was over.

When the New Year dawned, 5th Para Division had been in action in the Ardennes for more than a fortnight. When it had been called upon to advance it had done so, when ordered to hold, it had held without yielding. Its positions

were then threatened when the left flank Division crumpled under American assault and every man was needed to form a front against the attacking Americans. The Para Anti-tank Battalion which had entered the combat zone only days earlier, together with 13th Jaeger Regiment, were both put in to restore the situation, It was a new role for the anti-tank battalion but one not un-expected. The unit had been subjected to continuous fighter-bomber attack as it had moved forward to take its place in the line. As a result of those low-level, rocket attacks it had lost both its guns and transport. Now the gunners would fight as infantry. These two units were the last upon which 5th Para Division could call.

It had reached the end of its tether. The Fallschirm-jaeger formation could do no more than defend itself against the Americans who could put into battle units all of which were fully equipped and most of which were fresh. The villages which the Division had fought so hard to capture in the first days of the Ardennes offensive were lost, one after another, in furious battles against over-whelming odds. Under US pressure the Jaeger regiments were forced apart and on 9 January, a concerted attack surrounded 5th Para Division. Only a handful of sub-units escaped from the encirclement and subsequent destruc-tion, and fought their way through the American lines. These remnants were then gathered together and sent to hold the line at Prum in the Eifel where, in early March, two Divisions of Patton's Third Army struck them. Against so overwhelming a force the Jaeger defence could not last long and on 10 March, what remained of 5th Para was outflanked, surrounded and captured at Adenau. The few groups managing to escape this fate, were then regrouped and continued to fight until the end of April, when the final few survivors of 5th Para Division also passed into captivity.

General Heilmann, the divisional commander, wrote of his men and of the battles they had fought, and the emotion he felt is evident in his words. 'Despite misery, suffering and pain the Division remained strong at heart. . . . Field Marshal Model praised it in a special Order. . . . *En route* to close one breach near Dueren the Jaeger, who were foot marching because there was no petrol for the trucks, were ordered to turn about and march back into another threatened sector in the Eifel. . . . The 5th Para, sacrificed by the General Staff, carried out that task. In the general collapse on the left bank of the Rhine it was 5th Para Division in the north and 3rd Para in the south, that were not allowed to pull back across the river. The Division was surrounded and captured. Some units were able to save themselves and in the Harz mountains in the heart of Germany, those last remnants stood and fought to the end.

The 5th Para tasted both victory and defeat. It was truly no shame to submit to an enemy who could command such astronomical supplies of war material.'

The main body of 6th Para Division, which had been holding the northern sector of the Wesel bridgehead, crossed the Rhine on 9 March and took up defensive positions on the eastern bank. Left to form the rearguard was part of 18th Regiment and the Assault Battalion of First Para Army. Both crossed the river during the night of 10 March.

The positions which 6th Para held on the eastern bank were between Emmerich and Rees. The 18th Jaeger Regiment held the right flank. This was a formation so reduced in number – it had only two battalions left – that its strength had had to be made up with drafts from a Volksgrenadier Division. The left wing was held by 16th Jaeger Regiment whose numbers were increased by the remnants of 17th Regiment.

The Allies vaulted the Rhine on 24 March, and within a day the bridgeheads were expanding and forcing the Jaeger regiments north-eastwards. Under the US pressure contact was lost with 8th Para Division, the former left-flank neighbour and 6th Para had to fight its final battles with that flank wide open.

The retreat north-eastwards brought the Division to a defensive position behind the Twente Canal in Holland where it faced British and Canadian forces. Tank attacks by units of Montgomery's Army Group at the beginning of April, smashed the German defence on the line of the Twente Canal and under that pressure the Para Division pulled back, first to a line Zutphen to Deventer and then to one between Amersfoort and Putten. The Jaeger were still holding these positions when the surrender of all troops in north-west Germany brought the war to an end in that region.

This account of the fighting between the Maas and the Rhine cannot be completed without a quote from Heinz Bosch who wrote the definitive work on the battles between those two great rivers. In describing the Fallschirmjaeger in those operations he wrote, 'Those Jaeger who had actually jumped by parachute into battle, were only a very small minority in the units which fought along the Lower Rhine for, since 1943, jump training had been almost completely halted. The dedication and respect for the traditions of the old Para units was sufficient to weld the volunteers from the Flak and other Luftwaffe groups into battleworthy Jaeger Divisions. The greatest number of the 18/20-year-old men who came up as reinforcements, used as substitutes for inadequate training and lack of combat experience a willingness to fight and superb morale.'

20. 'The Standard must still fly even though its bearer falls'
THE END IN ITALY, JANUARY-MAY 1945

The last winter of the war in Italy saw the Divisions of Army Group C bracing themselves to meet the Allied offensive that would come with the return of campaigning weather. The bitterness of the winter had closed down major operations, but 4th Para Division, stationed near Monte Castellone, carried out a series of deep penetration patrols. Quite early during standard reconnaissance missions it could be seen that American sentries were not as watchful as those of the Red Army and that even large groups of Jaeger could infiltrate the US lines with little difficulty.

Some Fallschirmjaeger patrols penetrated as deep as twelve miles (twenty kilometres) and many marched unchallenged along main roads. All of them found, during the nights and days spent behind the US lines, evidence of a build-up of supply dumps and artillery units. The Allied hosts facing Army Group C were preparing a vast and massive operation.

Intelligence assessments were that the first main blow would be made by British Eighth Army and that this would be followed by the US Fifth Army offensive. It was a source of surprised discussion at senior Command level in Italy why the two Allied armies did not strike together or, at least, in a rapid succession of blows. The pattern throughout the campaign had been a ponderous first strike followed only after a long interval of time by a second, thus allowing the Germans time to move units across the width of Italy to meet the new challenge. If Mark Clark, who had succeeded Alexander as Army Group Commander, ran true to form there would be time enough to switch forces despite Allied superiority in the air.

At the end of January, in response to Intelligence forecasts, 4th Para was moved from the Monte Castellone sector facing the Americans, to Imola on the Adriatic side where 1st Para was in position. The Para Corps was now positioned behind the River Senio ready to defend Bologna and the approaches to the River Po against any offensive by Eighth Army.

The military crises facing OKW in both the other theatres of operations demanded that Army Group C in Italy give up units to support both the eastern and western fronts. Following that reduction in strength of Tenth and Fourteenth Armies came the order from OKL that a 10th Para Division be created. Both Divisions of the Fallschirm Corps were to supply complete units so that the new formation would have a cadre of veteran soldiers around which the recruits could be grouped. From 4th Para the second battalion from both 10th and 11th Regiments together with the 3rd Battalion of 12th Regiment were taken. The 1st Para Division gave up 3rd Battalion from its 1st and 4th Regiments as well as 2nd Battalion of 3rd Regiment.

While 4th Para had been actively patrolling against the Americans, 1st Para had been fighting throughout January and February, to hold important peaks in the foothills of the Apennine mountains. Conducting a slow withdrawal in the face of British pressure, First Para then concentrated around Imola where it proposed to hold, in conjunction with the other units of Para Corps, the now imminent Allied spring offensive.

Mark Clark had planned a three-stage operation. The first stage would be to capture Bologna. The offensive would develop, in its second stage, to become a general advance; the third stage would be the fast pursuit by the Allies of the remnants of Army Group C, so as to intercept these before they could reach the safety of the Alps.

For the operation Eighth Army fielded four Corps. V, X and XIII British and the Polish II Corps. The Americans had two Corps: II and IV. To back up the operations by the Allied armies High Command gave orders to put the partisan forces of northern Italy into action. They would delay the German forces' retreat. Operation 'Grapeshot', was to open on 9 April, with a converging thrust by the two Allied armies, to meet at Bondeno, twelve miles (twenty kilometres) to the north-west of Ferrara. The next advance, to Verona, would cut the German Army Group from its bases and begin to roll up its battle line.

The task of German Tenth Army, of which I Para Corps formed part, was to hold a line running from

Bologna, via Tossignano, Castel Bolognese and Bagnocavallo to the southern shore of Lake Comacchio. The area was not really suited for defence. There were several rivers which would delay but not halt Eighth Army's thrust. Only the Po would form a strong and defendable barrier and the German commanders in Italy sought permission to pull back across that river in good time so as to allow them to ferry the heavy weapons and equipment across to the northern bank. The answer from Fuehrerhauptquartier was the expected one. The Army Group would stand and fight where it was. No retreat would be countenanced. This was a sentence of death or captivity. The Jaeger would have to carry out a fighting retreat back to a major river that had only a limited number of crossing-points. The units had little transport and could move only on foot. The danger existed that they would be caught by Allied armour before they reached the Po.

On 9 April, following an aerial bombardment and an artillery barrage as violent as that at El Alamein, the British infantry crossed the Senio, climbed its high northern bank and moved into the smoke and destruction which were the product of the two bombardments. Under Eighth Army's assault the German 76th Corps, holding the Senio line, reeled back and then began to retreat. That movement uncovered the flank of I Para Corps, which was then forced to conform, retreating slowly and leaving small rearguards to hold the impetuous British drive. By 11 April, the front of Tenth Army had been pierced at a number of places and its Corps had been forced back behind the River Reno.

On 16 April, an attack by the New Zealanders and the Poles overrolled 992nd Grenadier Regiment and a battle group from 4th Para Division was rushed forward to close the gap where once the Grenadiers had held post. To carry out an advance immediately after reaching the battle zone, with no opportunity to reconnoitre, meant that the battle group was advancing blindly into the unknown. Perhaps,

Left: In an advanced position in the front line a Fallschirmjaeger keeps watch. To hand is an MG42 on a bipod mount and an MP38/40. (Brian L. Davis)

not quite unknown, for what was known for certain was that a clash between it and the advancing enemy force was inevitable. Outside Imola the leading files of Jaeger saw coming towards them scout cars and troop-carrying vehicles. An apron of mines hastily buried in the surface of the country road destroyed two of the scout cars and as the New Zealanders jumped from the trucks to engage the Paras, they were caught in machine-gun cross-fire and a hail of mortar bombs. The Jaeger officers accepted that they could not hold the position for any length of time; their mission was to delay the Allied advance and this they did.

As swiftly as they had moved into battle the Paras disengaged and during the succeeding days fought a number of similar delaying actions. Soon they were behind the River Quaderna. There were now only a few more minor waterways to defend before they had the Po at their back. On 20 April, I Para Corps issued orders to its subordinate units that they were to cross that river with the intention of reaching a defence line, the 'Blue Line', based on a series of fortifications dating from the First World War. On 23 April, Heidrich, the Corps Commander, called his divisional commanders to a conference at his headquarters near Felonica. His detailed analysis left them in no doubt as to the gravity of the situation which faced them. Hitler's refusal to allow the armies to pull back across the Po in good time had had the feared result. There was no way to get the heavy equipment ferried across the river. There were scarcely enough rafts to carry the Jaeger. Those who could swim would be expected to do so, but each man would be issued with a truck tyre to support him during his crossing. Heidrich did not need to emphasise that there would be no movement by day. Every German soldier knew that the Allies had air superiority and that the fighter-bombers or rocket-firing Spitfires attacked anything which moved. The crossing would be made during the night of 24/25 April. Destruction was ordered of anything that could not be taken. Only ambulances were to be spared and if possible ferried across to the northern bank. Both Divisions would leave rearguards which would hold a perimeter on the south bank of the Po until last light on the 25th. Then they, covered by the fire of German artillery on the north bank, would cross the river.

The passage of the main body and the rearguard was completed but not without loss. The number of crossing-points was limited and the number of roads along which Tenth Army could retreat to the Po, even fewer. Into that handful of country roads guns, tanks, trucks and carts were crammed in a slow-moving mass. Inevitably, Eighth Army's Divisions caught up with the almost immobile columns and shot them to pieces. Jaeger units, trapped in the carnage, turned back towards the sounds of battle, intending to fight for a breathing-space against the advancing enemy. In some places their efforts were little more than forlorn hopes and were crushed immediately. At others, skill and ability was able to call a halt, albeit a temporary one, to the close pursuit.

'I was in a Heavy Weapons Company. Before we crossed the Po we fired off every round and then blew out the gun barrels. The crossing was a well-conducted exercise with guides to show the way to the embarkation points, with units knowing on which ferry or raft they would sail, with guides on the far bank and a hot meal before the march to defensive positions behind the river.'

With his two Fallschirmjaeger Divisions now over the Po, Heidrich set them off on a march into the mountains to the 'Blue Line' positions. This move took both formations on a north-westerly march away from Eighth Army's sector and into that of US Fifth Army. The predominant thought in the mind of all the Para commanders was how long the units holding the Po line could resist the Allied assaults. Once the Americans and British had crossed the river their vehicles could speed across the Plain of Lombardy and fulfill Mark Clark's intention of trapping Army Group C before it reached the Alps. Unless the Po line were held for a long time, no matter how fast the Jaeger marched they would not be able to outpace the Allied armour.

The Para Divisions set out for their objective. The 4th Division, which had reached Padua, then divided into three groups. One was to gain Rovereto via Vicenza, the second to march via Bassano to Trient, while the third was to reach Belluno via Feltre. The 1st Para was to move as a whole force via Vicenza and Schio to Rovereto. The orders to reach the 'Blue Line' could not be met. The US 88th Division, which had spearheaded Fifth Army's advance in Operations 'Grapeshot', since the offensive opened on 14 April, reached Verona. The Jaeger rearguards there, which sought to halt the 88th's advance, were swept away as the 'Clover Leaf' Division struck then with considerable force. The pursuit of the Fallschirmjaeger by the 88th was relentless and at times, using side-roads or moving across country, the American infantry intercepted the Jaeger units before they could take up defensive positions.

The surrender in Italy came into effect on 2 May, but this was not known to the men of the 88th unitl a delegation of Para officers came into the lines of 351st Infantry Regiment with the news that hostilities had ceased at 14.00 hours that day. With the signing of the document of surrender, two of the most senior Para Divisions were now out of a war, which was still being fought and would continue to be fought for another week on the Eastern and Western Fronts.

21. 'Do you see in the east the blood-red dawn'

THE END IN THE EAST, JANUARY-MAY 1945

By the beginning of 1945, the cancer that was the Eastern Front had reached the terminal stage. The war between Russia and Germany still held, in 1945, the importance it had held since the first day of Operation 'Barbarossa' in June 1941, and it is surprising, considering that priority, to learn that only two Para Divisions fought there in 1945, both of them newly raised and neither at full strength.

The first of that pair of Divisions fought in northern Germany guarding the approaches to Berlin. The second was put into action in southern Austria.

The 9th Para Division was raised in February 1945, and its constituent regiments: 25th, 26th, and 27th, were ordered to concentrate in an area to the south of Stettin on the Baltic. This was an order which could not be quickly fulfilled given the military situation of the time. The Soviet offensive along the River Oder had smashed the German defences and the Jaeger of the future 9th Division, often in battalion groups or even smaller detachments, were fighting hard to stem the Soviet advance. It took time before the scattered Para units could be brought together so as to create a whole Division.

Of its three regiments, the 25th was interesting in that it contained battalions which had no Luftwaffe origins. The 1st was made up of the survivors of one of Skorzeny's special commando groups and the 2nd was from the Brandenburg Division. Skorzeny, whom we have met in the rescue of Mussolini, was authorized by the most senior SS commanders to raise units which would be Germany's answer to the British commandos. One of the first of these was 500 Para which was followed by 502 Special Services Battalion. The successes achieved by that unit led Skorzeny to create other formations; at first anti-partisan battalions to counter Russian guerrilla detachments and then, as the Allies approached the Reich, the German partisan units – Wehrwolf.

The Brandenburg Division had grown out of Germany's principal counter-Intelligence organization and as it expanded from Company, through battalion to divisional status, a number of specialist units had been formed,

among which was the Parachute Battalion, raised in February 1944. That formation had a short life and did not fight as a single unit. The sole occasion on which all the Companies took part in a mission, was in August 1944, at Bucharest. Only hours before their aircraft touched-down the Roumanian Government switched its allegiance to Russia. Within the short duration of the Brandenburg flight the German Army had changed from being Roumania's ally to her enemy. When the battalion landed it was surrounded and taken prisoner. Those Brandenburg Para battalion detachments that formed part of 25th Para Regiment, were made up of men from the Training Depot, from convalescents and those who had been on special, small-unit missions when the battalion flew to Roumania.

With such unusual groups constituting the 1st and 2nd Battalions, it is not surprising that the 25th Regiment carried, upon its raising in January 1944, the distinction, 'zbV', the initials of a military designation, 'for special purposes'. In January it was sent to hold the bridgeheads on the east bank of the River Oder and was involved in heavy fighting around Dramburg throughout that month and during February when the 1st and 2nd Battalions were removed from the regiment and posted to strenthen the defence of the beleagured city of Breslau.

The 26th Regiment, which was also raised in January 1945, contained two battalions which carried the names of their commanders. Both units had seen service during the Battle of the Bulge. The three battalions of the regiment did not fight as a single unit, but during the battles along the Oder were put in separately against Rokossovsky's 2nd White Russian Front which was advancing upon Stettin.

The greatest number of men in 27th Regiment were taken from three tank-busting battalions which had themselves been created from a nucleus made up of the remnants of the former Jaeger Regiment 16, fleshed out with volunteers and a Replacement and Training regiment. In common with the other units of 9th Para Division, the battalions of 27th Regiment were often seconded to Army Divisions as replacement for the losses which those formations had suffered. Their Jaeger identity could not be easily maintained under such conditions. The bitterness of the fighting on the Eastern Front in those first months of 1945, is shown by the fact that in 27th Regiment battalion strengths shrank to 80 men and in the other regiments were only a little higher.

It was not until 8 April that the Jaeger battalions, could be taken from the line and grouped to form a complete Division. It was first employed to help contain the bridgehead which Zhukov's troops had gained on the west bank of the Oder and out of which the Red Army's major offensive exploded on 16 April with Berlin as the common objective of Zhukov's and Koviev's Red Army Fronts.

It was the terrible fate of 9th Para that it was carrying out a regrouping of its units when the massive Soviet artillery barrage opened. This was the heaviest bombardment of the Second World War in any theatre of operations; a hurricane of fire to which the German artillery, outnumbered by 10 to 1, could make no effective reply. The weight and duration of the Russian bombardment crushed the German defence and the swift follow-up by motorized, cavalry and infantry units rolled over many German formations while they were still shocked from the artillery's fury. The 2nd Battalion of 27th Regiment and 3rd Battalion of 26th Regiment were wiped out in their positions.

Under this unequal pressure the Division pulled back to a line Straussberg–Muenchberg and it was there that the full force of massed Russian tank forces struck it. Under the massive Red Army blows the 9th Para Division fragmented. The 26th Regiment, holding the left flank, was flung north-eastwards, 25th Regiment retreated into north Berlin and the remaining sub-units came under the command of 61st Panzer Corps. As part of that formation the Jaeger conducted a fighting withdrawal into the southern suburbs of Berlin. Within days the city had been surrounded. During the days of fighting which followed the units of 9th Para, in their respective sectors, were slowly forced back as the defence perimeter contracted under the Soviet assault. In the last week of April the survivors of the young Division were grouped in the city centre to help defend the bunker in which Adolf Hitler was conducting the defence of the city.

The battle for Berlin, although of short duration, was hard and furiously fought. It was the case of fragments of German units, with little or no artillery or Panzer support, fighting against the Red Army's masses which had those things in abundance. For the duration of the battle for Berlin the Jaeger of 9th Division fought the same type of battle as that which 1st Para Division had fought at Cassino – small groups of determined men attacking at close-quarters enemy armour as it came crunching its way

across the rubble of ruined houses.

On 2 May, Berlin was surrendered by the military commandant, General Weidling, and the 9th Division Jaeger, together with the other survivors of the battle, passed into captivity. The 26th Regiment, which had been forced back northwards and which had, therefore, not taken part in the battle, finished the war fighting against the Anglo-American forces on a front extending from Wittstock to Schleswig-Holstein.

To close this account of the Para groups on the northern sector of the Eastern Front in 1945, there remains the story of the two battalions detached from Division and sent in to strengthen the garrison at Breslau.

The defence of that city was a more than usually staunch one. Many Gauleiters, the governors of provinces, made only token resistance when the Allies advanced upon their provincial capitals. Gauleiter Hanke of Breslau determined to hold his city and thereby prevent the Russians from using it as a base for their assault upon Berlin. The so-called 'Fortress Breslau' was surrounded soon after the opening of the Soviet offensive on 12 January and as the fighting intensified and casualties mounted there was a real danger that the defenders would soon be too few in number to hold the Red Army's assaults. To build up the garrison's strength and to equip it with first-class units, High Command ordered that the 2nd Battalion of 25th Para Regiment, whose members were principally drawn from the Brandenburg Division, should be sent to Breslau.

On 28 February, the 2nd Battalion was flown into the beleagured city, and formed part of a regimental Battle Group. Within weeks mounting losses among the Breslau garrison required that fresh reinforcements be sent. The 3rd Battalion of 25th Regiment was flown in. The flight was particularly hazardous. The Red Army, aware that the aircraft using the city's airport, were bringing in supplies and reinforcements, concentrated their attacks to capture it. When the airport fell the Red Army Commander might well have thought he had cut the city off from the air, but the defenders used the wide Kaiserstrasse as a runway and it was upon the explosion-pocked surface of that street that the machines carrying 3rd Battalion landed. That unit was soon incorporated into the same regimental battle group as 2nd Battalion and together they formed one of the strong bastions of Breslau's defence.

The Red Army attacks increased in number and weight as it sought to take the city. The Jaeger fought out battles at street level and below the streets; in the city's sewers. But however determined, however staunch their defence of Breslau, there could be only one outcome. The city fell on 6 May, having endured encirclement since January. The part played by the two Para battalions – numbered as 67 and 68 in the garrison's order of battle – cannot be described in detail because any records which might have been kept vanished when the Red Army entered the city on 7 May. The defence of 'Cassino on the Oder', as the Nazi propagandists had called the battle, was at an end and the harshest conditions in Soviet prison-camps was the lot of those who surrendered.

There is a memorial to a Para Division near the small market town of Feldbach in Austria's province of Styria. Standing on an open stretch of country, the memorial looks eastward across the dark forested, rolling hills out of which the Red Army's Corps and Divisions stormed in the last months of the war. The memorial commemorates the units of 10th Para Division, whose life was brief but whose gallant actions were so memorable as to be commemorated in enduring stone.

The 10th was created out of cadres taken from I Para Corps' 1st and 4th Divisions in northern Italy. The units which had been detached to help create the 10th Para Division did not take their heavy weapons units with them. They had been assured that these would join in Holland, the proposed concentration area, for Luftwaffe High Command intended to employ the 10th in northwest Europe. Those units did not reach the Netherlands. The capitulation of the Hungarian Army opened a large gap on the right flank of Army Group South through which came flooding the armour, cavalry and infantry of Marshal Tolbhukin's 3rd Ukrainian Front. These armies smashed through the ineffectual Eastern Defence Positions and advanced swiftly for Army Group South had no reserves which could be put in to hold the Soviet drive. Orders went out from Army Group High Command that every available unit was to be flung into the gap and among those which were intercepted and deflected eastwards were the Jaeger groups heading for Holland. The trains carrying them were halted and re-routed. The journey was slow, delayed as it was by frequent Allied air attacks so that it was not until 3 April that the first detachments began to arrive in the newly designated concentration area between Bruck an der Mur and the Styrian provincial capital, Graz.

The Jaeger regiments were to have had the standard support units, but these latter had arrived without heavy weapons and could be equipped with only part of their requirements. Men to flesh out the regiments around the 1st and 4th Division cadres, were taken from a number of Luftwaffe flying and ground formations – all of whom had varying experiences of warfare, but none of it in fighting the type of action which the veterans had in abundance. To them were added non-German units; soldiers of the former 14th SS Grenadier Division (1st Galician).

It is customary, when new and major formations are raised, for their constituent formations to spend time together, learning to collaborate with other groups. That 'shake-down' period was denied 10th Para Division; the military crisis did not permit it. Units arriving in the concentration area were sent up the line with minimal delay. This was particularly the case with 2nd Battalion of the divisional artillery regiment. In early April its Companies arrived at Graz main station and moved by road into the areas of Gratwein and Gratkorn, two villages just to the north of the city. Within hours of its arrival, Sixth Army ordered the battalion into battle, not as an artillery group but as infantry.

The armour and Guards infantry formations of Tolbhukin's Front had struck down the seam between the left wing of Second Panzer Army and the right wing of Sixth Army. Soviet tanks, infantry and cavalry were sweeping through the gap, forcing apart the two hard-pressed armies. Every available unit was needed to seal off the Red penetrations. It was to help deal with this crisis that 2nd Artillery Battalion was ordered into battle. The move towards the combat area was made under the attacks of swarms of Red Air Force aircraft which bombed and strafed anything that moved on the roads or in the fields. Just outside Feldbach the trucks carrying the battalion halted and the former Para artillerymen, now Para Jaeger, took up defensive positions on each side of the secondary road which runs, twisting from the village of Gnas, a few kilometres this side of the Hungarian frontier. Although the field of fire was good and observation was excellent in the clear, spring afternoon, there were many routes by which the Red Army could move towards the Jaeger positions and the battalion had too few men to cover all the avenues of approach.

The first hint that a Soviet attack was imminent came with an increase in Red Air force activity. Then the fighters departed and the Jaeger saw, driving along the road, as if on manoeuvres, a double column of tanks, chiefly T34s and JS machines. These deployed off the road and into a wood when the 88s of an Army battery opened fire. There was a short period of waiting and then masses of Russian infantry were seen in the woods. These formed into the classic Red Army 'wave' formation and began to advance towards the Jaeger. Fast-firing MG 42s and light mortars broke up the first charge. Another succeeded it, then a third came in and was destroyed in its turn. While the Red Army infantry was fighting its way forward, the Stormovik aircraft came back and attacked the artillery battery. The German guns lay silent. The T34s came back on to the road again, formed up and were about to advance when the 88s resumed firing. The tanks ran the gauntlet until they reached open country into which they could deploy in a long wave, advancing across the fields and up the slope towards the thin line of Jaeger. MG fire shot down the infantry supporting the armour and then it was a matter of using Panzerfausts, Panzerschreck projectors and explosive charges against the tank mass. The T34s pulled back, but the Jaeger knew that this failed assault would be the first of a series which would be maintained until the Soviets had forced a breakthrough. This forecast was correct and under the subsequent attacks from the air, from the regiments of Katyusha rocket artillery and from waves of Red armour and infantry, the battalion was crushed. Its few survivors struggled back to the concentration area to find that the other divisional units had been moved and were now fighting to the south-west of Vienna.

The memorial at Feldbach commemorates the stand by 2nd Battalion during those April days of 1945. The remainder of the Division, meanwhile, had arrived at St Poelten, in the Danube valley, where the 30th Jaeger Regiment, together with a battalion from 28th and 29th Regiments was contesting the Red Army's advance on that sector. The Red Army's attacks concentrated around the small town of Rothau which was defended tenaciously by the 1st Battalion of 30th Regiment until 18 April, when a Soviet outflanking movement forced a retreat southwards to the Buchberg, a dominating height and the principal objective of the Russian attack. The battle at times was hand-to-hand as the Jaeger struggled against the Red Army assaults. An understanding can be gained of the intensity of the fighting and the overwhelming masses of *matériel* which the Red Army could employ on just this small sector, from the regimental record which states that fourteen Russian tanks were destroyed in a single hour by just one Company.

The Jaeger were relieved from the line on 27 April, having held their positions on each side of Marktl throughout four days and nights of bitter conflict. Leaving 30th Regiment to fight on along the Danube, the rest of 10th Para Division, was moved by rail to Bruenn in Sudetenland, where German Eighth Army was embattled. In the Sudetenland, too, the regiments experienced the bitterness of being committed piecemeal to battle against an enemy superior in numbers and fire-power. As fast as the individual battalions were put in they were cut to pieces, making it impossible for the Division to be employed as a whole. There were actions not just against the Red Army but also against partisans who suddenly became more active and aggressive. The final stand of the remnants of 10th Para came at Bistric, to the north of Bruenn, where waves of tanks and infantry, crushing the last desperate resistance, overran and destroyed the

decimated battalions. Those who survived passed into prisoner-of-war camps.

The final account in this story is that of the last days of 30th Para Regiment which had been left behind in Lower Austria. The orders received by the regimental commander were to bring his unit into the Bruenn area, but the railway link between Austria and Czechoslovakia had been cut by the Red Army. The commander set his battalions foot-marching towards the objective, but then learned that the end of the war was imminent. He changed the direction of the march westwards so as to reach that area of Austria where the American Army was positioned and it was to them that he surrendered. Under the terms agreed by the Allies, it was the nation against which a German unit was fighting at the end of the war that would take it prisoner. Under that agreement the Jaeger of 30th Regiment were handed over to become prisoners of the Red Army, a fate shared already by the rest of 10th Para Division.

This catalogue of the war on the Eastern Front concludes with the operations conducted by a battle group which we had met in the Ardennes campaign, when it was commanded by Colonel von der Heydte.

His group had been almost totally destroyed in the fighting during December 1944. Less than 100 Jaeger fought their way through the American encirclement to reach the German lines; the greatest number, including the Battle Group Commander were taken prisoner.

The remnant was reinforced, regouped as 57th Jaeger Battalion and posted to the Eastern Front where it served as part of 'Grossdeutschland' Corps. The heavy losses which 57th battalion suffered during the battles in Lower Silesia so weakened it that it had to be posted away from 'Grossdeutschland' and it was then absorbed into 1st Division of the 'Hermann Goering' Para Panzer Corps. Together with that Division the battalion, under the command of Captain Later, took part in one of the last victories achieved by the German Army on the Eastern Front during the Second World War.

During the early stages of the offensive which the Red Army had opened in March 1945, Soviet tank forces swept westwards across Saxony heading towards Dresden. Near Koenigsbrueck the armoured hosts, perhaps over-confident by the weakness of the opposition it was encountering, drove across the front of the 'Hermann Goering' Division. To present an open flank was a serious tactical mistake against a German formation so skilled in battle. The 'Para Panzer Division' roared into action and when, after days of battle, the Russian tank thrust had been flung back, 1st Polish Division, one of its élite units, had been destroyed as a fighting force.

By that stage of the war units on the Eastern Front were fighting individual battles against overwhelming and frightful odds. The respite gained from the success at Koenigsbrueck did not last long, and the battalion conducted a fighting retreat across Germany until the last days of the war when, north of Dresden, and as part of the 'Hermann Goering' Division, its survivors surrendered to the Russians.

Left: A Fallschirmjaeger NCO carrying a flare pistol during a training exercise. Note the signal flare cartridge belt he is carrying.

Epilogue

On 9 May 1945, the Third Reich died and with its death the Second World War in Europe came to an end. Logically, therefore, the story of the German airborne forces at war should end at that date. It does not, for a spirit once inspired does not expire with signatures scrawled on pieces of paper. The spirit survives, takes on another form and is re-directed into fresh endeavours.

Thus the German Fallschirmjaeger returned from the prison-camps, from the solitary confinements of Siberian *gutags* to a Germany which was no longer that from which they had marched out years earlier. It was a ruined Fatherland, defeated and occupied. It would have been easy and understandable for each Jaeger to have concentrated on his own personal fate, but that sense of comradeship and loyalty which Student and the early senior commanders had bred, lifted the Jaeger out of personal interest and into common concern for their less fortunate comrades.

Those whose former homes were now in an eastern bloc country were helped to resettle in the west; those who had suffered severe disability were tended by their former comrades. It is easy to see why their most commonly reproduced motif shows a scene on the Eastern Front in winter in which a wounded Jaeger is being carried to safety on the back one of one his comrades. It was that spirit of selflessness, of dedication and concern which bound the former paratroops in those first bitter, post-war years.

As Germany grew in prosperity and confidence, the German Fallschrimjaeger organization inspired other bodies; the limbless, the blind, those who had been driven out of their ancestral homes and the war widows. This concentration of strength has won for those upon whom the disfiguring hand of war had left the deepest scars, the power to demand – not to beg for, but to demand adequate compensation. One recent statistic shows that there are still in Germany more war widows than there are students, more war disabled than there are soldiers in the army of the Federal Republic. It was for those in need

that the German National Fallschirmjaeger Association went into a battle as hard as any that its members had fought during the war. They fought and won but then, as an élite force, they were accustomed to taking on great odds and emerging from the struggle victorious.

Among the men of élite units there is an awareness of the ability which they have both as individuals and as members of an élite unit. It is an awareness that does not manifest itself in self-congratulatory songs or speeches. Good wine needs no bush and good units no fanfares. Nor is the awareness among the men of such a force shown in arrogant display, but in a quiet pride of a duty well done, of being better than the standard unit, in things though trivial to those who cannot enter that circle of excellence and remain, therefore, untouched by its magic.

Such seemingly trivial things; the distinctive slow marching pace of the French Foreign Legion is at one and the same time both reassuring to its friends and menacing to its enemies. The battle-cry of the British airborne, 'Whaho Mahomed!', has the ability to raise the tiredest trooper in the most fororn hope as readily as does the sound of 'The Black Bear' revive the Highland soldier and inspire him to greater endeavours. The German Fallschirmjaeger who had had that same spirit in war, brought it into peace-time endeavours and have retained it for more than four decades.

I have known the Jaeger since I fought them on the hillsides of Tunisia and became eventually their prisoner. Liberated from a German prison-camp I met them again in Italy and across the many years of post-war life they have become true and valued friends.

They and I are now old in years, but in my memory is the sound of their strong and confident voices singing as the trucks carried them into captivity at the end of the campaign in Tunisia. It is a memory so enduring that now at their reunions, when the Fallschirmjaeger song is sung, I do not see the greying heads of those around the table, but the young warriors who were my opponents so many years ago and whose deeds I have endeavoured to describe in this book.

Fallschirmjaeger Formations and Units

In this section of the book the major airborne formations from Army down to Division will be detailed. Previous chapters have shown that pre-war development of the airborne arm was from an amalgamation of individual sub-units into battalions and then into regiments which were grouped to become the Luftwaffe's 7th Flieger Division. Concurrent with that development was the conversion of the Army's 22nd Division from being an infantry division to becoming an air landing formation.

The German forces were so structured that two Divisions combined to form a Corps and those formations named above united to become XI Flieger Corps. During the course of the war the number of Para Divisions was increased so that by the end of hostilities eleven were on establishment. As more and more Divisions were created the need arose to form new Flieger Corps. XI Corps was renumbered to become I Para Corps and II Corps was created in May 1944.

The table of establishments in German military organization laid down that a force of two or more Corps required an Army structure. Discussions which had begun during November 1943, reached the stage by March 1944, where OKL could order the Airborne Army to be created. The Directive was all-embracing for included within Army's area of control were not only the Para Corps and their Divisions, but all independent formations, training schools and other establishments which had been, hiterto, not directly under Para control.

FIRST (FALLSCHIRM) PARATROOP ARMY

The raising of First Paratroop Army was completed by the end of August 1944, and on 4 September, the first units of the new army went into the Line on the Western Front where they served without a break until the general capitulation in May 1945, There were occasions during that long period of combat when it became absolutely essential to detach units to serve on the other battle fronts but the need to hold the west could only permit such small units as individual regiments or battalions to be taken. By that late stage of the war it was difficult to take a complete Division out of the Line to meet a crisis on even another sector of the Western Front and certainly out of the question to detach one for service in another theatre of operations. Thanks to the very flexible organization of the German military system and to the high combat abilities of the Jaeger, such sub-units as could be spared were able to meet and overcome potentially critical situations.

THE PARA CORPS

First Paratroop Army controlled two Corps. The first of these had been numbered, originally, XI Flieger Corps, and had had 7th Flieger Division and 22nd Infantry Divisions on its order of battle. Among the Corps troops on establishment was an Assault Regiment, together with the usual medical, signals and supply detachments. There was also a liaison group for the Transport aircraft Squadron as well as a glider squadron, Reinforcement and Training Depots. Corps remained in control of its Divisions until the beginning of 1944, when the raising of new Fallschirm-

jaeger Divisions required the creation of a second Corps.

In January 1944 XI Flieger Corps, which formed the nucleus of the Airborne Army, was renumbered to become 1 Para Corps and controlled 1st and 2nd Divisions under command. Its theatre of operations was Italy. At the same time plans were put in hand for a second Para Corps to adminster 3rd and 5th Para Divisions, stationed in France. On 12 May 1944, II Para Corps was established.

The Para Divisions

The original major airborne formation was numbered and titled, 7th Flieger Division. Orders to create it were issued early in 1938, and although the raising had not been fully completed at the time of the Munich crisis in September of that year, the 7th was alerted and ordered to undertake an airlanding operation in the Sudetenland area of Czechoslovakia. A political compromise ended that crisis and made the operation redundant, nevertheless, High Command mounted an airlanding exercise to occupy the Freudenthal airfield.

At Hitler's birthday parade on 20 April 1939, Fallschirmjaeger units took part for the first time and the excellence of their turn-out, the precision of their marching as well as that *élan* which accompanies élite formations, impressed all those who watched the parade. As yet only part of one regiment had been created, but work was begun on a second so that by June and July 1939, the 1st and 2nd Battalions of that Regiment, respectively, had been raised.

War came in September of that year. The 7th was not used in a Para role during the fighting in Poland, but in the campaigns fought between 1940 and 1943, there were many oppportunities for its units to show their special qualities. The OKL decision of that year to increase the number of Para Divisions brought about a change in 7th Flieger Division's number and description. In April 1943, it became 1st Fallschirmjaeger Division. By that time, too, the divisional order of battle shown on page 12 had also undergone a change. The units on the establishment of the new formation were: Divisional Headquarters with Major-General Heidrich commanding; Jaeger Regiments 1, 3 and 4, two battalions of Para Artillery Regiment No. 1 and the usual divisional services.

In January 1943, OKW issued orders that a second Fallschirmjaeger Division be raised, but it was not until March that the first units were formed around a nucleus composed of recruit volunteers stiffened with experienced men drawn from the remnants of several airborne units which had been mauled in battle. Included among those fragments were men of 2nd and 4th Battalions of the Air Landing Assault Regiment, the 100th Special Services Battalion and 2nd Jaeger Regiment. Others of those splinter groups were men of Ramcke's Para Brigade who had either escaped to Europe when Panzer Army Africa surrendered or else who had been convalescent in Germany. Command of 2nd Division was given to Major-General Ramcke and within months, thanks to his tireless efforts it was ready for action. The order of battle was Jaeger Regiments 2, 6 and 7 together with the usual services. In July 1943, the 2nd Fallschirmjaeger Division became one of the two major formations of XI Flieger Corps, later I Para Corps.

The 3rd Fallschirmjaeger Division was the second of the airborne units to be raised during the expansion year of 1943. Following the usual practice, the cadres around which the Division was created were drawn from the existing airborne regiments as well as from 1st Replacement and Training Regiment and an NCO Training School. The divisional ancillary units began to concentrate at the end of 1943 and shortly, thereafter, Jaeger Regiments Nos. 5, 8 and 9 were formed and grouped inside the divisional organization. The 3rd Division, under its commander, Major-General Schimpf, was ready for action.

The next Para formation, also created during 1943, was 4th Fallschirmjaeger Division, for whose raising orders were issued on 4 October 1943. The Jaeger regiments for the new formation were 10th, 11th and 12th. To bring them up to strength volunteers were accepted not only from certain non-Para Luftwaffe units, but also from the Italian airborne Division 'Folgore'. The units of that formation served as a complete component within 4th Division and were not broken up among the other rifle regiments. These Italian sub-units were accepted because 4th Fallschirmjaeger Division was raised in Italy and at a time when it seemed likely that the Anglo-American invasion would advance swiftly up the Italian peninsula. Any reliable and loyal unit would be acceptable. Folgore was both.

The next wave of Fallschirmjaeger Divisions came in the following year as a result of efforts made by the German Government to increase the number of its military units. The 5th Division was raised during April 1944, around a nucleus of existing paratroop detachments which had been seconded for that purpose. The divisional Jaeger regiments were each constructed around the third battalions of the 3rd and 4th Regiments of 1st Fallscirmjaeger Division. The artillery and other divisional services were created around cadres drawn from other para regiments.

The 6th Fallschirmjaeger Division was another Para unit raised during April 1944. The 2nd Battalion of 5th Regiment was the cadre around which 16th Jaeger Regiment was formed, while convalescent veterans of 17th and 18th Regiments were the nucleus around which volunteer recruits were grouped.

Five months after Luftwaffe High Command had directed that 5th and 6th Divisions be raised, orders came for a new wave of Para Divisions to be formed. The 7th Fallschirmjaeger Division was created by an OKW order under which a number of independent paratroop units serving on the Western Front were to be amalgamated into three regiments, named, initially, after their commanders. Because the greatest number of its soldiers were from training schools or were without battle experience, the veterans of von der Heydte's 6th Regiment were posted to it. The new Division received the number '7' in October, thereby initiating the first stage of an Order that an 8th, 9th and 10th Division be raised. OKL declared that the Jaeger regiments would no longer bear the commander's name but were given the numbers 19, 20 and 21 respectively. It was not until December 1944, however, that the 7th Fallschirmjaeger Division went into its first action, to hold the Venlo bridgehead on the west bank of the River Maas.

The 8th Division was also created out of a collection of fragments and by 15 January 1945, only two of its Jaeger regiments had been formed. The third was taken away even while the Division was being formed and was posted to reinforce 2nd Fallschirmjaeger Division.

Goering's Order dated 24 September 1944, that a new wave of three Para Divisions be raised, was first revoked in December and then re-issued in January 1945. It was, therefore, not until that month that work began to create 9th Division. Its three Jaeger regiments were fresh troops grouped around cadres of veteran officers and men, of whom the most experienced were the survivors of Skorzeny's special commando group and others from the Army's élite 'Brandenburg' Division.

Like the 9th Division, the order to raise 10th Fallschirmjaeger Division, was at first countermanded and not reinstated until February 1945. Cadres for the new Division were drawn from the 1st and 4th Divisions, both of which were serving with I Para Corps in Italy. The 28th Jaeger Regiment was formed round the third battalions of 4th and 12th Regiments. The 29th Regiment was formed from the second battalions of the 3rd and 4th Regiments. The 3rd Battalion of 1st Regiment and the 2nd Battalion of 10th Regiment formed the cadre for 30th Regiment. The men required to flesh out these regimental cadres were drawn from air and ground crews who had no aircraft to fly or to service, as well as the permanent staffs of a number of Luftwaffe training establishments.

1st Fallschirmjaeger Division

The 1st Fallschirmjaeger Dvision was created out of 7th Flieger Division during April 1943.
Divisional Commander Major-General Heidrich
Fallschirmjaeger Regiment No. 1 Lieutenant-Colonel Schulz
1st Battalion Major von der Schulenburg
2nd Battalion Major Groschke
3rd Battalion Captain Becker
Fallschirmjaeger Regiment No. 3 Lieutenant-Colonel Heilmann
1st Battalion Major Bohmler
2nd Battalion Major Rau
3rd Battalion Major Kratzert
Fallschirmjaeger Regiment No. 4 Lieutenant-Colonel Walther
1st Battalion Major Egger
2nd Battalion Captain Vosshage
3rd Battalion Major Grassmel
Fallschirm Artillery Regiment No. 1 Major Schram
Fallschirm Anti-tank Battalion No. 1
Fallschirm Engineer Battalion No. 1
Fallschirm Signals Battalion No. 1
Fallschirm Machine-gun Battalion No. 1
Fallschirm Medical Battalion No. 1

2nd Fallschirmjaeger Division

The Division was raised in Brittany in 1943.
Divisional Commander Lieutenant-General Ramcke
Fallschirmjaeger Regiment No. 2 Lieutenant-Colonel Kroh
1st Battalion Captain Schwaiger
2nd Battalion Major Pietzonka
3rd Battalion Captain Zimmermann
Fallschirmjaeger Regiment No. 6 Major Liebach
1st Battalion Captain Tannert

2nd Battalion Major Gericke
3rd Battalion Captain Pelz
Fallschirmjaeger Regiment No. 7 Colonel Straub
1st Battalion Major Herrmann
2nd Battalion Major Becker
3rd Battalion Major Huebner
Fallschirm Artillery Regiment No. 2
Fallschirm Anti-tank Battalion No. 2
Fallschirm Engineer Battalion No. 2
Fallschirm Signals Battalion No. 2
Fallschirm Medical Battalion No. 2
Fallschirm Services Units
The Fallschirm Anti-aircraft and Fallschirm Mortar Battalion together with the Replacement Battalion, all numbered 2, were not raised until the beginning of 1944.

3rd Fallschirmjaeger Division
Raised in France during the last months of 1943.
Divisional Commander Major-General Schimpf
Fallschirmjaeger Regiment No. 8 Major Liebach
1st Battalion
2nd Battalion
3rd Battalion
Fallschirmjaeger Regiment No. 9 Major Stephani
1st Battalion
2nd Battalion
3rd Battalion
Fallschirm Artillery Regiment No. 3
Fallschirm Anti-tank Battalion No. 3
Fallschirm Engineer Battalion No. 3
Fallschirm Anti-aircraft Battalion No. 3
Fallschirm Mortar Battalion No. 3
Fallschirm Signals Battalion No. 3
Fallschirmjaeger Regiment No. 5 should have formed part of the Division, but this was sent to Africa and lost there. A re-constituted 5th regiment was taken on establishment during March 1944; its commander was Major Becker.

4th Fallschirmjaeger Division
The Division was raised in Italy during November/December 1943.
Divisional Commander Major-General Trettner
Fallschirmjaeger Regiment No. 10 Colonel Fuchs
1st Battalion Captain Kuehne
2nd Battalion Major Hoppe
3rd Battalion Major Grundmann
Fallschirmjaeger Regiment No. 11 Major Gericke
1st Battalion Captain Ruthe
2nd Battalion Lieutenant Engelhardt
3rd Battalion Captain Wolf
Fallschirmjaeger Regiment No. 12 (The Assault Regiment) Major Timm
1st Battalion Captain Toschka
2nd Battalion Captain Hauber
3rd Battalion Captain Genz
Fallschirm Artillery Regiment No. 4
Fallschirm Engineer Battalion No. 4
Fallschirm Anti-tank Battalion No. 4
Fallschirm Anti-aircraft Battalion No. 4

Fallschirm Signals Battalion No. 4
The 4th Fallschirmjaeger Division also contained units from the two Italian Para Divisions 'Folgore' and 'Demgo'.

5th Fallschirmjaeger Division
The 5th Division was raised in France in April 1944.
Divisional Commander Lieutenant-General Wilke
Fallschirmjaeger Regiment No. 13 Major von der Schulenburg.
1st Battalion Captain Gebert
2nd Battalion Major Meuth
3rd Battalion Captain Schulz
Fallschirmjaeger Regiment No. 14 Major Noster
1st Battalion Captain Schmidt
2nd Battalion Captain Sauer
3rd Battalion Captain Meissner
Fallschirmjaeger Regiment No. 15 Major Groschke
1st Battalion Major Leimbach
2nd Battalion Captain Hoffmann
3rd Battalion Captain Meyer
Fallschirm Artillery Regiment No. 5
Fallschirm Anti-tank Battalion No. 5
Fallschirm Engineer Battalion No. 5
Fallschirm Mortar Battalion No. 5
Fallschirm Anti-aircraft Battalion No. 5
Fallschirm Signals Battalion No. 5

6th Fallschirmjaeger Division
The 6th Division was raised in the areas of Metz and Nancy in April 1944.
Divisional Commander Major-General von Heyking
Fallschirmjaeger Regiment No. 16 Lieutenant-Colonel Schirmer
1st Battalion
2nd Battalion
3rd Battalion
Fallschirmjaeger Regiment No. 17
1st Battalion
2nd Battalion
3rd Battalion
Fallschirmjaeger Regiment No. 18
1st Battalion
2nd Battalion
3rd Battalion
Fallschirm Artillery Regiment No. 6
Fallschirm Anti-tank Battalion No. 6
Fallschirm Mortar Battalion No. 6
Fallschirm Anti-aircraft Battalion No. 6
Fallschirm Engineer Battalion No. 6
Fallschirm Signals Battalion No. 6
Replacement Battalion
Reconnaissance Company

The re-raised 6th Fallschirmjaeger Division
The losses which the original 6th Division had suffered during the fighting in France and Belgium required that it be re-raised. This took place during the last months of 1944 in the Kleve area of the Rhineland.
Divisional Commander Major-General Plocher
Fallschirmjaeger Regiment No. 16 Colonel Dorn
1st Battalion Major Geppert

3rd Battalion Lieutenant-Colonel von Mehrhardt
There was no 2nd Battalion
Fallschirmjaeger Regiment No. 17 Colonel Vetter
1st Battalion Captain Blume
2nd Battalion Captain Weilbacher
3rd Battalion Major Sautter
Fallschirmjaeger Regiment No. 18 Major Witzig
1st Battalion Major Bilogan
2nd Battalion Captain Liebe
3rd Battalion Lieutenant Weber
Fallschirm Artillery Regiment and the other divisional units as previously shown.

In the last two monhs of the war, OKL ordered that an 11th Fallschirmajeger Division be created. Once again, the personnel for this new formation came from the survivors and splinter groups of units which had been smashed in furious and unequal battles, as well as men from training establishments and replacement depots. The administrative difficulties connected with the creation of a major formation, together with the catastrophic military situation, so delayed the raising of 11th Division that it did not go into battle as a single entity. Instead regiments or even individual battalions of the Division were given the tasks of closing a breach or of leading an attack. The active service life of the 11th Fallschirmjaeger Division, the last to be raised, was brief but bloody.

Mention was made above that in certain military circumstances individual regiments were detached from their parent bodies and given special tasks to fulfill. I do not intend to detail the formations undertaking such missions. Details of their operations have already been included in the chronological history of the war.

The following lists of unit establishments give the names, so far as it has been possible to establish these, of the officers commanding regiments and/or battalions within the divisions. Some names occur more than once. This reflects the promotions which took place within the officer corps of the Fallschirmjaeger arm of service.

1st Fallschirmjaeger Division, 1944
This Order of Battle is for the 1st Division during the period February to May 1944, when it fought in the Cassino battles. During this period there was movement among the commanding officers at both regimental and battalion level. These are NOT shown here.
Divisional Commander Lieutenant-General Heidrich
Fallschirmjaeger Regiment No. 1 Colonel Schulz
1st Battalion Major von der Schulenburg
2nd Battalion Major Groschke
3rd Battalion Major Becker
The 3rd Battalion, which had been destroyed in the fighting, was re-raised. Captain Folster
Fallschirmjaeger Regiment No. 3 Colonel Heilmann
1st Battalion Major Bohmler
2nd Battalion Captain Foltin
3rd Battalion Major Kratzert
The re-raised 3rd Battalion Captain Liebscher
Fallschirmjaeger Regiment No. 4 Colonel Walther
1st Battalion Captain Beyer

2nd Battalion Captain Huebner
3rd Battalion Major Grassmel
The other divisional units as previously shown.

7th Fallschirmjaeger Division
The 7th Division was created out of Para unit remnants grouped under the command of Lieutenant-General Erdmann, Chief of Staff to Colonel-General Student. The task of this *ad hoc* formation was to build a defensive front along the Albert Canal, in September 1944. The conversion of 7th Fallschirmjaeger Division took place in October 1944, and in December of that year the Order of Battle was:
Divisional Commander Lieutenant-General Erdmann
Fallschirmjaeger Regiment No. 19 Colonel Menzel
1st Battalion Major Pralle
2nd Battalion Captain Wegenich
3rd Battalion Captain Diehl
Fallschirmjaeger Regiment No. 20 Lieutenant-Colonel Grassmel
1st Battalion Captain Bayer
2nd Battalion Major von Keisenberg
3rd Battalion Captain Gramse
Fallschirmjaeger Regiment No. 21 Colonel Loytweg-Hardegg
1st Battalion Captain Hoffmann
2nd Battalion Captain Jaeger
2rd Battalion Captain Ewald
Fallschirm Artillery Regiment No. 7
Fallschirm Anti-tank Battalion No. 7
Fallschirm Engineer Battalion No. 7
Fallschirm Mortar Battalion
Fallschirm Signals Battalion No. 7
Divisional units.

8th Fallschirmjaeger Division
The Division was ordered to be raised in September 1944, but it was not until January 1945 that Major-General Wadehn received the confirmatory order.
Divisional Commander Major-General Wadehn
Fallschirmjaeger Regiment No. 22 Lieutenant-Colonel von der Tanne
1st Battalion Major Wiedemann
2nd Battalion Captain Adrian
3rd Battalion
Fallschirmjaeger Regiment No. 23 did not serve with 8th Division but with 2nd Division with effect from November 1944.
Fallschirmjaeger Regiment No. 24 Lieutenant-Colonel Huebner
1st Battalion Captain Uferkamp
2nd Battalion Captain Strohlke
3rd Battalion Captain Fischer
The only other divisional units which came on to strength were the Engineer Battalion No. 8, the Replacement Battalion and the divisional supply units. All other groups were planned but were never taken on strength.

9th Fallschirmjaeger Division
The Order to raise the 9th Division, which had been issued in September 1944, was withdrawn and not re-issued until January 1945. The Division was formed in the area south of Stettin.
Divisional Commander Lieutenant-General Wilke
Fallschirmjaeger Regiment No. 25 Major Schact

1st Battalion
2nd Battalion
3rd Battalion
Fallschirmjaeger Regiment No. 26 Major Brede
1st Battalion
2nd Battalion
3rd Battalion
Fallschirmjaeger Regiment No. 27 Major Abratis
1st Battalion
2nd Battalion
3rd Battalion
Fallschirm Artillery Regiment No. 9
Fallschirm Anti-tank Battalion No. 9
Fallschirm Engineer Battalion No. 9
Fallschirm Anti-aircraft Battalion No. 9
Fallschirm Signals Battalion No. 9

10th Fallschirmjaeger Division

The 10th Fallschirmjaeger Division was ordered to be raised in September 1944, but the order was cancelled and not withdrawn until February 1945. The Division was ordered to concentrate in the Dutch/German frontier area, but that was changed and the units were grouped in eastern Austria.

Divisional Commander Colonel von Hoffmann
Fallschirmjaeger Regiment No. 28 Major Schmucker
1st Battalion Captain Klein-Bolting
2nd Battalion Captain Merkel
3rd Batalion Captain Cairies
Fallschirmjaeger Regiment No. 29 Major Genz
1st Battalion Major Liebscher
2nd Battalion Captain Moller-Astheimer
3rd Battalion Captain Engelhardt
Fallschirmjaeger Regiment No. 30 Lieutenant-Colonel Wolff
1st Battalion Captain Plate
2nd Battalion Captain Molt
3rd Battalion Lieutenant Mueller
Fallschirm Artillery Regiment No. 10
Fallschirm Engineer Battalion No. 10
Fallschirm Anti-tank Battalion No. 10

11th Fallschirmjaeger Division

The 11th Fallschirmjaeger Division was ordered to be raised by the Luftwaffe High Command. The order was issued in March 1945, and the establishment was to consist of Fallschirmjaeger Regiments 37, 38 and 39. Command of the new Division was invested in Colonel Gericke and the concentration area was western Holland. The military situation did not allow the Division to be raised and the units fought as battle groups.

Left: The Fallschirmjaeger combat uniform was distinctive, the special helmet to the smock and gauntlets. Here a paratrooper proudly displays the Iron Cross awards, both Second and First Class. (Brian L. Davis)

Below: Harness fit was important; the jarring effect when the parachute opened needed to be distributed evenly about the torso to avoid broken bones. Here a senior NCO is checking the fit of a recruit's harness. (M. Klein)

Uniforms, Equipment and Weapons

UNIFORM

The most distinctive pieces of Fallschirmjaeger uniform were the helmet, the smock or overalls and the rubber pads worn at knee and elbow.

The helmet, practical in design, was modelled on the standard issue steel helmet, but without the neck and side shields. The inside of the rimless helmet had thick rubber padding, and to hold it in position it was fitted with a chinstrap which divided so as to pass in front of and behind each ear. On the helmet's left side a Luftwaffe eagle was displayed. A cloth cover was fitted with a band into which camouflage material could be fitted. The original helmet cover was blue-grey, but later in the war was of camouflage pattern.

Battledress was a green, later camouflage patterned, loose smock or overalls of waterproof gaberdine. These garments, which were worn over equipment for the jump, were usually removed as soon as possible after landing and then worn under the equipment. The smock extended down the thighs and was front-fastened by press-studs, later by zip-fasteners. To hold the smock in position or to prevent it riding up, the early pattern had short legs permanently fastened at the crutch. This was later discontinued in favour of a press-stud fastening at the crutch. The garment had long sleeves fastening at the wrist. Rank insignia in the shape of large-size 'wings' was worn on the upper arm. The Luftwaffe eagle was worn on the right breast. The smock had four large pockets: two on the chest and two on the thigh, each of which was closed by zip-fastener.

Trousers were blue-grey, loose fitting and gathered at the ankle so that they fitted into the tops of the lace-up boots. On the outside of each trouser leg was a deep pocket. A smaller pocket, fitted below the right knee, held a gravity-knife.

Para boots came above the ankle, to which they gave support. The first pattern boots laced up the side not the front, to cut down the risk of fouling the parachute lines or canopy. After the Crete operation boots were issued with front lacing. The soles were made of thick, chevron-ridged rubber and were not intended for long marches.

In addition to the combat dress described above, there was a standard uniform, a five-button jacket, open-necked and worn with a collar and tie. Collar patches were in yellow, the Fallschirmjaeger Arm of Service colour. On this tunic was worn a cuff band, dark-green for Divisional units and light-green for regiments. There was also a cuff title for those who had fought in Crete and yet another when 5th Regiment was transferred to the Hermann Goering Division. The former 5th Jaeger then wore the cuff title of their new formation on their jump smocks.

Worn on the left breast pocket of the standard uniform jacket was the parachutist's badge. This depicted a golden coloured, diving eagle set inside a wreath of oak and bay of oxydized silver colour. In its claws the eagle held a swastika. This badge was awarded to the Jaeger after he had completed his six qualifying jumps.

Unusually, the Fallschirmjaeger were authorized to wear a parade version pattern of the jump smock and para harness.

With this pattern smock, shirt collar and tie, medals and decorations were worn, as were cloth ammunition bandoliers. Gloves were parade pattern. Boots worn with this special dress were not the lace-up type, but the standard German marching boots. This parade pattern Fallschirmjaeger uniform was first worn publicly on the occasion of Hitler's birthday on 20 April 1939.

The Luftwaffe method of distinguishing élite formations was to authorize its officers and men to wear a cuff title. The one issued to Fallschirmjaeger units was in green with Gothic lettering. To further distinguish between units, all ranks of 1st and 2nd Jaeger regiments wore a light green band. The other units of the 7th Flieger Division carried a dark green band. In accordance with standard practice, a cuff title which identified the unit was worn on the right sleeve. Upon the declaration of war, however, orders were issued that Fallschirmjaeger units would no longer carry this distinctive mark. Even so, there were occasions during the war when cuff titles were issued as campaign decorations, and certain Jaeger were eligible to wear these. The first campaign distinction was the cuff band awarded for Crete. This was white with the word 'KRETA' set between two stylized palm emblems, the whole embroidered in yellow. The second was the cuff band bestowed for service in Africa; in this case the background was khaki-brown, with the word 'AFRIKA' in silver thread set between two palm trees of the same coloured thread. Those Jaeger who were eligible for both awards wore them, Africa above Crete, on the lower left sleeve.

When the 5th Regiment, in Tunisia, was transferred *en bloc* to the 'Hermann Goering' Division, its officers and men were issued with the cuff band of that formation. This was dark blue with Gothic lettering in grey (silver thread for officers). As a badge identifying a unit, the title was worn on the right sleeve.

THE PARACHUTE

The parachute with which the Fallschirmjaeger were first equipped was a development of the Italian 'Salvatore' type. In this the canopy was carried folded in a pack on the soldier's back and released by a cord extending from the back pack to a static line inside the aircraft.

There are two standard ways in which a parachute canopy is capable of being released. One is by a static line and the other by a rip-cord which the parachutist himself pulls. The Para commanders' insistence that their men be in the air for the minimum time possible meant that a static line had to be used. One thousand feet (300 metres), was the lowest height at which a rip-cord operated parachute would completely open, whereas using a static line the Jaeger could jump with safety at an operational height of 300 feet (91 metres). Indeed landings at much lower levels were successfully carried out during the Second World War, some from as low as 200 feet (60 metres.)

The first parachute type on issue to the German airborne forces was the RZ1. This made of silk panels forming a 28-feet diameter canopy, an area of 648 square feet, and attached by suspension lines to a pair of short straps. These joined to form a

single support strap attached to the back of the harness so that the Jaeger seemed to be suspended from a single cord. The German paratrooper could not reach the rigging lines by which he might have controlled the drop, but hung in a diagonal position, facing downwards with both hands free. For the short time that he was in the air he used arms and legs to bring him to a good landing position in the direction of drift. Much of the shock of landing was absorbed by a forward roll, during which knees and elbows were protected by thick rubber pads and his hands by gauntlets. Unfastening the thick waist-belt released the Jaeger from his harness and canopy.

The RZ1 parachute was designed for a rapid and total un-folding of the canopy. The abrupt shock when it opened exerted a pressure upon the body which was countered only when the jumper assumed a horizontal position with arms and legs outstretched. The harness had to be tight fitting; a loose one could cause injury by not distributing the strain evenly. The tightness of the harness and the force with which the canopy opened meant that no weapons could be inserted between the overalls and the harness straps.

The RZ1 equipment, thus, had two disadvantages. A tight harness and the need to adopt an abnormal position in the air upon leaving the aircraft. To achieve that position the Jaeger had to stand at the exit door, feet braced in the corners, with his toes on the sill and with his hands gripping each side of the door frame. The head had to be inclined slightly upwards. When the time came to jump his hands and feet pushed hard against the fuselage projecting him into the aircraft's slip-stream. As he leaped the 20-foot-long static line ripped open the back pack and the slip-stream withdrew the canopy. With the aircraft flying at approximately 100mph the first 90 feet of the jump were a free fall until the 'chute opened and the rate of descent slowed to sixteen feet per second.

The tight harness and the need to have both hands free to propel himself out of the machine meant that the Jaeger could carry no rifle, machine-pistol or machine-gun in his hands, and the tightness of the harness meant that these could not be carried beneath the harness straps. Weapons were carried in a container which is described below. Although no long-range firearm was carried, each man had a pistol, usually some grenades and a gravity-knife which was less a weapon than an instrument to cut the rigging lines in an emergency.

The RZ1 was already obsolescent when war broke out in September 1939, and the first operational use showed up design defects which had not been apparent or had been ignored on peace-time training exercises. The RZ16, which succeeded it was introduced early in 1940, but proved unsatisfactory and was replaced, first of all in the following year by the RZ20, and then by other models. These were usually only modifications of harness design. The RZ20, which was first used operationally in Crete, had an improved release buckle. It was the RZ20 with which the Fallschirmjaeger were equipped for the rest of the war although other designs were produced. The RZ36 was a break from standard design, with the canopy squared off and subsequently reshaped to a triangular form. By this time the design of the canopy was academic – the Fallschirmjaeger were making no more operational drops although it is known that Lieutenant-Colonel von der Heydte used a triangular chute for the Ardennes

operation. There were attempts by OKL to change the canopy colour from white to something less distinctive, but this necessary innovation brought about an immediate loss in Jaeger morale. A rumour spread that the chemicals used to dye the silk had an adverse effect upon the swift and smooth unfolding of the canopy. In vain the Para officers sought to demonstrate that the rumour was untrue. They were not believed and attempts to alter the basic colour were abandoned. Weapons containers and supply canisters continued to be dropped using coloured parachutes.

One interesting point about Jaeger parachutes is that each man packed his own. It was, thus, his life that hung upon the care and attention with which he carried out the packing.

CONTAINERS

Because the Jaeger carried no rifle or machine-pistol when he jumped, these and other weapons had to be dropped with the men. The containers were, initially, of different sizes, but were standardized after the Crete operation to become a bevel-edged box, five feet long and sixteen inches across. The full-length lid was held in place by clips and secured by four straps which passed round the container. At one end was fastened a parachute, either an old one of standard design or a special dropping pattern. The latter was such that the container fell at an approximate speed of 26 feet per second. Thus it would already be on the ground when the Jaeger arrived. The other end of the box was fitted with a screw-on, corrugated, metal alloy cushion, some eighteen inches deep, which crumpled upon landing and absorbed much of the shock of impact.

The container carried 260lb of weapons or supplies and since the contents were not standard there were few internal fittings to hold them in place, but one internal fitting was a special container hung within the container by means of straps. To prevent damage the inside of the container was padded using foam rubber or felt pieces. A platoon of 43 Jaeger needed, in an initial drop, no fewer than fourteen containers, and coloured stripes or bands were used to aid unit identification. Once located and opened the boxes could be moved using either four carrying handles, two on each side, or a small, balloon-wheeled bogie which was fitted inside the container.

Lack of space inside the aircraft carrying the Jaeger meant that the boxes had to be carried in special racks adapted for the purpose inside the bomb-bays or else under its wings. Recovery of the containers after a mission was considered vital and teams of men were employed to search for and retrieve as many as could be found. Orders and directives from Luftwaffe Headquarters indicated that the containers were often kept, illegally, by other finders – invariably non-Jaeger personnel – as mobile cupboards to hold personal property.

It will be appreciated that the first task of the Jaeger upon landing was to retrieve the containers, open them and arm themselves, for until they did they were almost defenceless. The absolute necessity of finding the containers was the flaw in German airborne procedures and one for which the Jaeger paid heavily. It only needed for some of the containers to be lost or for enemy fire to prevent their retrieval and defeat was almost inevitable. Although later developments sought to overcome the problem of carrying weapons during a drop, it was never fully mastered and in the last German parachute mission, in the

Ardennes in December 1944, it was the loss of the weapons containers which prevented von der Heydte's battle group from achieving its given task.

One feature of air drops was the 'provisions bomb', carried in bomb-racks and shaped like conventional bombs. These were six feet long and eighteen inches in diameter. One end held the parachute but there were no shock absorbers at the other end. The rations which Jaeger took into battle were expected to last for two to three days. Included among the foodstuffs were sliced and wrapped 'Wittler' bread, a sort of semi-hard biscuit, chocolate containing Cola and Caffeine to prevent drowsiness, boiled sweets and biscuits. There were certain tablets supplied to produce energy among which were Dextro-energen and Pervitin, a Benzedrine-type of preparation to maintain alertness, but with the side-effect of producing intense thirst.

TRANSPORT: AIRCRAFT AND GLIDERS

Although the German airborne forces used a variety of aircraft in their operations it is with the Junkers 52, that they are most closely identified. Indeed it might almost be claimed that the Ju 52 was tailor-made for airborne operations.

This 3-engined, all-metal machine, with an overall length of 62 feet and a wing span of 96 feet, was the work-horse of the Luftwaffe, capable of use in a variety of roles. It was not an elegant aircraft but was robust and very distinctive, having a corrugated aluminium fuselage, fixed undercarriage and square-tipped wings.

There was a low-set door on the port side of the machine through which the Jaeger jumped or through which cargo was loaded. No provision was made to shift heavy loads from the ground into the cargo space and these had to be manhandled, a serious handicap which slowed down loading and unloading, particularly under fire. In addition to the fuselage cargo space of just under 600 cubic feet, additional freight could be carried in the bomb-bay or under the wings.

The Ju 52 had begun life as a long-range, passenger aircraft in service with Lufthansa, and in common with most commercial aeroplanes of that period was tri-motored, this being seen as a necessary safety measure. The three BMW radial engines, each producing 830hp, gave the aircraft a maximum speed of 172mph and a range of nearly 700 miles. One of the special features of the Ju 52 were the full-span flaps on the trailing edge of the wings which enabled the machine to take off or land in a very short distance.

When used for a para drop all superfluous interior fittings were removed and replaced by small canvas seats on which the Jaeger sat. Most former Fallschirmjaeger to whom I have spoken or with whom I have corresponded have mentioned the high level of noise inside the machine. The aircraft's metal fuselage acted as a sort of sounding-board for the three engines whose noise almost deafened the Jaeger. Small wonder that signals had to be given by klaxon or by lights. Vocal orders would have gone unheard in the din of the echoing metal box which was the Ju 52.

When the commanders of the Para force studied the tactics which would be employed, it was clear to them that a para drop suffered from two disadvantages. One was that the Jaeger would be dispersed over a wide area and, secondly, that they would arrive on the ground unarmed. Some operations demanded an armed and concentrated group. Gliders were the obvious answer

and in the early 1930s Germany had a force of skilled pilots most of whom had been trained to use their aircraft in a commercial role. The Third Reich intended to use freight gliders in the same way as trucks are used today, to move heavy loads across the length and breadth of Germany, cheaply, rapidly and efficiently.

Since evidence had shown that gliders were capable of carrying heavy loads, it followed that they could also carry armed men. A specially designed machine to meet the demands of the Para commanders was produced by the German Research Institute for Gliding. The DFS 230, a fabric-covered, tubular fuselage, carried a pilot, a co-pilot and eight Jaeger. These sat straddling a wooden bench which ran down the centre of the machine. On touch-down the perspex cockpit cover was ejected allowing the pilot and co-pilot to join the assault. The Jaeger left the aircraft through a pair of doors, one port and one starboard. The machine, with a total weight of one ton, could carry as an alternative to the Jaeger one ton of supplies.

The DFS 230 had a wing span of just over 72 feet and a length of 37 feet. The maximum speed at which it could be towed was 100mph and once released from the tug aircraft the glider sank at the rate of 240 feet per minute although this could be increased dramatically. In the chapter dealing with the 9th Para Division in action, mention is made of the airlanding by two Jaeger battalions in Breslau during February 1945. Research and experiment by the Para Instruction Battalion showed that it was possible to bring the glider down at a very steep angle for a very short landing. The principle was that the machines were towed in at a height, in excess of 10,000 feet, and for them to be released so as to glide towards the target slowly losing height. Above the target area a tail parachute was activated and the machine was put into an almost vertical dive. The parachute kept the descent speed to just above 100mph. At 800 feet the pilot levelled out, lowered the flaps and after a quick circuit landed the machine using nose-mounted retro-rockets if necessary to cut down the length of the landing run.

Using such tactics the two battalions of Jaeger reinforced the Breslau garrison by landing on the city's Kaiserstrasse. What the feelings of the Paras must have been can only be imagined, but it must have been alarming to sit huddled in a blanket against the extreme cold, and then to descend almost vertically through the dark night and into the fiery destruction which was Breslau at that stage of the war. This was the last glider operation of the German airborne forces and it was a remarkable demonstration of ability on the part of the pilots and of courage on the part of the Jaeger.

There were other gliders which had, in theory, been constructed for airborne operations, chiefly to bring in support weapons. Of these the Gotha Go 242 was also used at Breslau, but it came into service too late to be effective as an airborne weapon. The Me 321 was a giant glider designed to carry up to 20 tons of supplies, or a Panzer or 130 troops. This monstrous machine could best be towed by a 'troika' of three tug aircraft, an operation which required great skill on the part of all the pilots. The fitting of rockets to assist take-off eased the strain on the tug aircraft, but these were often not available and so the Me 321 was fitted with six engines, a not altogether satisfactory solution to the problem.

PISTOLS

The principal pistol with which the German Armed Forces were issued was the Pistole 08, the Luger, although this began to be phased out when the Walther P38 was adopted during 1940. In addition to these German-made weapons, large numbers of captured FN Browning pistols were taken into service and used under the term P640(b). The Walther pistol was a semi-automatic weapon with a grip magazine feed. It was recoil operated, the breech mechanism sliding to the rear after each round had been ·fired.

Calibre	9mm
Barrel length	4³/₄ inches
Weight	2lb 5oz (loaded)
Magazine	8 rounds

The Kampfpistole

The Kampfpistole and its later variant, the Sturmpistole, were both versions of the standard signal flare pistol. In the case of the Kampfpistole the barrel was rifled, and the ammunition fired included message grenades, smoke grenades and parachute flares as well as explosive grenades. The Sturmpistole was developed from the Kampfpistole to project anti-tank grenades. In order to take 22mm missiles, a rifled insert was fitted into the weapon's barrel. To give stability when firing, a folding stock was fitted above the pistol grip. A sight was fitted on top of the barrel.

The MP40 (Schmeisser) Machine-Pistol

A blow-back operated machine-pistol, this was developed from the MP38, which had been introduced into the German service in response to demands for a light, mobile, fast-firing weapon. The Schmeisser was widely used by Fallschirmjaeger units, which had a higher than normal establishment of these weapons. The MP40 should have been phased out of general service by 1943, when the Sturmgewehr was introduced, but insufficient new

Right: The Kampfpistole.

Below: The MP43.

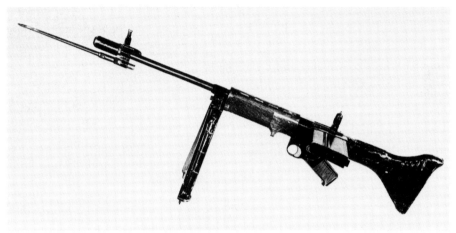

weapons had been produced and the MP40 remained on standard issue until the end of the war.

The defects in the Schmeisser were that it could not fire single rounds and that it had no safety catch, but merely a notch into which the cocking handle fitted. Late examples incorporated a two-piece cocking handle, which locked the bolt in the closed position. The advantages of the weapon were that it could easily be stripped down into three principal parts: barrel, body and firing mechanism. This latter was a firing-pin attached to a telescopic spring. It used plastic for lightness and had a skeleton butt, which folded under the body of the weapon.

Calibre	9mm
Barrel length	9.9 inches
Overall length	33½ inches
Weight	9lb without magazines
Magazine	32 rounds
Rate of fire	500rpm cyclic, 150rpm practical
Sights	109 yards with battle sight, 219 yards with folding rear sight.

The Fallschirmgewehr 42 Automatic Rifle

The FG42, of which there were several variants, combined the long-range performance of a standard rifle with the high rate of fire of a light machine-gun. This gas-operated, automatic rifle, specially designed, developed and produced for Fallschirmjaeger, could be used as a light machine-gun or a machine pistol. The weapon had a permanently attached folding bipod and permanently fitted bayonet. The FG42, was not long in service and was superseded very quickly by better, fast-firing weapons.

Calibre	7.9mm
Overall length	44 inches (with bayonet)
Weight	9lb
Magazine	20 rounds in a magazine held in a horizontal position of the left of the receiver
Sights	Graduated from 1099 to 1310 yards

The MP43 Machine-Pistol

This was a gas-operated machine-pistol produced almost entirely of stamped metal parts, in those times a revolutionary process in arms production. Hitler, who did not have to use the gun in action, approved of it and had it produced in large numbers; veteran soldiers found it heavy and unreliable.

Calibre	7.9mm (short version of rifle ammunition)
Length	37 inches
Weight	11lb
Magazine	38 rounds in a curved magazine
Sights	876 yards; leaf rear sight

The MG34 Machine-Gun
The standard German machine-gun, used as a LMG on a bipod or as a heavy machine-gun with tripod mounting. The action was operated by short recoil, assisted by muzzle blast. The belt-fed weapon was air cooled.

Calibre   7.92mm
Length   48 inches
Weight   26½lb (bipod mounted)
    72lb (tripod mounted)
Rate of fire   900rpm (cyclic)
    100/120rpm as LMG
    300rpm as HMG
Range   600/800 yards as LMG
    2,500 yards as HMG

The MG42 Machine-Gun
This weapon was intended to replace the MG34 and was very similar in length, weight and range. It had no provision to fire single shots.

Rate of fire   1,200 to 1,400rpm (cyclic)
    250rpm as LMG
    500rpm as HMG

The extremely rapid rate of fire of the MG42 gave it a characteristic sound unlike any other machine-gun in service – the Red Army called it the 'Hitler saw'.

The Panzerfaust
The Panzerfaust 30 and those which succeeded it in service consisted of a steel launching-tube containing a percussion-fired

Right: The MG34 mounted on a tripod for use in the heavy machine-gun role.

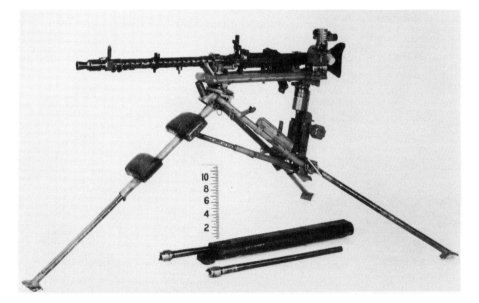

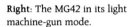

Right: The MG42 in its light machine-gun mode.

Right: The Panzerfaust. A page from instruction manual.

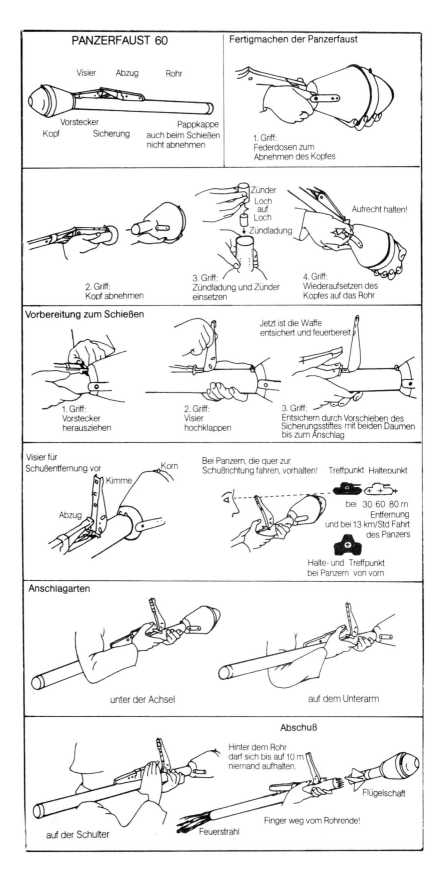

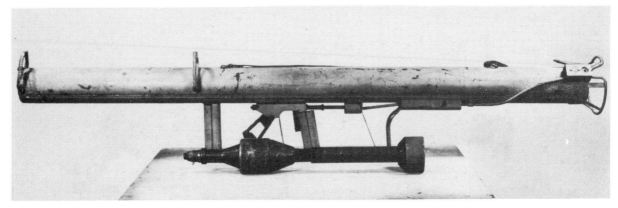

Above: The Panzerschreck.

Right: The Rocketenwerfer 43.

propellent charge. A hollow-charge anti-tank grenade was fired from the tube and a penetration of just over 200mm was obtained. Range was about 30 yards. This one-shot weapon had a weight of 11lb and an overall length of 41 inches. The sighting was crude, the back sight being merely a vertical piece of metal which was lined up with the nose of the bomb. The Panzerfaust 60 had an improved sight, a longer range and was 13½lb in weight. The Panzerfaust 100 was larger in size than its predecessors and was sighted up to 150 metres.

The Panzerschreck

This weapon fired a hollow-charge rocket projectile from a steel tube which was fitted with a front and back sight, a cocking lever and a trigger to activate an electrical firing mechanism. A steel shield, which clamped round the barrel, protected the firer from the effects of the blast flame and a small window allowed him to see and to aim at the target. Unlike the Panzerfaust the Panzerschreck could be re-used and it required a team of two, one to load and one to fire. The Panzerschreck projectile was a

7lb, hollow-charge rocket which had a propellant in the tail tube, a fuze in the nose and a circular tail fin.

Raketenwerfer 43 or Pueppchen

This was a heavier version of the Panzerschreck and was mounted on a single trail, two-wheeled carriage. The piece was fitted with a protective shield and had a hinged breechblock and striker mechanism. The Pueppchen could be neither traversed nor elevated mechanically. The piece had to be pointed at the target and held at the required elevation.

Calibre	88mm
Length	9 feet 2 inches
Weight	270lb
Range	765 yards

Mortars

The paratroop version of the 81mm mortar was the standard issue weapon but with a shortened barrel. It was an attempt to combine the power of the standard mortar with the mobility and lightness of a smaller weapon.

Above: The 81mm mortar.

Below: The 120mm mortar here on its wheeled carriage.

Calibre	81mm
Total weight	62lb
Max traverse	10°
Elevation	47°–88°
Max range	1,200 yards

The 105mm Nebelwerfer was an enlarged version of the standard 81mm mortar and was originally intended for firing smoke or gas shells. It was used principally to fire a 16lb high-explosive bomb.

Calibre	10.5cm
Total weight	231lb
Max traverse	13°
Elevation	45°–80°
Range	3,300 yards

12cm Granatenwerfer 42

This was a copy of the standard Russian mortar. Although conventional in design, having a tube, base-plate and bipod, it was unusual in that it could be fitted with a wheeled carriage.

Calibre	12cm
Weight of shell	35lb
Total weight	616lb
Traverse	16°
Elevation	45°–85°
Range	6,600 yards

The long range and heavy shell of this mortar gave it a power equivalent of a 105mm field howitzer.

Anti-tank Guns

The paratroop version of the Pz B 41, high-velocity, tapered-bore anti-tank gun was in service until the introduction of the rocket weapons, Panzerfaust and Panzerschreck. In 1943 the B 41 was phased out. The basic difference between the paratroop version of this weapon and that in standard use with the Army was that the Fallschirmjaegers' weapon had no gun shield, was fitted on a light alloy cradle and its tubular mount was fitted with balloon-tyred wheels.

Calibre	28mm

Weight   260lb (in action)
Muzzle velocity   4,600fps
Traverse   90°
Elevation   −45°−+45°

The gun fired HE and AP ammunition which would penetrate 53mm at 400 yards at 30°.

The 75mm LG 40

This gun required no recoil mechanism. The breech was designed to eliminate recoil by emitting part of the propellant gases to the rear through a Venturi tube which extended from the rear of the breech. Weight was reduced by making the carriage and wheels of alloy. Guns of this type could be broken down into two parts and parachute-dropped in wicker baskets.

Calibre   75mm
Length of tube   45½ inches

Right: The Pz B 41 high-velocity, tapered-bore anti-tank gun.

Weight in action 321lb
Range   8,900 yards
Shells   12lb HE, 15lb AP, 10lb hollow-charge.

The hollow-charge grenade penetrated 50mm at 30°.

The 10.5cm LG 40

This was a heavier version of the 75mm LG 40.

Calibre   105mm
Length of tube   75 inches
Weight in action 855lb
Range   8,694 yards
Shells   32½lb HE, 26lb hollow-charge

In addition to these weapons, there was also on issue the standard Gewehr 98 rifle and the stick hand-grenade. Hollow-charge grenades of the type used at Eben Emael have been described in the text.

Right: The 10.5cm LG 40 recoilless gun.

Chronology of Airborne Operations

1939

14 Sept   Ground operations by 3rd Battalion, 1st Regiment at Sucha, in Poland.

24 Sept   Ground operations by 2nd Battalion, 1st Regiment at Vola Gulovska, Poland.

1940

9 April   Parachute operation by 1st Battalion, 1st Regiment to capture Oslo airfield, Norway, and the Falster-Fuenen bridge in Denmark.

14 April   Parachute operation by 1st Battalion, 1st Regiment to capture the Donbas railway junction, Norway.

10 May   Combined parachute and glider assault to take out the fortress of Eben Emael, and the Albert Canal bridges by the Assault Regiment. Air landings in Holland by other units of 7th Flieger and 22nd Air Landing Divisions.

14 May   Parachute operation by 1st Battalion, 1st Regiment and Alpine troops at Narvik, Norway.

1941

26 April   Parachute operation by 2nd Jaeger Regiment to seize the bridge across the Corinth Canal, Greece.

20 May–2 June   Parachute, glider and airlanding assault by 7th Flieger Division and Corps troops together with 5th Alpine Division to capture Crete.

From Sept   Units of 7th Flieger Division sent to the Leningrad and Volkhov sectors of Eastern Front.

1942

From June   Operations by 'Ramcke Brigade' in the Western Desert.

From Oct   Return to the Rzhev sector of the Eastern Front by units of 1st Para Division (formerly 7th Flieger).

From Nov   The 5th Para Regiment and Para Corps Engineer Battalion in action in Tunisia where they fought until the end of the war in Africa in May 1943.

1943

12 July   The bulk of 1st Para Division parachuted into the Catania sector of Sicily.

26 July   Air transport of 2nd Para Division and Corps HQ from southern France to Rome following the Italian collapse.

Sept   Parachute operation by 4th Battalion of the Assault Regiment to take out the headquarters of the Italian Army in Monte Rotondo.

The 1st Para Division in action in Apulia and 2nd Para Division in the Rome area.

The Para Training Battalion made a glider landing to release Mussolini.

The 2nd Battalion made a parachute drop to capture the island of Elba.

Oct   The 2nd Para Division in action on the Eastern Front at Zhitomir.

Nov   Parachute operation by 1st Battalion, 2nd Para Regiment to capture the island of Leros.

The 2nd Division airlanded in Kirovgrad.

1944

From Jan   The 1st Para Division in action at Monte Cassino in Italy, the 4th Para Division and the Training Battalion in action at Anzio.

May   The SS 500th Para Battalion made an unsuccessful glider and parachute drop to capture Marshal Tito, at Drvar in Yugoslavia.

6 June   Para Regiment No. 6 in action at Carentan.

From June   II Para Corps, 3rd and 5th Para Divisions in action in Normandy. The 2nd Para Division, excluding 6th Regiment, in action in Brest area.

Autumn   I Para Corps, 1st and 4th Divisions, in action in Central Italy.

Operations against the Allied airlandings at Arnhem.

Individual Para units in action at Vilna and Kauen (Lithuania) on Eastern Front.

The newly raised Para battalion of 'Brandenburg' Division was surrounded and taken prisoner as it airlanded at Bucharest airfield.

Dec   The last parachute drop by Fallschirmjaeger during the Second World War. A battle group under the command of Lieutenant Colonel von der Heydte dropped during the Battle of the Bulge, but failed to cut the Eupen–Malmédy road.

The 3rd and 5th Para Divisions in action during the Battle of the Bulge.

1945

Jan   The 7th Para Division in Operation 'Nordwind', along the Rhine.

From Feb   The First Para Army in action during the defensive battles between the Maas and the Rhine, until the end of the war.

28th Feb   A parachute battalion flown into the city of Breslau surrounded by the Red Army.

From Feb   The 9th and 10th Para Divisions in action on the Eastern Front (Austria, Berlin, Czechoslovakia), until the end of the war.

The 1st and 4th Para Divisions in action in northern Italy until the end of the war.

Select Bibliography

English-language published works

2nd Army, *Account of Operations of 2nd British Army in Europe 1944/45.* HQ 2nd Army, 1945

Barclay, *History of 53rd Welsh Division in the Second World War.* W. Clowes & Son, 1956.

Blake, G., *Mountain and Flood: The History of 52nd Division.* Jackson & Co., 1962.

Bielefeld and Essame, *Battle for Normandy.* Batsford.

US Army, *Conquer: The History of 9th Army, 1944/45.* Infantry Journal, Washington 1947.

Gill and Groves, *Club Route in Europe: A history of 30 Corps in the European Campaign.* Printed in Germany, 1946.

– *A History of 15th Scottish Division, 1939–1945.* Blackwood, 1948.

Jackson, C., North, J. *Operations of 8th Corps, North West Europe, 1944/45.* BAOR, 1946; HMSO 1953.

3rd Armored Division, *Spearhead in the West: A History of 3nd US Armored Division.* Infantry Journal, Washington, 1945.

German published works

Arbeitskreis der 56 ID, *Geschichte der 56 ID.* Podzum, 1955.

Austermann, H, *Von Eben Emael bis Edwechter Damm. Fallsch. Pionier,* Holzminden, 1971.

Busch, E. D., *Die Fallschirmjaeger Chronik.* Podzun-Pallas Verlag, 1983.

Euler, H., *Die Entscheidungsschlacht an Rhein und Ruhr, 1945.* Motorbuchverlag, 1980.

Goetzel, *Generaloberst Kurt Student und seine Fallschirmjaeger.* Podzun Verlag, 1971

Gericke, *Hurra! Wir springen.* Motz & Co. Verlag, 1942.

Heydte, F. von der, *Muss ich sterben, will ich fallen.* Vowinckel, 1987.

Jacobsen, H., *Fall Gelb: Der Kampf um den deutschen Operations-plan zum Westangriff, 1940.* Steiner, 1957.

Klietmann, H. *Die Waffen SS: Eine Dokumentation.* Podzun Verlag, 1964.

OKW, *Kriegstagebuch des OKW, 1940–45.* Bernhard & Graefe, 1940.

Ritgen, H. *Die Geschichtes d. Panzer Lehr Division im West, 1944/45.* Podzun 1964.

Michelsen u Sleepenbeck *Niederreinnisches Land im Kriege.* Boss Verlag, Kleve, 1964.

Winterstein, E., *General Meindl und seine Flieger.* Bund deutsch. Fallschirmjaeger, 1974.

Meyer, H., *Kriegsgeschichte der 12 SS Panzer Division 'Hitler Youth'.* Munin Verlag, 1982.

Journals

Der deutsche Fallschirmjaeger Signal Der Freiwillige Letters from and interviews with men of the German Paratroop organization.

Unpublished material

A. G. 'B', *Kriegstagebuch,* various dates.

BAOR, *Intelligence Reviews,* 1944, 1945

Criegern, *Die Kampfe des 84 A. Korps in der Normandie von der allierten Landung bis zum 17 Juni 1944.*

6th Canadian Armoured Brigade, *War Diary,* 1944/5.

7te Armee, *Kriegstagebuch,* 1944.

8th Corps, *War Diary,* 1944/5.

21st Army Group, *War Diary,* 1944/5.

Index